THE SOCIOLOGY OF DISABILITY: EUROPE AND THE MAJORITY WORLD

Edited by
Colin Barnes and Geof Mercer

The Disability Press
Leeds

First published 2005
The Disability Press
Centre for Disability Studies
School of Sociology and Social Policy
University of Leeds
Leeds LS2 9JT.

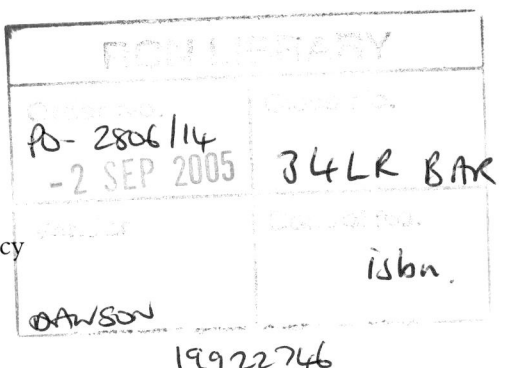

© The Disability Press 2005/ Colin Barnes & Geoffrey Mercer, selection and editorial matter; individual chapters, the contributors.

Produced by Media Services at the University of Leeds.

All rights reserved. No part of this book may be reprinted or reproduced or utilised in any form by any electronic, mechanical, or other means, now known or hereafter invented, including photocopying and recording, or in any information storage or retrieval system, without permission in writing from the publishers.

British Library Cataloguing in Publication Data
A catalogue record for this book is available from the British Library

Library of Congress Cataloguing in Publication Data
A catalogue record of this book has been requested

ISBN 0-9549026-0-2 (pbk)

Contents

The Disability Press — v

Acknowledgements — vi

Contributors — vii

1. Understanding Impairment and Disability: towards an international perspective – *Colin Barnes and Geof Mercer* — 1

2. We're all Europeans now! The social model of disability and European social policy – *Mark Priestley* — 17

3. Personal Assistance Reforms in Sweden: breaking the assumption of dependency? – *Susanne Berg* — 32

4. Pupil or 'Patient': difference, disability and education in France – *Felicity Armstrong* — 49

5. Disabled Peoples' International: Europe and the social model of disability – *Rachel Hurst* — 65

6. Dismantling Barriers to Transport by Law: the European journey – *Anna Lawson and Bryan Matthews* — 80

7. Disabled People and the European Union: equal citizens? – *Hannah Morgan and Helen Stalford* — 98

8. One World, One People, One Struggle? Towards the global implementation of the social model of disability – *Alison Sheldon* — 115

9. Finally Included on the Development Agenda? A review of official disability and development policies – *Bill Albert* — 131

10. Definitions of Disability and Disability Policy in Egypt – *Heba Hagrass* — 148

11. An Evaluation of the Impact of Medical Services Provided by General Hospitals Compared with Services Aligned to a Social Model Perspective at a Spinal Cord Injury Centre in Bangladesh – *A. K. M. Momin* — 163

12. 'Food' or 'Thought'? The social model and the majority world – *Tara Flood* — 180

13. Disability and Rehabilitation: reflections on working for the World Health Organization – *Enrico Pupulin* — 193

Index — 209

The Disability Press

The Disability Press aims to provide an alternative outlet for work in the field of 'disability studies'. It draws inspiration from the work of all those countless disabled individuals and their allies who have, over the years, struggled to place 'disability' on to the political agenda. The establishment of The Disability Press is a testament to the growing recognition of 'disability' as an equal opportunities and human rights issue within the social sciences and more widely in society.

The Centre for Disability Studies at the University of Leeds has provided funding for this volume. We also wish to record our thanks to the School of Sociology and Social Policy at the University of Leeds for its continuing support.

Colin Barnes and Geof Mercer

Acknowledgements

This is the third volume that we have edited based on contributions to a seminar series on 'Implementing the Social Model of Disability: from Theory to Practice' organised by the Centre for Disability Studies (CDS) at the University of Leeds. The first and second volumes, *Implementing the Social Model of Disability: Theory and Research* and *Disability Policy and Practice: Applying the Social Model* were published in 2004 by The Disability Press.

We wish to thank the Economic and Social Research Council for a grant to help with this series, and also to the participants and particularly those presenting papers at the fifth and sixth seminars on which this volume is based.

Once again, we want to record our special debt to Marie Ross for her expert support and skills in preparing the collection for publication and more specifically in producing the Index.

Contributors

Bill Albert is a member of the British Council of Disabled People's International Committee and a consultant and trainer on disability and development.

Felicity Armstrong is a Senior Lecturer in Inclusive Education and Course Leader for the MA in Inclusive Education at the Institute of Education, University of London.

Colin Barnes is Professor of Disability Studies at the Centre for Disability Studies, School of Sociology and Social Policy, University of Leeds.

Susanne Berg is a disabled activist and consultant from Stockholm, Sweden. She is currently working for Stockholm's Independent Living Institute.

Tara Flood is Information and Publications Co-ordinator at Disability Awareness in Action, the international information and research network on disability and human rights.

Heba Hagrass studied Anthropology and Sociology at the American University of Cairo and is currently undertaking a PhD in the Centre for Disability Studies at the University of Leeds.

Rachel Hurst is Director of Disability Awareness in Action, the international information and research network on disability and human rights.

Anna Lawson is a Lecturer at the School of Law and a member of the Centre for Disability Studies at the University of Leeds.

Brian Matthews is a Research Fellow in the Institute for Transport Studies at the University of Leeds. His main interests are in the economic analysis of transport policy.

Geof Mercer teaches and undertakes research in the School of Sociology and Social Policy and the Centre for Disability Studies at the University of Leeds.

A.K.M. Momin is a disability activist and involved in setting up Bangladesh's first treatment and rehabilitation centre for people with spinal cord lesion and academic institute for rehabilitation professionals.

Hannah Morgan is a Lecturer in Applied Social Science at Lancaster University.

Enrico Pupulin was formerly the Co-ordinator of Disability and Rehabilitation at the World Health Organization, and is currently Professor of Epidemiology at the University of Modena in Italy.

Mark Priestley is a Reader in Disability Studies at the Centre for Disability Studies at the University of Leeds, and administrator of the international e-mail discussion group disability@jiscmail.ac.uk.

Alison Sheldon is a Teaching Fellow in the Centre for Disability Studies at the University of Leeds.

Helen Stalford is a Senior Lecturer in Law at the University of Liverpool. She has research interests in EU free movement law and the concept of EU citizenship.

CHAPTER 1

Understanding Impairment and Disability: towards an international perspective

Colin Barnes and Geof Mercer

Despite recent attempts to construct a universal language of disability (Üstün et al. 2001), to be designated 'disabled' in the wealthier 'developed' or 'minority world' nations in North America, Europe, and Australasia often carries with it a different set of meanings and experiences to those encountered by people who acquire this label in the poorer countries of the 'developing' or 'majority world' in, for example, Africa and Asia (Coleridge 1993; Ingstad and Whyte 1995; Ingstad 2001). Notwithstanding such international variation, the experience of disability is interwoven in most societies with multiple deprivations and disadvantages (WHO 2001; Barnes and Mercer 2003). Hence, the growth of political activism amongst disabled people and their organisations across the globe since the 1960s has concentrated on campaigns to overturn their social exclusion and oppression and achieve 'independent living' (Driedger 1989; Charlton 1998).

The chapters in this book explore selected aspects of these developments with particular emphasis on the contribution of the 'social model of disability' that was constructed during the 1970s by disabled activists. The social model approach shifted the attention away from the functional limitations and psychological 'loss' stressed by the dominant individual or medical approach to 'disability' or the ways in which physical and social environments excluded individuals with impairments from participation in mainstream society (UPIAS 1976; Oliver 1983). It offered a socio-political analysis of the discriminatory structures and processes that impact on the lives of people with impairments. Its early adoption in 1981, albeit in a modified form, by Disabled Peoples' International (DPI) signalled its widening significance for disabled people, not just in Europe but in majority world countries (Driedger 1989).

The contributors to this volume present detailed studies of these issues from a variety of countries and perspectives. In order to provide further context for their analyses, this introduction offers a critical overview of the global production of impairment and disability.

Impairment: prevalence and origins

In their efforts to direct attention towards the economic, political and cultural aspects of the disability experience early advocates of a social model approach highlighted a conceptual distinction between impairment and disability. Initially, social model writers accepted the contemporary medical definition of impairment, typically equating it with functional limitations. In contrast, disability refers to the social exclusion and oppression experienced by people with accredited impairments (UPIAS 1976), with a particular stress on significant historical and cross-cultural differences. Although not of the same interest to early social model advocates, the definition of impairment is also influenced by socio-cultural factors, as illustrated by changing and contested notions of 'mental illness' and 'learning difficulties'. While not denying the relevance of a medical focus on treating impairment for some disabled people, the social model emphasises the need for political action and social change to remove 'disabling' barriers (Barnes and Mercer 2003).

This conflicts with the traditional approach among health and social welfare professionals which regards impairment as the underlying cause of 'disability'. In the World Health Organization's (WHO 1980) highly influential formulation, the *International Classification of Impairments, Disabilities and Handicaps* (ICIDH), 'impairment' is defined as the biological condition, 'disability' as the ensuing functional limitation, and 'handicap' as the social consequences of impairment and disability. This approach underpinned international league tables compiled by the United Nations on the prevalence of 'disability' (UN 1990). Even then, international comparisons are made problematic because of the different meanings given to impairment and disability between societies and the sometimes stark differences in methods of data collection and processing. For instance, some nations relied on professional diagnoses and research whilst others were based on lay responses.

Setting aside these concerns, the UN figures indicate that most of the world's disabled population live in the poorer nations of the majority world, although the incidence of reported impairment (broadly functional limitations) is higher in wealthier countries. There are three major reasons for this. First, in richer societies the longer life expectancy and much larger proportion of people over fifty years old are linked directly with higher (age-related) rates of impairment. Second, these countries have more extensive health and support services, which typically produce a higher survival rate among people born with impairments and those who acquire them later in life. Third, some conditions such as dyslexia are classified as an impairment in highly industrialised economies although in more rural majority world countries these are often not considered a 'functional limitation' and therefore not recorded as an impairment to anything like the same degree (Coleridge 1993).

There are other noteworthy patterns between majority world countries. For example, a higher level of impairment is reported in more urbanised areas. This is probably because they contain more medical rehabilitation and support services, while there is also a greater risk of injury through pollution, traffic and work accidents, and perhaps more possibilities for a person with an impairment to earn a living, including begging. Again, there is often an association with gender, 'race' and ethnicity, because of the marked differences in the geographical distribution and quality of medical services. Thus, over recent decades in South Africa, this has meant that a spinally injured white person was ten times more likely to survive into late middle age than a black person with a similar condition (Coleridge 1993).

Furthermore, the disparity in wealth between the 'developed' and 'developing' world has widened steadily. Some estimates suggest that in 1820 the gap between the world's richest and poorest nation was approximately three to one, but by 1992 this had risen to a staggering seventy-two to one (Giddens 2001: 70). Much impairment across the world is the outcome of such skewed and exploitative economic and social development. Specific diseases once common but now rarely recorded in industrialised countries remain widespread and in some cases are increasing in other parts of the world. For example, there were over 100,000 new cases of polio in 'developing' countries in 1994 (Stone 1999a: 5), and in India, the prevalence of polio and blindness is at least four times higher among people who are below the poverty line compared with those who are above it (Ghia 2001: 29). More than 30 per cent of the population in some villages in Zaire are affected by 'river blindness' (Coleridge 1993). Such experiences underpin the demand for public health and medical-related interventions to complement the struggle against social and environmental barriers by disability activists (WHO 2001). Whereas lifestyle choices such as diet, lack of exercise, consumption of alcohol and smoking are ranked as significant causes of impairments in wealthier nations (Gray 2001), around three-quarters of India's 60 million disabled people live in areas where public amenities like clean water, electricity, sanitation, and medical services are in very short supply (Ghia 2001). Disabled women and children in majority world states are especially vulnerable and frequently experience higher levels of poverty and impairment (S. Miles 1996; UN ESCAP 2003). Some critics have calculated that as much as half the impairment in the majority world could be prevented by the introduction of effective policies to reduce poverty and malnutrition, improve sanitation, drinking water and working conditions (Charlton 1998).

The lack of funding to counter these sources of impairment is further exacerbated by the policies of international financial institutions such as the World Bank and International Monetary Fund that force governments to cut back on public services to service enormous international debts. Moreover, access to medical and rehabilitation services is often dependent on the ability to pay and this poses major problems for disabled people and their families. There is also an acute shortage of trained medical personnel that is made worse by the active 'poaching' of qualified staff by richer nations, with no financial compensation for poorer countries to educate and train new staff. As a result, only one per cent of disabled people in 'developing' nations have access to any form of rehabilitation or disability related services (WHO 2001). This contrasts starkly with the much higher proportion of financial and human resources in 'developed countries' that is channelled into medical services, including preventive medicine. However, the latter has attracted considerable criticism from disabled people where it has led to policies supporting euthanasia, selective abortion, eugenics and other attacks on their human rights.

Needless to say, poverty and the lack of an adequate health and social care infrastructure are neither peculiar to majority world states nor the only factors leading to impairment (Abberley 1987). A fuller set of 'causes' includes natural disasters (earthquakes, floods), by-products of economic development (industrial accidents and pollution), and specific cultural practices (such as female genital mutilation). Civil wars, often fanned by the international arms trade, have resulted in an unprecedented growth in civilians and military personnel with impairments. In Cambodia, an estimated 100,000 people lost limbs as a direct result of the combatants' use of landmines (UNESCO 1995). There was a similar growth in the number of people with impairments associated with the civil war in Rwanda, with claims that a strategy of maiming rather than killing people helps undermine resistance both economically and psychologically because 'disabled people remain far more visible than the dead' (Coleridge 1993: 107).

Socio-cultural perceptions of impairment

Social research studies illustrate how perceptions of individual health, well-being, competence and ability differ conspicuously between cultures. While most include notions of what is 'normal' and or 'ideal', the body-mind split has been a particular feature of western, scientific medical thinking. What rank as acceptable individual attributes, and what 'difference' justifies an individual's social exclusion also diverge significantly (Hanks and Hanks 1980; Scheer and Groce 1988; Miles 1992, 1995; Ingstad and Whyte 1995).

These cultural differences have generated competing explanations. To understand the significance of impairment and how and why certain individuals and groups are considered 'abnormal' or 'incompetent' and how control and resistance is exercised, it is necessary to explore these issues within specific cultural contexts. According to Mary Douglas (1966), responses to perceived physical, sensory or cognitive difference involve deep-seated psychological fears of 'anomaly'. This denotes a connection between perceptions of impairment and a non-human 'liminal' status. Cultures deal with assumed ambiguity by either attempting to control it in some way or by adopting it as ritual. Examples include the Nuer practice of regarding 'monstrous' births as baby hippopotamuses accidentally born to humans. The Nuer's response is to return them to 'the river where they belong' (Douglas 1966: 39). Nevertheless, infanticide for those born with perceived impairments is far from typical of traditional cultures (Charlton 1998).

Ida Nicolaison (1995) identifies notions of 'humanity' and 'personhood' as key concepts in understanding how different cultures create their own complex hierarchies to locate individuals. She shows how, among the Punan Bah of Central Borneo, only a relatively narrow set of conditions, notably epilepsy, 'madness' and severe birth defects, denote a non-human status that warrants social exclusion. In addition, the notion of 'personhood' is used to distinguish between specific roles or rankings. This encompasses expectations of what it means to be a child or adult, man or woman. Whereas in most western societies personhood is equated with adult employment, in China it has been traditionally linked to marriage, parenthood and lineage (Stone 1999b).

Other interpretations accord religious ideas a crucial role in determining what is considered socially acceptable, particularly in non-western cultures. However, there is no consensus among major religions such as Buddhism, Hinduism and Islam on the 'correct' way to regard impairment. In societies where these religions hold sway impairments are widely regarded as 'misfortunes, sent by deity, fate, karma; and often associated with parental sin' (Miles 1995: 52). These produce often very different social responses to the individual with an impairment and their family. However, social research in poorer societies has concentrated on responses to impairment in small-scale, rural-based groups, where religious beliefs may exert a stronger influence compared with those living in urban environments (Scheer and Groce 1988; Ingstad and Whyte 1995).

These examples illustrate the diversity of cultural responses to people with designated impairments in 'developing' societies (Kisanji 1993). Certainly, perceived impairment does not necessarily lead to social exclusion. Among the Masai people of Kenya, people with physical impairments may marry, become parents and participate in all communal activities (Talle 1995). More broadly across different cultures, the range of social statuses of people with physical impairments stretches from 'pariah', because the individual is deemed an economic or moral liability or threat, through 'limited participation', where the individual is granted selected social or other concessions, to 'laissez-faire', where some people enjoy opportunities to acquire prestige and wealth (Hanks and Hanks 1980).

Disability and globalisation in an unequal world
In order to understand this complex relationship between impairment and disability in the 21st century, comparative studies must also be located within a broader materialist analysis. Over the last few decades, the process of globalisation has intensified, with a gathering internationalisation of economic, political and cultural structures and processes, stimulated by the rapid spread of new information and communication technologies. These trends have been complemented by the dramatic growth of trans-national corporations like Coca Cola, General Motors and Exxon, which have become richer than many majority world states. This signifies a significant extension of the capitalist world order (Held et al. 1999).

This is where terms such as 'developed' and 'developing' countries tend to obscure the reasons underlying the vast inequalities of wealth between 'rich' and 'poor' nations, and the international dissemination of western institutions and practices. Most importantly, they conceal the extent to which the 'developed' world 'underdevelops' the majority world by exercising its overwhelming economic and political power (Hoogvelt 1976, 1997). Even so, the polarisation of countries into either the majority or minority world grouping is not always straightforward, just as the expansion of the European Union into eastern and southern Europe is bringing together countries at very different 'stages of development'.

Nevertheless, the spread of industrial capitalism has typically forced changes in traditional approaches to impairment and disability. For example, its impact on the Punah Bah economy and culture has been dramatic. The arrival of international logging companies has brought very different approaches to work and wage labour which conflict with established understandings of personhood and the status of people with accredited impairments. Furthermore, smaller family units have been replacing the typical extended household, leading to a reduced capacity to support dependent members. Overall, 'capitalist' values are beginning to 'imperceptibly permeate the Punan Bah view of themselves and the world' (Nicolaisen 1995: 54). In a similar fashion, the exposure of Masai society to market forces has undermined traditional support networks for people with impairments (Talle 1995). This process has been considerably heightened by the growing influence of 'scientific medicine' and the western mass media in promoting a contrary perception understanding of 'able-bodied normalcy' (Coleridge 1993; Charlton 1998).

The impact of industrial capitalism on the majority world has been particularly severe among disabled people. There is a lack of appropriate support systems ranging from technical aids and equipment such as brailling machines, wheelchairs and prostheses, as well as sign language interpreters, to an inaccessible built environment, housing and transport systems. Even where appropriate support is available it is often too expensive for most potential users. Moreover, the likelihood of early changes being introduced is remote exactly because the disabling barriers are so extensive and entrenched and there are very few resources to fund the necessary changes (Charlton 1998).

Education is widely presented as a way of addressing the problem of poverty and social exclusion. Yet in many majority world states disabled children, most often girls, are routinely denied formal schooling (UNESCO 1995; UN ESCAP 2003). Even then, western-style education may have unintended consequences for disabled children. For example, the emphasis on literacy and numeracy for economic and social success can lead to the labelling of some children as 'educationally backward' and their marginalisation from environments even where these attributes are not vital to an individual's life chances (Kalyanpur 1996; S.Miles 1996).

The experience of social exclusion in developing countries has generated widespread political activism amongst disabled people (Jayasooria and Ooi 1994). International contacts in the 1980s had a particularly galvanising effect for many disabled activists and disability rights organisations. This was particularly evident at the inaugural meeting of Disabled Peoples' International, the world's first international organisation controlled and run exclusively by disabled people, in Singapore in 1981 (DPI 1982). As the disabled activist Joshua Malinga from Zimbabwe reported: 'When I went to Singapore I was a conservative, but when I returned I was very radical' (quoted in Charlton 1998: 133).

The growing international interest in disability issues and policy can be traced back to the 1970s and the UN's *Declaration of the Rights of Mentally Retarded Persons* (1971) and the *Declaration of the Rights of Disabled Persons* (1975). These were followed by the designation of 1981 as the 'International Year of Disabled Persons' (IYDP) and 1983-92 the 'Decade for Disabled Persons'. However, the apparent radical thrust of these initiatives has been weakened by the continuing influence of conventional individualistic notions of disability and medical rehabilitation (Barnes and Mercer 2003). Nonetheless, since the 1990s, anti-discrimination legislation for disabled people has been enacted in countries as diverse as the United States and China. Another decisive initiative was the United Nations' *Standard Rules on the Equalization of Opportunities for People with Disabilities* (UN 1993). It comprises twenty-three rules to facilitate full participation and equality for 'persons with disabilities'. These cover aspects of daily living including awareness raising, medical and support services, education, employment, leisure and cultural activities. More recently, the WHO's (1999) revised definition of disablement - the 'International Classification of Functioning, Disability and Health' – has been associated with an 'environmental turn' in international disability policy (Tøssebro 2004). However, the rhetoric from international organisations still outruns policy implementation at national levels, not least because majority world governments have insufficient resources to bring about radical changes.

Disability and the European Union

The prospect of the transfer of social model thinking into national policy practice has also been enhanced by its adoption by the Commission of the European Communities (2003). It expresses a commitment to removing 'the environmental barriers in society which prevent the full participation of people with disabilities in society' (p. 4). However, it remains to be seen how far individual Member States follow this up with specific initiatives, particularly as the widening of EU membership into eastern and southern Europe has brought together very different traditions in disability policy.

Organisations of disabled people have campaigned for the EU to take action on disability rights since the 1980s, ranging from the setting up of the European Network for Independent Living in 1989 to holding a Disabled People's Parliament in 1993. The EU has also been sensitive to international developments, particularly the UN's (1993) *Standard Rules on the Equalization of Opportunities for People with Disabilities*. Action very much followed a legal route with the representation of disability as a human rights issue, although the early EU emphasis was on measures to enable a disabled person to enter and retain employment. The inclusion of disability in the Treaty of Amsterdam in 1997 as one of the grounds for challenging discrimination proved crucial. This was reinforced by the Framework Equal Treatment Directive (FETD) in 2000 which required those states which had not already done so to introduce anti-discrimination legislation by 2006. For disabled people's organisations, the aim has been to emulate the EU's 'Race Directive' which extended beyond employment into such areas as education, housing, social protection, goods and services. However, the disability remit does now include indirect discrimination and requires 'reasonable accommodation' to be made for disabled people. It remains to be seen how the courts interpret this formulation on removing disabling barriers.

The widening of the disability remit is evident in the EU Disability Strategy with its goal of achieving a 'society open and accessible to all'. This stresses:

- co-operation between the Commission and the Member States;
- full participation of people with disabilities;
- mainstreaming disability in policy formulation.

In accordance with the principle of 'subsidiarity', the EU Commission is accorded a significant facilitative role in promoting disability awareness whilst policy responsibility is exercised at the national level. This has led to the inclusion of disability in National Action Plans, and initiatives such as an annual 'European Day of Disabled People', National Information Days on disability issues, and the 2003 European Year of Disabled People.

The involvement of disabled people in policy making and implementation has been highlighted as part of a wider attempt to promote a more active civil society and new processes of governance across the EU. The (EU funded) European Disability Forum, was set up as an umbrella organisation with the largest (in terms of membership) 'disability' organisation 'representing' each Member State. This disregards basic questions about whether these organisations are controlled by disabled people, and whether they accept a primary focus on removing disabling social barriers rather than individual rehabilitation. Disabled people's organisations are also participants in the EQUAL initiative (2000-2006) that is charged with producing new ideas on job creation and social inclusion. This raises important questions about how far there is a 'European way' of approaching disability and the extent and direction of disabled people's influence in reforming national institutions, structures and processes so as to enhance the social inclusion of disabled people in each Member State.

Furthermore, a specific Unit for the Integration of People with Disabilities has been charged with mainstreaming disability issues into Commission activities beyond its current focus on employment and training. This is evident in a growing focus on accessibility in the built environment, with technical standards drawn up for work, leisure and educational environments, amidst a general promotion of 'universal design' or 'Accessibility for All'.

Such initiatives open the way for a policy convergence on disability across Member States. At present, the contrasting economic and socio-cultural traditions are represented in very different social policy regimes. For the majority, medical and allied health and social welfare professionals have defined the needs of disabled people in ways that have perpetuated a view of their 'personal tragedy' and social dependence (Barnes and Mercer 2003). In EU terms, achieving political agreement on the eligibility of citizens for social security and other benefits is confounded by the many different national definitions of a disabled person. In contrast, the social model literature has stressed the identification and removal of the barriers to social inclusion as opposed to defining a disabled person.

Notwithstanding the EU's endorsement of the social model, and attempts to find mechanisms to generate appropriate 'good practice', very different national practices abound, with stark contrasts in 'mainstreaming' services as opposed to 'special provision'. The recognition of the human rights of disabled people still leaves them at the mercy of resource allocation, with states excused action on the grounds of too many demands on their scarce resources. There is, as the contributors to this collection demonstrate, a long way to go before equality of opportunity and equal treatment for people with designated impairments are the norm rather than the exception whether in the EU or the majority world.

The organisation of the chapters

This book contains contributions from academics, researchers and activists that explore the impact of social model inspired thinking in Europe and the majority world. In Chapter 2, Mark Priestley examines the various ways in which social model thinking has become more visible in policy documents produced by the European Union. He argues that despite a shift in emphasis towards explicit recognition of disabled people's rights, specific policies have yet to materialise with which to make the vision of an inclusive Europe a reality. This, he maintains, is due to the disparate histories and characteristics of Member States and their respective economic, political and welfare concerns. His analysis raises major questions about the complex interplay between EU disability policy, national interests, and disability activism within an increasingly global economy characterised by market forces and economic and social inequality.

In Chapter 3, Susanne Berg analyses how economic considerations play a crucial role in the development of personal assistance reforms in Sweden – a country renowned for its communitarian welfare policies. Employing a social model interpretation as her starting point, she shows how the Swedish 'relational' model of disability that underpins welfare policy for disabled people in general and personal assistance reforms in particular, actually re-enforces rather than challenges conventional notions of disabled people's economic and social dependence.

Sensitive to the challenges of exploring different cultural contexts Felicity Armstrong analyses education policy for children with impairments in France through both a medical and a social model lens in Chapter 4. Her overview of the historical and philosophical foundations upon which French policy rests and broad brush account of current educational practices demonstrates how social exclusion remains the norm rather than the exception. She argues that used together the medical and social models enable us to identify the distinctions and overlaps in culturally embedded systems and practices, struggle and realignment.

In a similar vein, Rachel Hurst in Chapter 5 warns against confusing the social model as an analytical tool and the actions needed for meaningful social change, and the political struggle for rights. She provides a brief sketch of the role of the social model within the British disabled people's movement and on Disabled Peoples' International, Europe. She argues that, when coupled with an approach to disability as a human rights issue, these offer a much more positive political programme than the deficit models of disability that characterise European policy statements. However, further advances are threatened by a range of factors, from bioethics and eugenics to the silencing of the voices of disabled people.

In Chapter 6, Anna Lawson and Bryan Matthews draw attention to the problem of inaccessible transport across Europe. They illustrate how, over the last decade, some progress has been made in terms of the acknowledgement of, and tentative efforts to overcome, the difficulties encountered by disabled people when using public transport systems in European states both by policy makers and the transport industry. In a critical evaluation of these measures from a social model perspective, they argue that the full force of the law is urgently needed to hasten the pace of change.

Hannah Morgan and Helen Stalford address issues pertaining to the freedom of movement within and between European states and its links to paid employment in their discussion of the barriers to disabled people's equal status as European citizens in Chapter 7. They examine the limitations of current thinking in this regard and argue for a broader rights based approach. This should extend beyond the economic imperative of the free movement of labour towards a more inclusive and positive declaration of the needs of disabled Europeans which values their direct and indirect participation in the economy.

Alison Sheldon, in Chapter 8, signals a shift in focus in this volume towards 'developing' countries or the 'majority world'. She explores a radical political economy approach that takes account of the increasing influence of globalisation on disability. This suggests a close relationship between disability and uneven economic development. When informed by a social model approach, it underscores the significance of a materialist analysis of disability in the majority world in contrast to the dominant concern with cultural factors and differences. Sheldon suggests a 'systemic solution' that will encompass both the exclusion of disabled people and the poverty of majority world people generally.

In Chapter 9, Bill Albert provides a critical evaluation of the various policy documents that have emerged from international aid agencies.

Albert's primary concern is with the complex relationship between disability and development, and he acknowledges that some limited progress has been made in recognising disability as a human rights issue in official documents. Nevertheless, policy implementation is basically locked into a traditional individualistic welfare approach that has limited relevance for furthering the demand for a wider human rights agenda.

In Chapter 10, Heba Hagrass provides a socio-political analysis of impairment and disability in Egypt. She shows how economic and cultural factors are major causes of impairment in Egypt, but argues that whereas social interaction between disabled and non-disabled people takes many forms it is often less harsh than widely imagined. Moreover, Egyptian legislation and policy are firmly grounded in an individualistic deficit model of disability, and she contends that the impetus for change must be given more support by the international community of disability activists and scholars.

A comparative analysis of the services for people with spinal cord injury in Bangladesh is provided by A. K. M. Momin in Chapter 11. His contribution provides a graphic account of provision and support for people with spinal injuries provided by the Centre for the Rehabilitation of the Paralysed (CRP) and general hospitals in Bangladesh. His study demonstrates how the combination of a medical and social model approach to rehabilitation, as provided by the CRP, the only unit of its kind in Bangladesh, offers clear benefits for spinal cord injured people, but that a chronic shortage of resources means that they are only available to a fraction of those who need them.

In Chapter 12, Tara Flood discusses some of the criticisms of social model thinking in majority world contexts. By tracing socio-political interpretations of disability within the international disabled people's movement, Flood shows how the social model/social action mantra as used by disabled activists has had a particularly meaningful impact on user-led community based rehabilitation projects in majority world states such as Mexico, South Africa, Cambodia and India.

The relationship between CBR and social model thinking is a key theme in Chapter 13 by Enrico Pupulin, based on his experience as the Chief Medical Officer of the WHO's Disability and Rehabilitation Team. Pupulin describes how the socio-political or social model approach to disability rose to prominence, albeit gradually through the 1990s, culminating in initiatives such as *Rethinking Care from the Perspective of Disabled People* (WHO 2001).

Taken together these chapters illustrate how far, and in what ways, the socio-political or social model approach to addressing and explaining the problems encountered by disabled people in both developed and developing nations is timely and appropriate. There can be little doubt that at the start of the 21st century:

> Overall, the politics of impairment is inseparable from the politics of global poverty and inequality, and the social, economic, political and cultural changes resulting from capitalist industrialisation and globalisation. It is particularly important given that these developments will almost certainly have profound implications for everyone whether a disabled person or not, and regardless of whether they live in the minority or majority world (Barnes and Mercer 2003: 149).

Bibliography

Abberley, P. 1987: The concept of oppression and the development of a social theory of disability. ***Disability, Handicap and Society***, 2 (1), 5-19.

Barnes, C. and Mercer, G. 2003: ***Disability***. Cambridge: Polity.

Charlton, J. I. 1998: ***Nothing About Us Without Us: Disability Oppression and Empowerment***. Berkeley: University of California Press.

Coleridge, P. 1993: ***Disability, Liberation and Development***. Oxford: Oxfam Publications.

Commission of the European Communities 2003: ***Equal opportunities for people with disabilities: A European Action Plan***. Brussels: COM/2003/650 final.

Douglas, M. 1966: ***Purity and Danger***. London: Routledge and Kegan Paul.

DPI 1982: ***Proceedings of the First World Congress***. Singapore: Disabled Peoples' International. Available on: www.leeds.ac.uk/disability-studies/archiveuk/index

Driedger, D. 1989: ***The Last Civil Rights Movement. Disabled Peoples' International***. London: Hurst and Company.

Ghia, A. 2001: Marginalization and disability: experiences from the Third World. In M. Priestley (ed.), ***Disability and the Life Course***. Cambridge: Cambridge University Press.

Giddens, A. 2001: ***Sociology***, 4th edn. Cambridge: Polity.

Gray, A. (ed.) 2001: ***World Health and Disease***. 3rd edn. Buckingham: Open University Press.

Hanks, J. and Hanks, L. 1980: The Physically Handicapped in Certain Non-Occidental Societies. In W. Philips and J. Rosenberg (eds), *Social Scientists and the Physically Handicapped*. London: Arno Press.

Held, D. et al., 1999: *Global Transformation: Politics, Economics and Culture*. Cambridge: Polity.

Hoogvelt, A.M. 1976: *The Sociology of Developing Societies*. London: Macmillan.

Hoogvelt, A.M. 1997: *Globalisation and the Postcolonial World: the new political economy of development*. Basingstoke: Macmillan.

Ingstad, B. 2001: Disability in the Developing World. In G. L. Albrecht, K.D. Seelman and M. Bury (eds), *Handbook of Disability Studies*. London: Sage.

Ingstad, B. and Whyte, S.R. (eds) 1995: *Disability and Culture*. Berkeley: University of California Press.

Jayasooria, D. and Ooi, G. 1994: Disabled Peoples Movement in Malaysia. *Disability and Society*, 9 (1), 97-100.

Kalyanpur, M. 1996: The influences of Western special education on community-based services in India. *Disability and Society*, 11 (2), 249-69.

Kisanji, J. 1993: Growing up disabled. In P. Zinkin and H. McConachie (eds), *Disabled Children in Developing Countries*. London: MacKeith Press.

Miles, M. 1992: Concepts of Mental Retardation in Pakistan: towards cross-cultural and historical perspectives. *Disability, Handicap and Society*, 7(3) 233-55.

Miles, M. 1995: Disability in an eastern religious context: historical perspectives. *Disability and Society*, 10 (1), 49-69.

Miles, S. 1996: Engaging with the disability rights movement: the experience of community-based rehabilitation in Southern Africa. *Disability and Society*, 11 (4), 501-17.

Nicolaisen, I. 1995: Persons and Nonpersons: disability and personhood among the Punan Bah of Central Borneo. In B. Ingstad and S. R. Whyte (eds), *Disability and Culture*. Berkeley: University of California Press.

Oliver, M. 1983: *Social Work with Disabled People*. Basingstoke: Macmillan.

Scheer, J. and Groce, N. 1988: Impairment as a Human Constant: Cross-Cultural and Historical Perspectives on Variation. *Journal of Social Issues*. 44 (1), 23-37.

Stone, E. 1999a: Disability and development in the majority world. In E.Stone (ed.), *Disability and Development*. Leeds: The Disability Press.

Stone, E. 1999b: Modern slogan, ancient script: impairment and disability in the Chinese language. In M.Corker and S.French (eds), *Disability Discourse*. Buckingham: Open University Press.

Talle, A. 1995: A Child is a Child: Disability and Equality among the Kenya Masai. In B.Ingstad and S.R. Whyte (eds), *Disability and Culture*. Berkeley: University of California Press.

Tøssebro, J. 2004: Introduction to the Special Issue: Understanding Disability, *Scandinavian Journal of Disability Research*, 2 (1) 3-7.

UN ESCAP 2003: *Final Report, UN ESCAP Workshop on Women and Disability* (18-22 August and 13 October 2003), Bangkok: Thailand (Available on: http://www.worldenable.net/wadbangkok2003/recommendations.htm (site accessed 9 January, 2005).

UNESCO 1995: *Overcoming Obstacles to the Integration of Disabled People*. London: Disability Awareness in Action.

UN 1971: *Declaration of the Rights of Mentally Retarded Persons*. New York: United Nations.

UN 1975: *Declaration of the Rights of Disabled Persons*. New York: United Nations.

UN 1990: *Disability Statistics Compendium*. New York: United Nations Statistics Office.

UN 1993: *Standard Rules on the Equalization of Opportunities for Persons with Disabilities*. New York: United Nations.

UPIAS 1976: *Fundamental Principles of Disability*. London: Union of the Physically Impaired Against Segregation. Also available on: www.leeds.ac.uk/disability-studies/archiveuk/index

Üstün, B., et al. (eds) 2001: *Disability and Culture: Universalism and Diversity, ICIDH-2*. Seattle: Hogref and Huber.

WHO 1980: *International Classification of Impairments, Disabilities and Handicaps*. Geneva: World Health Organization.

WHO 1999: *International Classification of Functioning and Disability, Beta-2 draft, Short Version*. Geneva: World Health Organization.

WHO 2001: *Rethinking Care from the Perspective of Disabled People*. Geneva: World Health Organization.

CHAPTER 2

We're all Europeans now! The social model of disability and European social policy

Mark Priestley

There has been a dramatic shift of thinking about disability in European social policy circles. For years social model perspectives remained a fringe concern, advocated by European disability activists on the international stage yet at the margins of the European policy community. By contrast, there is now much talk of the 'social model'. Indeed, according to the latest European Union (EU) Action Plan there is even an 'EU social model of disability':

> The EU also sees disability as a social construct. The EU social model of disability stresses the environmental barriers in society which prevent the full participation of people with disabilities in society. These barriers must be removed (Commission of the European Communities 2003: 4)

The discussion in this chapter introduces two key questions. First, to what extent has social model thinking influenced the European social policy agenda? For example, do moves towards a rights-based policy framework really reflect a 'social model' perspective on disability? Second, how useful is the social model in providing a framework for European policy convergence; and how useful is it in explaining the situation of disabled people in an increasingly diverse range of member states?

The language of the social model is often associated with developments in Britain, and regarded by many in other European countries as a rather British concept (although there is wide agreement that disabled people's exclusion has some social causes). To recap, the traditional view of disability was to assume that people with accredited impairment would be unable to perform 'normal' activities and social roles. From this perspective, disability was seen as an individual problem caused by impairment. The solution for policy makers was either to treat the person (through medicine and rehabilitation) or to compensate them for their 'limitation' (by arranging less valued social roles such as sheltered employment, residential care, etc.). From a social model perspective, there is no necessary causal relationship between acquiring impairment (whatever that is) and becoming disabled. Lack of participation and equality can then be attributed to limitations within society rather than within the individual. Disability can be examined as a social problem caused by social structures, social relationships and social processes. To use a familiar example:

> In our view, it is society which disables... Disability is something imposed on top of our impairments, by the way we are unnecessarily isolated and excluded from full participation in society. Disabled people are therefore an oppressed group in society (Union of Physically Impaired Against Segregation/Disability Alliance 1976: 3).

There are four key points here. First, although some people may experience impairments, disability is something different. Second, disability is about exclusion from full participation in society. Third, this exclusion is not inevitable (i.e. we could imagine a society where people with impairments were not 'disabled'). Fourth, it makes sense to think of disabled people as an oppressed social group. Disability in this sense is 'the loss or limitation of opportunities to take part in the normal life of the community on an equal level with others due to physical and social barriers' (Disabled Peoples' International 1982). To summarise:

> disability, according to the social model, is all the things that impose restrictions on disabled people; ranging from individual prejudice to institutional discrimination, from inaccessible buildings to unusable transport systems, from segregated education to excluding work arrangements, and so on. Further, the consequences of this failure do not simply and randomly fall on individuals but systematically upon disabled people as a group who experience this failure as discrimination institutionalised throughout society (Oliver 1996: 33).

So, how has this kind of social model approach influenced policy making within the European Union?

Early developments in European disability policy

The policy agenda for the European Community was, from the outset, preoccupied with creating the economic and monetary conditions for a single market (i.e. the free movement of capital, labour and products between member states). However, there was also recognition that relevant social actions would be required to achieve these ends, and disability was not entirely overlooked. Thus, in seeking to promote 'full and better employment' and an 'improvement of living and working conditions', the Council Resolution of 21 January 1974 concerning a social action programme recommended 'a programme for the vocational and social integration of handicapped persons', including a comparative review of national policies in this area. The European Commission proposed using the European Social Fund for an action programme concerning disabled workers and, later the same year this was established in the Council Resolution of 27 June 1974. This Resolution outlined for the first time a wider social goal for policy intervention:

> The general aim of Community efforts on behalf of the handicapped must be to help these people to become capable of leading a normal independent life fully integrated into society. This general aim applies to all age groups, all types of handicaps and all rehabilitation measures (Council of the European Communities 1974).

Although framed within a rehabilitation paradigm (using medico-functional definitions of accredited impairment rather than a social model approach) the programme also recognised the need for wider public action. By the end of the 1970s then, the emerging European disability agenda acknowledged certain social goals (such as independence and full integration) but remained driven by individual model definitions, a rehabilitation approach, and a primary focus on employment.

The end of the first action programme and the International Year of Disabled People (IYDP) provided opportunities to broaden this agenda at the political level. For example, the European Parliament Resolution of 11 March 1981 affirmed a commitment to promote social and economic integration for disabled people, in addition to their vocational integration. There were also first signs of a more socio-economic understanding of disability, evidenced in acknowledgement that disabled people are amongst those most adversely affected by the economic cycle of a capitalist free market. In this context, it is worth noting that the re-evaluation of European disability policy, prompted by IYDP in 1981, occurred in the wake of widespread economic downturn affecting member states during the late 1970s. Thus, the Council Resolution of 21 December 1981 on the social integration of disabled people articulated concerns that disabled people should not be disproportionately disadvantaged by adverse fluctuations in the European economy (particularly in relation to their employment).

By the mid 1980s, and with the growing influence of the international disabled people's movement, a broadening social analysis was becoming more clearly articulated. The 1986 'Recommendation on the Employment of Disabled People in the European Community' (86/379/EEC) benchmarks two persistent themes – the preoccupation with employment and the emergence of a rights-based approach. The Recommendation was based on the principle of 'fair opportunities' for disabled people within a European labour market, via state measures on non-discrimination and positive action. This suggested targeted measures such as job creation, sheltered employment, vocational training, guidance, and compensatory social security arrangements. But it also acknowledged the need for a more enabling environment, in terms of accessible housing, transport, workplaces, information, and social research. Significantly, there were by now explicit references to active consultation with disabled people and their organisations.

On the political and rhetorical level then, there had been something of a shift in policy focus, between the late 1970s and the late 1980s, away from individualised rehabilitation and towards equal rights, participation and the socio-economic environment. In practice, European action programmes continued within the rather narrower HELIOS framework (although there were also a number of rather general positive statements around this time). By 1990, there had also been positive moves on education, such as the Council Resolution of 31 May 1990 'Concerning Integration of Children and Young People with Disabilities into Ordinary Systems of Education'. However, since Europe's primary area of competence remained centred on labour market regulation; it is perhaps unsurprising that actual policy development continued to emphasise employment.

From discrimination to a rights-based approach

Although disabled Europeans and their organisations had championed the social model on the international stage throughout the 1980s, it had not achieved any great prominence within the European Community. That is not to say that there was no interest in disabled people, simply that such attention was not focused through a social model lens (being more concerned with care, rehabilitation and vocational training). Although there were developments in the area of gender equality, disability (along with racism) did not yet figure prominently in such debates (Cunningham 1992).

However, in response to disabled people's increasing advocacy, and spurred by the United Nations' *Standard Rules on Equalization of Opportunities for Persons with Disabilities*, disability became a more prominent European theme by the early 1990s. In 1993 a Disabled People's Parliament was held to mark the first European Day of Disabled People, at which around 500 participants agreed recommendations to the Commission (*Report of the First European Disabled People's Parliament*, 3 December 1993). The resolution passed at that Parliament acknowledged that disabled people have equal shares in universal human rights but that they also experience discrimination in three ways – as a result of 'direct discrimination, indirect discrimination, and "unequal burdens" imposed by socially constructed barriers'. By comparison with official European policy statements, the claims of disabled people's organisations articulated a more explicit social model approach, with the conviction that:

> disabled people should be guaranteed equal opportunity through the elimination of all socially-determined barriers, be they physical, financial, social or psychological, which exclude or restrict full participation in society (Report of the First European Disabled People's Parliament, 3 December 1993).

Such statements clearly accord with the social model, in that they recognise discrimination on a number of levels; not simply in terms of individual rights, personal prejudice or direct discrimination but also in terms of social barriers arising indirectly from existing arrangements institutionalised within society.

The same resolution called on the Commission to act in specific areas: to amend the name of Directorate General V (to identify a remit for 'Equal Opportunities' as well as employment and social affairs); to establish a new sub-Directorate, including disabled staff, with responsibility for equal opportunities policy; to adopt and monitor the UN Standard Rules; and to produce legislation, 'including a comprehensive social policy initiative'. In addition, the Resolution called institutions of European governance to support studies on human rights; to adopt equal opportunities instruments on employment, contract compliance and funding criteria, and to ensure that a 'general anti-discrimination provision' was included in any revision of the Treaty on European Union. This was a broad and radical agenda, based largely on social model analysis, which challenged economic and cultural assumptions, demanded changes to decision-making institutions, and called for amendments to European law. In the light of its social model aspirations, it is interesting to examine what has happened to that agenda since 1993.

Perhaps the most high profile action has occurred in relation to the claim for a 'general anti-discrimination provision' in the Treaty on European Union. After 1993, disabled people and their allies become more politicised and more strategic; persuaded that progress at the European level could be most rapidly and symbolically advanced by legal recognition of discrimination at the highest level. There was already some sympathy within the European Commission for a general non-discrimination clause, bolstered by inter-governmental working groups under the Spanish presidency during 1995 (disabled people's organisations played a key role here, via the European Disability Forum and the Spanish National Council of Disabled People).

Since the campaign prioritised legal recognition, input was increasingly invited from those with legal expertise (particularly human rights lawyers). So, while the impetus arose from the self-advocacy of disabled people's organisations, grounded in a broadly 'social' approach, developments took an increasingly legalistic turn. This legal emphasis was evident in the report for the 1995 European Day of Disabled People, written by lawyers and providing detailed legal analysis of disabled people's omission from European Treaties, their rights as workers and consumers within the European Union, the inadequacy of those rights, and calls for greater legal protection (Degener et al. 1995).

After continuing pressure from disability organisations, disabled people were finally made 'visible' in the Amsterdam Treaty of 1997 (Whittle 1998, 2000). In summary, Article 13 of the amended Treaty empowered the Council to take action to combat discrimination on grounds of disability (along with discrimination on grounds of sex, racial or ethnic origin, religion or belief, age and sexual orientation). The inclusion of disability in this general clause conveyed a new competence to the European Community, permitting it to address disability discrimination, but did not immediately convey any new rights to disabled people. This legal recognition of disability discrimination was undoubtedly a landmark achievement, establishing disabled people's claims to full participation and equality as a legitimate concern of the European legislature and policy community. Yet, questions remain about the extent to which it represents progress in 'implementing the social model'.

There is a tendency in European social policy debates towards what is often called, within disability studies, a 'rights-based approach' (Mabbett 2003). While sharing similar sources of inspiration, the rights-based approach does not always accord with social model analysis. The social model (as defined by its early British authors) had focused on the structural basis for disabled people's collective oppression, arising from social relations of production and reproduction in modern capitalist societies. The implication was that real change could only be effected through political struggle to expose and challenge the disabling relationships and institutions that underpin such societies (Oliver 1990). By contrast, disability activists in North America had drawn more heavily on a 'minority group approach' that emphasised claims to civil rights using existing legal frameworks and constitutional law (Hahn 1986). As Liggett (1988: 271) points out, the rights-based approach implies that the 'legitimate demands' of disabled people for legal protection might be pursued within an existing political system, without overtly challenging the system itself.

Both social model and rights-based approaches recognise disability as a human rights issue, yet the social model suggests that disability is much more than this. However, there is often confusion and the social model has been exposed to numerous interpretations (Priestley 1998). Indeed, it is not uncommon to see conflations of terminology in which social model and rights-based approaches are used synonymously. As Finkelstein (2001: 1-2) notes:

> nowadays most people probably refer to the social model of disability in a much more vague, confused and sometimes totally alien way to the radical version that Mike [Oliver] developed. In recent times the social model of disability has even been so bent out of shape that it is confused with the 'rights' campaign agenda for legal safeguards.

That is not to say that advocates of social model analysis have not been strong advocates of civil rights and legal reform, quite the contrary (Barnes 1991). The point is simply that they are not the same thing. Indeed, it is precisely in revealing why legal safeguards alone cannot produce sufficient conditions for disabled people's full participation and equality that social model analyses are so useful (Young and Quibell 2000; Russell 2002). In order to understand disability, in the social model sense, it is necessary to look beyond the superstructure of civil society and legal institutions and to the social and economic relations that underpin inequality and social exclusion. In capitalist market economies (like the European single market) the social model demands a critical examination of the social relations of production and exchange, and the ways in which these create or sustain disability.

The narrower rights-based approach has proved a highly successful strategy, legitimising the concerns of disabled people and pushing disability up the European policy agenda by 1997, but constraints to its progress remain. For example, there is, as yet, no imperative to act on non-discrimination in relation to disability beyond employment (although there is in relation to sex or nationality). Any attempt by the European Council to adopt anti-discrimination legislation would require a unanimous vote by member states. In addition, any such measure would be limited to existing legal competence (which, for example, does not cover areas such as children's education or housing). In this sense, the high profile campaign for legal protection in the 1990s may have been inspired by disabled people's self-organisation and a social model analysis but would not necessarily be viewed as 'implementing the social model'. It is therefore important to think more carefully about the relevance of the 'social model' to European policy development.

In order to understand the development of a rights-based policy approach it is important to appreciate how rights figure more generally in European governance. As a benchmark, Article 6.1 of the Treaty on European Union asserts that:

> The Union is founded on the principles of liberty, democracy, respect for human rights and fundamental freedoms, and the rule of law, principles which are common to the Member States.

The founding Treaty of the European Economic Community, in 1957, contained no equivalent to a US 'Bill of Rights' and it was not until the Single European Treaty of 1987 that citizenship rights were introduced more explicitly. It is worth noting that such rights were accorded only to workers and consumers (the fundamental European freedoms are essentially the freedom to labour within a single market and the freedom to consume its products). It is perhaps unsurprising then that disability discrimination policy remained so centred on employment rights (Waddington 1995, 1997). However, the Council Decision to combat discrimination (2000-2006) certainly raised the profile of disability equality, and the Directive on Equal Treatment in Employment (2000) required legislative action by member states.

For disabled people's rights to be addressed more generally (and, in the social model sense, more structurally) we need to look beyond the rights-based policy initiatives. Social exclusion features high on the European social policy agenda; an agenda that envisages an active European welfare state, based on the values of solidarity and justice. Article 26 of the Charter of Fundamental Rights highlights the integration of disabled people directly and the EU Disability Strategy seeks 'a society open and accessible to all' - involving the removal of disabling barriers, the participation of disabled people, and the mainstreaming of disability policy. Such aspirations may be consistent with a broadly conceived social model approach but implementation demands substantial structural investment. While individual legal rights dominate the European policy headlines, there have also been moves to address the underlying issues.

The Action Plan following 2003 European Year of Disabled People continues to prioritise equal treatment in employment, but emphasises the wider mainstreaming of disability policies. Thus:

> Contributing to shaping society in a fully inclusive way is therefore the overall EU objective: in this respect, the fight against discrimination and the promotion of the participation of people with disabilities into economy and society play a fundamental role (European Commission 2003).

While legal strategies on human rights seek to engender 'respect for diversity', there is a 'social model' approach to removing environmental barriers and moves to mainstream disability concerns in the allocation of European structural funds. In this context, there may be some scope for misinterpretation, since the European Social Inclusion Process builds on a wider notion of a 'European social model' that is not specific to disability but aims to combat poverty and social exclusion more generally. The mechanisms involved can be regarded as a form of 'soft' policy (by comparison with rights-based legislation) and hinge on the Open Method of Co-ordination (OMC). This involves the negotiation of common objectives and indicators of social inclusion across a range of relevant areas (De la Porte, Pochet and Room 2001). At the central level, there is evidence that social model thinking has begun to influence European policy making. Yet, there remain questions about the opportunities for real change at the level of the member states, given the consensual nature of this process. However, for advocates of a (disability) social model, mainstreaming disability within the OMC process and its associated indicators, and campaigning for a comprehensive Disability

Directive in future, may be the most immediate ways forward at the present time.

One Europe, many countries

In this context, it is important to remember that European institutions of governance wield far less top-down authority than some Euro-sceptics would have us believe. Europe is a community of sovereign nation states and the overriding principle of subsidiarity places substantial limits on social policy implementation. As Mabbett (2003: 17) notes, 'subsidiarity may govern both the definition of disability and the determination of reasonable accommodation'. The initial Treaties of European Union conveyed only limited powers to tackle discrimination and, while the EU may now demand non-discrimination across a common labour market, many prerequisites to this (such as investments in education, housing, social security, and so on) are largely determined by individual member states (Machado and de Lorenzo 1997).

As a consequence, there remains much diversity in disability policies between different states. For example, Hvinden (2003) sees little evidence of convergence in key areas, like social security, that are already 'crowded' by the welfare regimes and traditions of individual states (Aarts, Burkhauser and de Yong 1998; van Oorschot and Hvinden, 2000, 2001; Mabbett 2003; Prinz 2003). By contrast, he argues that there is greater scope for convergence in new and relatively 'vacant' areas, such as European market regulation and anti-discrimination law. The more straightforward subsidiarity explanation is perhaps more convincing but, whatever the explanation, we must consider seriously whose Europe we are talking about if we are to pursue the political vision of 'an inclusive European society'. This by no means a straightforward task, given the political, economic and cultural diversity of states in the new Europe.

The initiation of European disability policy in the 1970s arose from co-operation between the six members of the original 'common market' (Belgium, West Germany, Luxembourg, France, Italy and the Netherlands), plus Denmark, Ireland and the United Kingdom (who joined in 1973). The three 'Southern' states of Greece, Spain and Portugal came to the table during a period of change in the 1980s, and a more disability critical agenda was well established when Austria, Finland and Sweden joined the EU in 1995. In addition to these 15 member states, the disability policy community has tended to include the non-member Nordic states of Iceland and Norway (for example, as members of the European Disability Forum).

With EU enlargement in 2004, there are new member states and applicant countries to consider, adding complexity and diversity. These include two more Southern states (Cyprus and Malta) together with eight Central and Eastern states (Czech Republic, Estonia, Hungary, Latvia, Lithuania, Poland, Slovakia and Slovenia). This latter group share many aspects of European culture and traditions, yet their past histories and political transitions in the post-Soviet era create particular economic and social circumstances. For example, Walsh (1997) notes how disabled people 'share the mixed fortunes' of the diverse countries in which they live (drawing attention to people with learning difficulties in Central and Eastern European countries) while Ursic shows how social transformation impacts indirectly on disabled people and the policies affecting them:

> Severe economic and political crises, reduction of social transfers, increasing unemployment – all this exerts a negative influence upon the chances for integration and full participation of the people with disabilities in social life (Ursic 1996: 91).

There are then a further applicant three countries that raise new questions about the vision of an inclusive European society. Although Bulgaria and Romania share many similarities with the Central and Eastern member states, the situation for disabled people in those countries, particularly children and adults with learning difficulties and psychiatric system users, remains challenging in the extreme (Rosenthal and Sundram, 2002). The new states and applicant countries face many barriers in harmonizing their disability policies and practices towards EU standards, and with limited economic resources to devote to that task. The addition of Turkey to the group of Southern states raises similar challenges, together with new questions about what a European identity or culture might mean.

Including the new states and the applicant countries brings the total number of countries participating in European disability policy up to 30, in which we can identify four broad groups: the traditional Western European nation states (former colonial powers and partners in post-war reconstruction); the Nordic countries (with their strong cultural links, attachment to civil society, and historic commitments to particular forms of welfare state provision); the Southern states (that had historically lower levels of industrialization and public welfare provision); and the Central and Eastern European states (associated through their recent history with the former Soviet Union). The variety of national conditions raises great challenges to implementing the social model. We will need to engage actively with these challenges if we are to further aspirations for 'an inclusive European society', and to comprehend what a 'European welfare state' might look like, or what might constitute the core 'European values' that underpin it.

Conclusions

For those of us in member states, EU policy and regulation will increasingly frame our measures of disability equality. To summarise, the historic policy focus on employment-related issues and legal protection reflects the economic foundations of the single market and the tendency to define European citizenship in terms of employment rights (Morgan and Stalford 2005, this volume, chapter 7). Policy initiatives have emerged in other areas but there has been little convergence due to entrenched national policies, the limited competence of the European Union and the principle of subsidiarity. In recent years there has been a shift, towards a more generic, rights-based approach, added to which the European Union, through the Commission and the Council of Ministers, has developed a vision of European society in which the social inclusion of disabled people now figures more explicitly than before.

Yet, as European integration and enlargement proceed, there is an increasing awareness of the tensions raised by different national priorities. There may be differences of emphasis about the kinds of issues that matter most - or about the ways in which these should be addressed - arising from local economic conditions, welfare regimes and histories of exclusion. In this context, we need to keep asking why we need a 'European' perspective on disability policy and whether this is possible in a diverse and enlarging Union. This, in turn, raises questions about priorities for action on disability, given the complex interplay between the single market, its institutions of governance, and the range of social and economic contexts across member states. We also need to look critically at how accountability to disabled people's movements can be maintained in these diverse contexts and at the European regional context.

Finally, we need to be acutely aware that the agenda for disability policy is not simply a European one. European developments will be influenced by global activism and techniques of governance, such as the emerging United Nations Convention, but we must also consider the role of Europe in the world. To what extent does the development of a European policy agenda cause us to look inward at the expense of a more global view on social inequality? In particular, how do we advance participation and equality for disabled people in Europe without adding cultural imperialism to the economic protectionism and exploitation that marginalises and disadvantages disabled people throughout the majority world?

Bibliography

Aarts, L., Burkhauser, R. and de Yong, P. 1998: Convergence: a comparison of European and United States disability policy. In T. Thomason, J. Burton and D. Hyatt (eds), *New Approaches to Disability in the Work Place*, IRRA Research Volume Ithaca, NY.: Cornell University Press.

Barnes, C. 1991: *Disabled People in Britain and Discrimination: a case for anti-discrimination legislation*. London: Hurst/BCODP.

Commission of the European Communities 2003: *Equal opportunities for people with disabilities: A European Action Plan*. Brussels: COM (2003) 650 final.

Council of the European Communities 1974: *Council Resolution of 21 January 1974, concerning a social action programme*.

Cunningham, S. 1992: The Development of Equal Opportunities Theory and Practice in the European Community. *Policy and Politics*, 20 (3), 177-189.

Disabled Peoples' International 1982: *Disabled Peoples' International: Proceedings of the First World Congress Singapore*. Singapore: DPI.

De la Porte, C., Pochet, C. and Room, G. 2001: Social Benchmarking, Policy-Making and the Instruments of New Governance, *Journal of European Social Policy*, 11 (4), 71-79.

Degener, T. et al. 1995: *Disabled Persons Status in the European Treaties, Invisible Citizens*. Report of the Third European Day of Disabled Persons, December 7, 1995. Secretariat of European Day of Disabled Persons 1995, Brussels.

European Commission 2003: *Equal opportunities for people with disabilities: a European action plan*. Communication of 30 October 2003 from the Commission to the Council, the European Parliament, the European Economic and Social Committee and the Committee of the Regions. COM/2003/0650 final.

Finkelstein, V. 2001: *The Social Model of Disability Repossessed*. Paper presented to Manchester Coalition of Disabled People, 1 December 2001. Available at: http://www.leeds.ac.uk/disability-studies/archiveuk/finkelstein/soc%20mod%20repossessed.pdf (accessed July 2003).

Hahn, H. 1986: Public support for rehabilitation programs: the analysis of US disability policy. *Disability, Handicap and Society*, 1(2), 121-137.

Hvinden, B. 2003: The uncertain convergence of disability policies in western Europe. *Social Policy and Administration*, 37(6), 609-624.

Liggett, H. 1988: Stars are not born: an interactive approach to the politics of disability. *Disability, Handicap and Society*, 3 (3), 263-275.

Mabbett, D. 2003: ***The Development of Rights-Based Social Policy in the European Union: the example of disability rights***. Brunel University. Available at: http://www.brunel.ac.uk/depts/govn/research/Development_of_Rights-based_Policy_Bham22Jan.doc (accessed July 2004).

Machado, S. and de Lorenzo, R. (eds) 1997: ***European Disability Law***. Madrid: Escuela Libre Editorial.

Oliver, M. 1990: ***The Politics of Disablement***. Basingstoke: Macmillan.

Oliver, M. 1996: ***Understanding Disability: from theory to practice***. Basingstoke: Macmillan.

Priestley, M. 1998: Constructions and creations: idealism, materialism and disability theory. *Disability and Society*, 13 (1), 75-94.

Prinz, C. (ed.) 2003: ***European Disability Pension Policies***. Aldershot: Ashgate.

Report of the First European Disabled People's Parliament (3 December 1993). Brussels: DPI-EC.

Rosenthal, E. and Sundram, C. J. 2002: International Human Rights in Mental Health Legislation. *New York Law School Journal of International and Comparative Law*, 21, 469-510.

Russell, M. 2002: What Disability Civil Rights Cannot Do: employment and political economy. *Disability and Society*, 17(2), 117-35.

Union of Physically Impaired Against Segregation/Disability Alliance. 1976: ***Fundamental Principles of Disability***. London: UPIAS/Disability Alliance.

Ursic, C. 1996: Social (and disability) policy in the new democracies of Europe (Slovenia by way of example). *Disability and Society*, 11(1), 91-105.

van Oorschot, W. and Hvinden, B. 2000: Introduction: Towards Convergence? Disability Policies in Europe. *European Journal of Social Security*, 2 (4), 293-302.

van Oorschot, W. and Hvinden, B. (eds) 2001: ***Disability Policies in European Countries***. The Hague: Kluwer Law International.

Waddington, L. 1995: *Disability, Employment* *Community*. London: Blackstone Press Ltd.

Waddington, L. 1997: The European Comm discrimination: Time to address the deficit of *Society*, 12 (3), 465-479.

Walsh, P. N. 1997: Old world - New territory: European perspec intellectual disability. *Journal of Intellectual Disability Research*, 41, 112-119.

Whittle, R. 1998: Disability Discrimination and the Amsterdam Treaty. *European Law Review*, 23 (1), 50.

Whittle, R. 2000: Disability Rights after Amsterdam: the way forward. *European Human Rights Law Review*, 1, 33-48.

Young, D. and Quibell, R. 2000: Why rights are never enough. *Disability and Society*, 15(5), 747-764.

CHAPTER 3

Personal Assistance Reforms in Sweden: breaking the assumption of dependency?

Susanne Berg

Introduction

In Sweden, personal assistance, and direct payments for such assistance, became a legislative right for a limited group of disabled people, through the enactment of the Support and Service Act, and the Support and Finance Act, in 1994. These legislative reforms were passed in 1993 to provide individual rights to ten different kinds of social services (SFS 1993: 387 section 9). This chapter focuses on one of these services, namely, personal assistance.

The paradigm shift, from dependency creating services in kind to 'independent living' cash payments, was not accepted by all political interests at the time and the future of the reforms is, therefore, hardly secure against tomorrow's political decisions. In the context of the Swedish welfare system, the goal of social justice is largely viewed in terms of the re-distribution of resources. More specifically, and in line with this general approach, the Swedish 'relative model of disability' has been developed to guide policy with respect to disabled people. This chapter will explore some of the main issues raised about the potential of the 1993 reforms to challenge the assumptions of dependency that surround disabled people.

In writing this chapter, use is made of various non-English, international sources that mostly use a different terminology to that advocated in Britain by organisations of disabled people (Oliver 1990). Furthermore, the discussion contains frequent excerpts from Swedish sources. These have been translated by the author, who has chosen to leave the Swedish terms *funktionshinder* and *handikapp* in direct quotations and elsewhere in the text. This is done because direct translation of Swedish terms can be rather confusing from a (British) social model perspective. *Funktionshinder* roughly corresponds with 'disability' as defined in the World Health Organization's (WHO 1980) *International Classification of Impairments, Disabilities and Handicaps* (ICIDH); while *handikapp* is equivalent to ICIDH's use of 'handicap'. Disability, according to ICIDH, is an incapacity, due to injury or disease, to perform activities in the manner or within the limits considered 'normal'. Handicap is the disadvantage an individual experiences when this incapacity prevents fulfilling of expected social roles.

Entitled consumers or empowered individuals?

The employment of personal assistants, and specifically using direct payments for this purpose, is a key issue for those promoting 'independent living' (Morris 1993) because, without it, disabled people who need help with everyday life activities, risk segregation and institutionalisation (Oliver 1990; Barnes 1991). Institutions are the 'ultimate human scrap-heaps' (UPIAS 1976:2) and disabled people fought against incarceration for decades (Hunt 1966) before the use of personal assistants for everyday tasks became a reality. In Sweden, the struggle for personal assistance was carried out, against a background of cluster housing and limiting home help services, in the 1980s. The hierarchic organisation of these developments prevented choice and control and made them into what the embryonic Swedish Independent Living Movement (ILM) defined as 'ambulatory' institutions (Ratzka 1986).

The assumption of dependency is the reason for, and the justification of, institutionalised services:

> When ... impairment means that there are things that someone cannot do for themselves, daily living tasks with which they need help, the assumption is that this person is 'dependent' (Morris 1993: 22).

Assumptions of dependency justify paternalism and communitarian-type services. Being classified as dependent implies that you are unable to make life choices and determine what is best for you. However, in contemporary society dependency is the norm and disabled people's dependency is not 'different in kind from the rest of the population but different in degree' (Oliver 1990: 84). To uphold control over disabled people, therefore, 'mainstream' society regards us, not as individuals with capacities, but as a group united by our incapacity thus separating us from non-disabled peers. The social model of disability challenges this assumption and contends that it is the organisation of services and wider societal structures that disables people with impairments. This approach underlines the contention that the individualistic medical model of disability correlates with the administrative paradigm for those in control of disability services and so justifies their continued power over disabled people (Finkelstein 1993).

While, in contrast, the ILM demands control and choice in everyday life as a human and civil right for disabled people (Ratzka 2003), and so embraces the full range of action to achieve those rights (Morris 1993). It is not therefore based on a single model of disability. Its philosophy therefore takes on different cloaks depending on the source of its advocacy. In the United States, where the ILM started, a key division exists between those concerned with service provision and those with civil rights.

> It is an interesting side note that many claim that California was the origin of both the demand for services and the fight for civil rights. They lump both together under the name of the Independent Living Movement. Others claim Massachusetts was the origin of both ... under the name of the Disability Rights Movement (Pfeiffer 1992: unpaged).

Once this split is recognised within the political struggle for political change, it is not surprising to find that arguments by supporters of the ILM range over both social justice and market discourses in promoting the importance of direct payments (Pearson 2000). Personal assistance is a 'bread and butter' issue and these tend to encourage a pragmatic stance. Ratzka (1986) applied a 'consumer perspective' from the start, and has been criticised for using this discourse without examining the possible consequences. This includes:

> a very real concern that responsibility for ensuring that needs are met will be abdicated to the vagaries of 'market forces' and the rationale of economic efficiency (Zarb 1989: 213).

At the same time, the source of this early criticism, Zarb, was one of the researchers on the British Council of Disabled People's study of cost and effectiveness of direct payments (Zarb and Nadash 1994), which incorporated arguments belonging to a market discourse.

Outside the group of disabled people who need personal assistance, empowerment through cash benefits remains a contentious issue between advocates for a more or less communitarian or autonomous principle behind organisation of social services. While, the communitarian view is based on a collectivistic ideal where the state impose certain moral principles on its citizens and so prevents undesirable life choices, the autonomous view is that the state should remain neutral to the life choices of its citizens (Rothstein 2002).

The conflict, between communitarian and autonomous ideals, is evident within debates on Swedish welfare (Rothstein 2002), where there has been a 'feminisation' of the social workforce and strong distributive trends (Esping-Andersen 1990). It also certainly exists between disabled people and non-disabled feminists (Morris 1991; Dalley 1996).

Disabled people view personal assistance and direct payments as the way of achieving empowerment for users of services. Feminists argue that direct payments will result in a flea market of 'care' that disempowers the predominantly female 'carers' and in the end destroys the quality of services provided (Ungerson 1997). However, many disabled activists are aware of the devastating effects that a totally free market can have on access to assistance. While maintaining that direct payments are 'about promoting collective responsibility for protecting individual rights' (Morris 1997: 60) some critics have expressed concerns over the trend towards turning personal assistance users into consumers.

A relative model for strategy and pragmatism

The legislative reforms implemented in 1994 are clearly located within the Swedish relative model of disability (Prop.1992/1993:159). Basically, the relative model can be described as a variant of ICIDH, subsequently revised as the *International Classification of Functioning, Disability and Health* (abbreviated as ICF) (WHO 1999). The Swedish terminology follows that of the original WHO scheme quite closely, although considerable confusion remains over the use of key terms such as 'disability' and 'handicap': for example, '*Funktionshinder* and *handikapp* are often used as synonyms' (Prop. 1992/1993:159: 52).

The relative model is usually said to date back to the 1960s, when Vilhelm Ekensteen's book - *On the back yard in the people's home* (1968) - was published. This appeared just two years after Paul Hunt's *Stigma* (1966), and also contains major criticisms of disabled people's socio-economic situation. However, the contributors to Hunt's anthology voice a perspective focused in disabled people's own experience, while Ekensteen, even though a disabled person active within disability politics discusses the issue from a general left-wing political perspective. Ekensteen's critique is above all concerned with the manifest inequalities within the division of welfare. His preferred remedy is a fairer distribution of income and wealth (Ekensteen 1968).

It can be argued that the differences between the social model and the relative model were present from the start. While the Union for the Physically Impaired Against Segregation (UPIAS 1976) continued with its development of the social interpretation of disability, the relative model quickly became integrated into the official disability policy of the Swedish state and annexed by the establishment. In 1976 the Official Parliamentary Report *Culture for Everybody* describes *handikapp* as follows:

> The word *handikapp* has different meanings. We use the word ... to characterise a person, who because of physical or psychological reasons, experiences more difficulties in daily life. Within this description lies the meaning that a *handikapp* is affected by the individual's living conditions, by the design of society ... it is not the injury itself we think of when we use the word ... but the consequences an injury can result in (SOU 1976:20: 45-50).

The social model clearly states that it is society that disables people with impairments; while in the Swedish viewpoint disability is relative, but remains fundamentally a consequence of injury or disease. Even if, the consequences can be limited and sometimes obliterated, the relative model does not cut the causality between impairment and disability as has been the case with the social model (Oliver 1990).

Instead, the relative model has been increasingly connected with ICIDH. Thus, Calais van Stokkom and Kebbon have claimed that 'a well-known application of the environmental relative' (1996: 35) model is also a feature of ICIDH since 'the individual is described in relation to the environment and its demands' (p. 37). The connection with ICIDH is reinforced and strengthened with its revision and reformulation as ICF. The Swedish Council for Working Life and Social Research (FAS), the main funding body for research in the area of disability, in its current programme for research on *funktionshinder* and *handikapp*, states that:

> the classification [has] now left an earlier hierarchical and disease orientated medical model of *funktionshinder*, which means that one identifies the problem within the individual ... Within another contrasting social model *funktionshinder* is mainly viewed as a socially created problem and principally a question of complete integration of individuals into society ... The present ICF is built on a combination of these two contradictory models, and tries to generate a more complex picture with an interactive model (FAS 2001: 17).

This move towards a more complex picture can, from a Swedish perspective, be traced back to Martin Söder's (1982) translation of ICIDH terminology. It has been argued that Söder was worried about the risk of socio-political passivity in a relative concept (Holme 1995). He believed that, if obstacles existed solely within the environment, very large, perhaps unreasonable levels of resources would be needed to achieve societal change at the expense of services aimed at individual needs. His aim with the recommended terminology was to identify needs or groups with special needs, to enable the channelling of resources to these groups, and to clarify the process creating these needs (Calais van Stokkom and Kebbon 1996).

Social justice as it is widely understood in Sweden is mainly concerned with promoting a more even distribution of income and wealth. From the start of modern welfare society in the 1930s, Keynesian economic theories encouraged the use of budget deficits to finance social reforms and create jobs in an expanding public sector (Esping-Andersen 1990; Holgersson 1992). This trend has been present throughout the development of the modern welfare state in Sweden. The primary remedy for social injustice and inequality has been policies to improve the distribution of resources through action in respect of the social insurance system, welfare benefits and social services.

This distributive paradigm underpins the relative model of disability, as this basically regards equality in terms of outcomes. This 'division of welfare' solution is certainly highlighted by Ekensteen (1968), who viewed disabled people as one of a number of vulnerable and disadvantaged groups, who are all referred to as *handikappade*.

> If the general public got its eyes opened to the principal similarity between the situation of physically *handikappade* and socially and economically *handikappade*, something would be won. People then would be freed from the fatal fixation with the seemingly inescapable role and identity, as *handikappade* and object for care, of the physically *handikappade*, i.e. in the conventional meaning *handikappade* (Ekensteen 1968: 30).

This also seems to be Söder's (1982) aim with his translation of terminology as a way of achieving a matrix of social reforms based on economic re-distribution.

The relative model offers a specific strategy rooted in pragmatism and flexibility, which places disability on an ever shifting line somewhere between the individual and the environment. It is a political tool to achieve rather than design social reforms. From a relative model perspective personal assistance through direct payments is a form of compensation for individual incapacities. It is also a compensation for obstacles of other kinds, not necessarily belonging to the personal sphere. The assumption of dependency is, therefore, not really questioned from a relative model perspective. And while reforms emphasising choice and control, as stressed by the ILM, can be argued from a relative model perspective, self-determination through choice and control is not necessarily an integral part of this approach.

Personal assistance in the Swedish reforms

Independent living as a legislative role-model
Independent living is unquestionably the philosophy behind the right to personal assistance in the 1994 reforms (Berg 2003). The Stockholm Co-operative of Independent Living (STIL) provided direct payments after reaching agreements with an increasing number of municipalities in the Stockholm area. Other Independent Living Co-operatives were up and running in different areas of the country. A direct payment for personal assistance was becoming a more widely accepted solution. Indeed, STIL was identified in the government bill as an 'interesting attempt to create alternatives to home help services and increase freedom of choice for disabled people' (Prop. 1992/1993:159: 45). Freedom of choice and integrity were emphasised as the most important concepts within disability policy.

> It is obvious that the welfare state sometimes has shown altogether too little consideration for the wishes of the individual. Also, disabled people and their families must gain greater control over their own lives (Prop. 1992/1993: 159: 43).

The philosophy behind independent living is indubitably centred on a concept of autonomy. At the core of the ILM, irrespective of other national differences, are principles such as self-determination, self-respect, peer support, empowerment and risk-taking (ILRU 1999). This individualistic view of rights and duties is thoroughly incompatible with the previous organisation of social services in Sweden. Historically, social services belonged to the 'care' category and were organised on communitarian ideas. However, during recent decades, there has been a shift towards a greater balance between communitarian and autonomous ideals (SOU 1990:44; Rothstein 2002).

This view of the relationship between democracy and societal organisation is echoed in the Parliamentary Report on which the government bill is based. It states that:
> every political system must find a point of balance between, on the one hand a collectivist democratic ideal protecting the rights of the majority to enforce their will, and on the other hand, a democratic ideal centred on the individual, which protects the right to self-determination (SOU 1991:46: 99).

The right to personal assistance might be taken from the ILM's concept of choice and control, but a closer investigation shows that both ideals of communitarian and autonomous services co-exist within the scope of reform. The law addresses the needs of a limited section within the disabled population, namely individuals assessed as having extensive and permanent impairments. The Minister responsible for this legislation stated that:
> the majority of persons with *funktionshinder* already should be able to have their needs for support and services satisfied within the framework of regulations contained within the more general legislation (Prop. 1992/1993:159: 54).

Personal assistance is, then, only granted to a smaller sub-group, those with essential needs of at least one of the following kind: 'help' with intimate hygiene, eating, dressing or undressing, communicating, or other essential needs which require thorough knowledge about the impairment. This means that the vast majority of disabled people still does not have any explicit right to choice and control, and receives services of the old custodial kind.

A continuing question is whether the right to choice and control in the Swedish reforms is intended to break the disabling assumption of dependency. Arguments for personal assistance given in the bill are found:
- in the area of integrity, as assistance in very private situations;
- in connection with compensatory measures on account of disease or impairment, as in rehabilitative training; and
- in connection with compensation for disabling barriers, as in avoiding isolation or enabling work or education (Prop 1992/1993:159).

The general argument from the individual to the societal levels is more compatible with the relative model of disability than it is with the social model's attack on assumptions of dependency and incapacity. These arguments also demonstrate the relative model's fondness for compensating needs, connected to all levels in the ICIDH, that is, impairment, disability and handicap, by measures contained within the welfare solution to the division of wealth.

When advocating for change, there is nothing as powerful as using an example of very bad practice, and this was provided by the Parliamentary Disability Commission's Status Report in 1990.

> In the interview enquiry, conducted by the Centre for Disability Research at Uppsala University on behalf of the Disability Commission, different obstacles for influence are listed. These comprise professionalism turning into paternalism, inflexible regulatory systems, the organisation of services, and social conceptions of *handikapp* (Prop. 1992/1993:159: 44).

Only eight percent of the respondents could decide who would provide services within the Swedish home help system. It is probably safe to say that evidence of poor standards within existing services is the main reason behind the demand for assistance, not an analysis of the disabling nature of the assumption of dependency, nor a will to provide autonomous services as a result of such analysis.

The fondness for communitarianism and the obsession with employment

Swedish politics exist within a culture of negotiation. Government bills are debated in parliamentary committees before reaching the final vote in the Chamber. The Parliamentary Committee for Social Affairs and Welfare dealt with several private member bills related to the government bill. The Private Member's Bill SoU18 by social democrats Bo Holmgren et al. (Bet. 1992/1993 SoU19) expresses support for reform but advocates above all the need to protect the general welfare system.

> [I]n countries which have chosen more selective politics, where special solutions for *handikappade* are prioritised at the expense of more universal measures, persons with *funktionshinder* are in a much worse situation than in Sweden (Bet. 1992/1993 SoU19).

Another Private Member's Bill So245 by social democrats Jan Andersson et al. (Bet. 1992/1993 SoU19) argued that 'freedom of choice' should not be simply a question of freedom for producers of services to choose. Instead the importance of co-operatives and experiences from disabled people's own projects like STIL and GIL should be disseminated (Bet. 1992/1993 SoU19).

Empowerment as promoted by the ILM is not really compatible with mainstream social democratic ideology. Admittedly, there was a group within social democracy in the beginning of the 1990s that called for 'self-empowerment', but this was very different from the concept of freedom of choice for the individual. 'Self-empowerment' was fundamentally concerned with the decentralisation of decision making that allowed small groups of workers control over their working conditions. It was about taking power together, as in a co-operative organisation (Trägårdh 1999), and the co-operative organisation of the Swedish ILM should not be underestimated. It possibly tipped the scale in favour of personal assistance more than once. The Parliamentary Committee, reflecting the Conservative-Liberal majority of the chamber, rejected the suggestions of these Private Members' Bills (1992/1993 SoU19).

The emphasis on employment and the labour market as central to the welfare state is a key factor underpinning the concept of 'self-empowerment'. Swedish style democracy is about power over working conditions, and this power is executed collectively. The organisation of work has been identified as the chief disabling mechanism in society (Oliver 1990; Gleeson 1997) and the importance of labour is not just emphasised within capitalism but also by the political left (Abberley 1997). Disabled people ousted from the labour market are perceived as burdens and this perception is the central basis for the assumption of dependency.

> One has sometimes described the dominant conception of persons with *funktionshinder* as an idea about 'eternal childhood'. They are perceived as children; dependent on the help and support of others and therefore incapable of self-determination and an independent life (SOU 1990:19, 372).

From the late 1960s onwards in Sweden, the responsibility for this 'burden' was shifted from the family to the social welfare system. A further contemporary political influence was created by the wave of female labour entering the labour market due to both economic and integrative forces (SOU 1990:44; Holgersson 1992). However, it is argued that, the male role (as primary provider) and the associated organisation of the labour market was never questioned or changed. The result was that when women entered the labour market they were mainly located within the newly organised public sector, which had taken over the 'caring' role of the family (SOU 1990:44). The stark divide between the private and public spheres was broken down but women continued to undertake the 'caring' tasks although now in a paid capacity.

It can be argued that the compensatory dimension to the Swedish welfare system allows its citizens to escape being economically dependent on the family but does little to break assumptions connected with dependent social roles. If this is true of policy measures for gender equality, it is also present in the 1994 reforms. Entry into the labour market is the main priority and the welfare system is the central means by which this is turned into reality.

The right to parenthood, and the right to associated supportive measures, displays in an interesting way the remaining assumptions connected with gender equality and disability, as well as the emphasis on employment. The reforms clearly state that personal assistance should not assume the ordinary duties connected to parenthood or the responsibilities of child-care and schools for disabled children. However, when a child has extensive 'care needs' then personal assistance should be granted.

> Both parents shall, if they want to, be able to remain in gainful employment, shall have the same possibilities as other parents to maintain friendships and cultivate interests outside the family (Prop. 1992/1993:159, 44).

It is clear that this 'parental assistance', to non-disabled parents, is aimed at alleviating the 'burden' of having a disabled child. The family unit is the priority and emphasis is placed on the importance of adapting this form of support to the individual family and in so doing provides parents with a decisive influence over the assistance given.

> The aim with assistance [in these cases] is often to satisfy parents' need for relief of care or to provide the family with possibilities to carry out activities in which the child does not participate (Prop. 1992/1993:159, 66).

Though the wording of the Swedish reforms is gender neutral, it is safe to say that this is a measure to prevent female economic dependency on male providers. It is another tool for eroding the barrier between the private and public spheres, while doing relatively little to alter traditional social roles (SOU 1990:44). Thus, it belongs to what feminists identify as the 'ideology of familism' in 'care' policies (Dalley 1996), which stresses the 'caring', nurturing role of women, or more correctly, non-disabled women. The reforms clearly aim to allow parents (mothers) the right to paid employment. A secondary aim is to give support to the family, so it will stay together and continue taking basic responsibility for a disabled child.

Disabling assumptions behind the reforms

The assumption of dependency around disabled people constitutes us as asexual, child-like, and therefore unfit for parenthood (Shakespeare et al. 1996). Thus, the question of disabled parents only entered the Swedish reform process after the Council of Legislation's review of the proposed reforms. And even then, it did not address the assistance needed to fulfil the parental role. Instead, the argument for granting personal assistance to disabled parents is based on the emotional and developmental needs of the child during its formative years.

> First, a child is gradually able to develop an understanding about her/himself and relate to other persons. It is, therefore, important for the child's development that it, during this time, can have its essential needs met by only a limited number of adults. If any of the parents have personal assistance, it is in my opinion natural that the assistant, if he or she is suited for this ... should also help the parent with the care he or she cannot provide him/herself. This does of course not exclude the possibility that the child may have need for other or additional support (Prop. 1992/1993:159, 66).

It is clear that parenthood is not expected of disabled people. Personal assistance is not granted for activities performed as a consequence of fulfilling the social role of being a 'caring' and 'competent' disabled parent. When a child is mature enough to be able to 'handle close relations outside a limited circle', or if disabled people do not have assistance needs (as defined by the legislation) except in their parental role, support is provided through the general welfare system (Prop.1992/1993,159). The reforms do not address the assumption of dependency in the context of a disabled person's right to parenthood. 'A child's need for care is principally not a task for the personal assistant of the parent' (Prop. 1992/1993:159, 178).

Another life situation where personal assistance was not considered necessary was 'old age':

> An important aim with personal assistance should be to achieve conditions for persons with extensive lifelong or prolonged *funktionshinder*, which are equivalent to those of people of a similar age. Therefore, I mean that the right to personal assistance should be limited to persons who have not reached the general retirement age, 65 years (Prop 1992/1993:159, 64).

The reasons for this are mainly economic – certainly at the time when the legislation was introduced. However, a survey, conducted for the National Board of Health and Welfare after the first five years of the reforms, showed that losing the right to personal assistance at the age of 65 'meant support of a lesser extent and lower quality for many of those concerned' (Prop. 2000/2001: 5, 9). One consequence was that further legislation was passed to grant those already receiving personal assistance the right to keep this after reaching 65 years, although it was limited to the existing level of support.

As has been shown, personal assistance in the 1994 reforms is not really intended for older (disabled) people, for disabled parents, or for disabled children, unless their 'care' need is extensive enough to disturb their parents' ability to work. It appears that the priority given to paid employment and labour market concerns extends to the area of disabled people of working age, while the assumption of dependency remains secure.

Conclusion

The social model, as outlined by UPIAS (1976), cut the causal link between impairment and disability and instead focused on analysing the 'disabling society'. This provided a mechanism for understanding where the responsibility lies for the social exclusion of people with impairments. It also emphasises that reforms must address disablement across all areas of social life. The Swedish relative model offers a different analytical approach. Responsibility for disablement is regarded as flexible and this highlights the potential value of limited reforms without contradicting assumptions within conventional explanations of disability.

Personal assistance, in the recent Swedish experience, is based on the relative model's flexible view, and aims at compensating assistance needs linked with all levels of the ICIDH: whether injury or disease, resulting functional incapacity, or disabling conditions due to environmental factors. While it is certainly true that personal assistance enables some disabled to board the 'accessible' subway in Stockholm, this does not address the basic assumptions of dependency directed at disabled people generally.

This assumption underpins a view of disabled people as child-like and incapable. It reinforces the principle of a need for 'care', as in 'taking care of' instead of 'caring for', and confirms orthodox ideals of service provision by a variety of (professional) experts. The ILM principle of self-determination has resulted in demands for services controlled and run by users is based on the opposite ideal of 'independence' and autonomy. As argued above, the Swedish right to personal assistance was enacted, not primarily as a right to self-determination for disabled people, but more as a necessary political remedy to the miserable conditions experienced by disabled people within the municipal home help services of the time. A general welfare system, built on a high taxation level, has to create sufficiently equal living conditions, otherwise the whole system risks losing its legitimacy. The reforms of 1994 bridged the welfare gap within social service provision for a specific section of the disabled population but did not break the underlying assumptions of dependence. Disabled people outside this 'privileged' minority are still receiving services based on traditional communitarian ideals.

Swedish welfare policy is built around an emphasis on employment and breaking down the wall between the private and public domains. Thus, it should not be surprising that legislation applied the same criteria when considering changes in the area of personal assistance. Consequently, personal assistance for disabled children is clearly aimed at making gainful employment possible for non-disabled parents (a gender issue), almost to the point of their self-determination being the priority. At the same time, personal assistance for disabled people is not regarded as a general, human right. In childhood, it does not replace measures within day care and schools; in parenthood, it is not granted as part of the parental role; and in older age, it is only provided at the level awarded when a person was sixty-five.

It can, therefore, be argued that the weakness of reforms based on the relative model and the continuing assumption of dependency may generate future problems. Compensating disabling barriers through personal assistance may lead to rocketing costs within the social security system. Continuing disabling mechanisms in the employment sector may prevent disabled people entering the labour market in spite of policy support and assistance. This creates a political climate where the value of reforms may be questioned. In the current economic context, where other groups such as older disabled people live under horrendous conditions, advocates of traditional communitarian services may gain general support. Whether disabled people in Sweden are moving forwards on the road to self-determination or going backwards towards the municipal scrap heap remains to be seen.

Bibliography

Abberley, P. 1997: The Limits of Classical Social Theory in the Analysis and Transformation of Disablement. In L. Barton and M. Oliver (eds.), ***Disability Studies: Past, Present and Future***. Leeds: The Disability Press.

Barnes, C. 1991: ***Disabled People in Britain and Discrimination***. London: Hurst and Co., in association with British Council of Organisation of Disabled People.

Berg, S. 2003: *Personal Assistance in Sweden*. Stockholm: Independent Living Institute (http://www.independentliving.org/docs/wrfmono.pdf) Accessed on 18.03.2004.

Bet. 1992/1993 SoU19: *Stöd och service till vissa funktionshindrade*, Stockholm: Rixlex (http://www.riksdagen.se/debatt/bet_yttr/index.asp) Accessed on 05.01.2004. (*Report from the Parliamentary Standing Committee for Social Affairs and Welfare*, 1992/1993 SoU19)

Calais van Stokkom, S. and Kebbon, L. 1996: Handikappbegreppet. In M. Tideman (ed.), *Funktionshinder & Handikapp*. Stockholm: Johansson & Skyttmo Förlag.

Dalley, G. 1996: *Ideologies of Caring: Rethinking Community and Collectivism*, (2nd edn.). Basingstoke: Macmillan.

Ekensteen, V. 1968: *På folkhemmets bakgård*. Stockholm: Verdandi Debatt. (On the backyard in the people's home).

Esping-Andersen, G. 1990: *The Three Worlds of Welfare Capitalism*. Princeton: Princeton University Press.

FAS 2001: *Program för forskning om funktionshinder och handikapp*. Stockholm: FAS. (http://www.fas.forskning.se/omfas/program/handikapp.pdf) Accessed on 23.02.2003.

Finkelstein, V. 1993: Disability: a social challenge or an administrative responsibility? In J. Swain, V. Finkelstein, S. French and M. Oliver (eds), *Disabling Barriers - Enabling Environments*. London: Sage. (http://www.leeds.ac.uk/disability-studies/archiveuk/archframe.htm) Accessed on 02.02.2002.

Gleeson, B. 1997: Disability history: a historical materialist view. *Disability and Society*, 12 (2), 179-202.

Holgersson, L. 1992: *Socialtjänst*, Sixth Rev.edn. Stockholm: Tidens förlag.

Holme, L. 1995: Begrepp om handikapp. En essä om det miljörelativa handikappbegreppet. In M. Tideman (ed.), *Handikapp - synsätt, principer, perspektiv*. Stockholm: Johansson & Skyttmo Förlag.

Hunt, P. 1966: *Stigma: The Experience of Disability*. London: Geoffrey Chapman.

ILRU 1999: *Washington Declaration*. Houston: Independent Living Research Utilization (http://www.ilru.org/summit/1-declaration.htm) Accessed on 24.03.2004.

Morris, J. 1991: *Pride against Prejudice*. London: Women's Press.

Morris, J. 1993: *Independent Lives? Community Care and Disabled People*. Basingstoke: Macmillan.
Morris, J. 1997: Care or Empowerment? A disability rights Perspective. *Social Policy and Administration*, 31 (1), 54-60.
Oliver, M. 1990: *The Politics of Disablement*. Basingstoke: Macmillan.
Pearson, C. 2000: Money Talks? Competing Discourses in the Implementation of Direct Payments. *Critical Social Policy*, 20 (4), 459-477.
Pfeiffer, D. 1992: Division in the Disability Community. In DPI's Independent Living Committee, *Resource Kit for Independent Living Tools for Power*. European Network on Independent Living (http://www.enil.eu.com/tools/tools.pdf) Accessed on 16.03.2004.
Prop. 1992/93:159: *Stöd och service till vissa funktionshindrade* Stockholm: Allmänna förlaget (*Government proposal 1992/93:159, Support and service to persons with certain functional impairments*).
Prop. 2000/2001: 5: *Personal Assistance to persons over 65* Stockholm: Rixlex (http://www.riksdagen.se/debatt/propositioner/index.asp) Accessed on 05.01.2004.
Ratzka, A.1986: *Independent Living and Attendant Care in Sweden: a consumer perspective*. Stockholm: Independent Living Institute (http://www.independentliving.org/docs/wrfmono.pdf) Accessed on 07.01.2002.
Ratzka, A. 2003: *Independent Living: A Personal Definition*. Stockholm: Independent Living Institute
(http://www.independentliving.org/def.html)
Accessed on 17.02.2003.
Rothstein, B. 2002: *Vad bör staten göra?* (2nd edn.). Stockholm: SNS Förlag.
SFS 1993:387: *Lag om stöd och service till vissa funktionshindrade*. Notisum (http://www.notisum.se/) Accessed on 24.02.2004. (*Support and Service Act, SFS 1993:387*)
Shakespeare, T., Gillespie-Sells, K. and Davies, D. 1996: *The Sexual Politics of Disability*. London: Cassell.
Söder, M. 1982: *Handikappbegreppet - en analys utifrån WHO:s terminologi och svensk debatt*, Stockholm: Socialdepartementet.
SOU 1976:20: *Kultur åt alla*, Stockholm: Allmänna Förlaget (*Report from Parliamentary Commission on Culture - Culture for Everybody*).
SOU 1990:44: *Demokrati och makt i Sverige*, Stockholm: Allmänna Förlaget (*Report from Parliamentary Commission on Democracy - Democracy and Power in Sweden*).

SOU 1991:46: ***Handikapp Välfärd Rättvisa***, Stockholm: Allmänna förlaget (*Report from Parliamentary Commission on Disability - Handicap Welfare Justice*).

Trägårdh, L. 1999: ***Bemäktiga individerna***. Stockholm: Independent Living Institute (http://www.independentliving.org/docs3/bemaktiga.pdf) Accessed on 29.03.2004.

Ungerson, C. 1997: Give Them the Money: Is Cash a Route to Empowerment? ***Social Policy and Administration***, 31 (1), 45-53.

UPIAS 1976: ***Policy Statement***. London: UPIAS. (http://www.leeds.ac.uk/disability-studies/archiveuk/archframe.htm) Accessed on 01.02.2002.

WHO 1980: ***International Classification of Impairments, Disabilities and Handicaps***. Geneva: World Health Organization.

WHO 1999: ***International Classification of Functioning, Disability and Health***. Geneva: World Health Organization.

Zarb, G. 1989: Independent Living and Attendant Care in Sweden: A Consumer Perspective. ***Disability, Handicap and Society***, 4 (2), 209-214.

Zarb, G. and Nadash, P. 1994: ***Cashing in on Independence: Comparing the Costs and Benefits of Cash and Services***. Belper: British Council of Organisations of Disabled People.

CHAPTER 4

Pupil or 'Patient': difference, disability and education in France

Felicity Armstrong

This chapter attempts to use the social model and the medical model as contrasting lenses through which to begin to analyse the French education system and how it responds to 'difference'. My starting point is an interest in the processes of exclusion and inclusion in education, in their many and disparate forms. These processes do not begin and end in easily identifiable ways. They are historically rooted and spread into all aspects of social, economic and political life, so it is impossible to draw a boundary around something called 'the education system' and to treat it as separate from the broader landscapes of social life. This is quite clearly demonstrated in France where some disabled children and young people are 'not counted' as being members of the education system at all. They are denied the social role of 'pupil' on the grounds of impairment and deficit-driven perceptions of difference. The French regional newspaper *la Dépêche du Midi* (26.01.03) challenges this exclusion of disabled people:

> Because of impairment, many children continue to experience forms of discrimination and rejection and their education is restricted and considered as of secondary importance. How can we energise the system and awake the collective conscience? Must we legally force institutions to practice integration? What is the credibility of a school which excludes (children) at the same time as it claims to be against exclusion?

Citing Charles Gardou, director of the department of education at the Université Lumière, Lyons, the article continues:

> Today there are 40,000 children who are not receiving education, which means that the right to education for all is not yet assured

in this country, for we are (locked into) a culture of *intention; we do not act*. What right have we to deprive anyone of the right to knowledge? We should allow every person to develop in their own way: two children who (happen to) have the same impairment, are not *the same*. Everybody is unique. (*my emphasis*)

Practices of removal

The act of assessment and diagnosis is a routine part of practices of removal and the construction of disabling barriers to participation in ordinary social life. These barriers are socially produced and spatially legitimated. They do not emanate from the characteristics of individual children or young people – on the contrary, they are derived from societal attitudes, power relations and particular constructions of privileged knowledge. They are linked to financial imperatives and bureaucratic rigmarole, to narrow constructions of normality embedded in psychological testing, to the design and organisation of the environment and to the shortcomings of education systems.

Although I focus particularly on the *external* structures and processes of exclusion here, the interpretation of the social model I am drawing on recognises the importance of the interplay between the 'public' and the 'private' which provides depth of meaning to the notion of exclusion. This relates to the social relational model of disability (Thomas 1999) described as including:

> both structural and psycho-emotional dimensions of disability (in which) disability is seen as a form of social oppression that operates at both the public and personal levels, affecting what people can *do* as well as who they can *be* (Reeve 2004:83).

In France – as elsewhere – the exclusion of disabled children and young people has a profound effect on what it means for those who make up the school population to be a pupil, or rather it defines what a school pupil can *be*. The values and assumptions underpinning the exclusion of any group of students for whatever reason, infuse the cultures, practices and student identities in all schools, implicitly and complicity, not least in terms of the imposition of particular versions of normality and particular models of humanity and citizenship.

> Disabled children are confronted on a daily basis with ways of speaking about disability that influence their experience and their sense of identity. Negative portrayals of disability abound and disabled children in particular have been subject to

institutional discourses of tragedy, medicalization and otherness (Priestley 1999: 93).

These processes affect the world-view of *all* members of the community, including those of pupils in schools in which disabled children are absent.

There is currently a major reappraisal of the education system taking place in France, encompassing a wide span of sectors including all age ranges and higher education, as well as its aims and values. In 1999 the 'plan Handiscol' - an initiative focusing on education and disabled children and adolescents - was established, managed by the ministère de l'éducation nationale (the Department of Education) in close collaboration with the ministère de l'Emploi et de la Solidarité (the Department of Employment and Solidarity). Its purpose is to improve the education system and, in particular, the widening the participation of disabled children and young people in ordinary education settings. This has provided a forum for debate and the development of policy, as well as more immediate initiatives such as the setting up of a national information helpline for the families of disabled children which provides information and advice about rights and services.

The Handiscol initiative has made an important contribution to the wider debate on issues relating to education and the rights of disabled children. This debate has clarified distinctions between a 'soft' approach which sees widening participation in ordinary schools as 'desirable' and the more deeply political position which problematizes issues in ways which are more challenging to dominant policies and assumptions. Plaisance (2005) cites the example of the position taken by the Association for Disabled Adults and Young People (Association pour adultes et jeunes handicapés - the APAJH) which has systematically opposed the way in which 'integration' has been presented in official texts in terms of being 'desirable' or something to be 'favoured' rather than as an obligation. The APAJH argues that disability issues should not be posed in terms of *integration*, which presupposes that a disabled person is an 'outsider' or 'comes from the outside', but that questions should be situated within a critical debate about exclusion. An important consequence of this is the affirmation of the right of education *for all*, and the obligation placed on schools to recognise this. This position necessarily poses the necessity of a concrete realisation of the fundamental principle of 'equalisation' at all levels, including in terms of support and the transformation of the environment (Plaisance 2005).

An important piece of legislation relating to disabled people is being discussed by parliament – the law concerning 'Equality of rights, opportunities, participation and citizenship of disabled people' (*Pour l'égalité des droits et des chances, la participation et la citoyenneté des personnes handicapées*). The proposals under discussion are based around 4 main principles:

- Freedom to choose for disabled people in terms of home, family, social and professional life so that their desires and aspirations are respected.
- The right to 'compensation' for 'the consequences whatever they are of disability' and to provide the financial conditions for disabled people to live autonomously 'with dignity'.
- The right to participate in social life, including providing access to education, employment, buildings and transport.
- The simplification of procedures and the setting up of a system of advice and personal guidance which will allow disabled children and their families straightforward access to new opportunities and possibilities.

If the changes in opportunities and practices which work their way into people's lives reflect the principles outlined above, they are to be welcomed. However, there are two important issues which require consideration. Firstly, it appears that although all children have a right to be enrolled in a school in their neighbourhood, it does not follow that they will not then be placed in a special school if there are 'explicit and recognised reasons for doing so'. Secondly, there are questions which need to be raised about the notion of compensation when this is couched in terms of offsetting the effects of impairment rather than removing the practical barriers to participation, although the proposals *are* explicitly concerned to 'compensate' for these by removing structural and financial barriers. One embedded assumption underpinning the notion of compensation for *impairment*, rather than in response to *institutionalised discrimination*, is that it locates the 'problem' within the individual rather than within society. Historically, this 'individual model' has been closely associated with segregated special education, and this is often still the case (Boxall 2002). There appears to be a blurring of the two positions in current debates: society has a duty to compensate individuals on the basis of their impairments *and* remove structural and financial barriers to participation.

In the sections which follow I will explain how I am interpreting the medical and social models of disability and examine their usefulness in understanding the history and processes of inclusion and exclusion in the French system. In the context of this chapter, 'implementing' the social model means using it as an approach to exploring and providing fresh insights for understanding and interpreting.

The advent of the medical

I will take as my starting point Bill Hughes' description of the medical model and its origins:

> For disabled people the legacy of modernity was one of invalidation. This originated in the processes that excluded 'impaired labour power' from the work-force and in medical systems of classification in which disability came to mean a 'faulty' or abnormal body. A disabled person was a victim of that cruel whim of nature or circumstance and became the kind of person that her body allowed her to be. The barriers to citizenship, to living a full and active life, were - tragically and unfortunately - physical and internal. The ontological essence of disability was impairment. For example, with respect to people with mobility impairments, the medical model suggests that 'their immobility is their own fault or the consequence of deviant corporeality which requires medical care, or, failing that, the application of charitable works' (Imrie 2000: 1652). (Hughes 2002: 63).

The history and organisation of responses to impairment in France in many ways demonstrate this description very clearly. With the development during the nineteenth century of modern, industrialised approaches to managing masses of people, and the rise and rise in the status of the physical sciences and the medical professions, the identification and care and control of those who were deemed 'unproductive', disturbing, destitute, criminal or sick, led to increasing numbers of people being brought together to be treated and managed.

Responses to disability, difference and non-conforming others have, historically, included the systematic segregation of groups of people from the rest of society. In 1793 Philippe Pinel released eighty-nine 'lunatics' from their shackles and began to 'treat' them, marking a move away from a purely custodial model towards a medical model of care and treatment. This event was symbolic in that it heralded an epoch of diagnosis and the categorization of conditions and impairments and the use of these categories as a basis for placement and therapy. The twin projects of management and care, which became increasingly mediated by the state, continue to coexist as social and political responses to difference in all so-called 'western' societies today. These responses are, in turn, formulated and rationed, explained and rationalised, according to changing values, variations in political climate and in the light of different agendas and decisions about the use of resources.

Pinel's work ushered in new practices of care and therapy, based on a changed perception of difference in which the person was no longer regarded as possibly dangerous, out-of-control, useless, the subject of derision, but as an individual human being whose difficulties could be reduced through the application of medicines and therapies (Armstrong 1996).

The importance of understanding historical developments with all their discontinuities and contradictions as one means of illuminating current practices and struggles cannot be underestimated. Today in France placements of children in particular institutions designated for some conditions or impairments may still require a medical prescription. Similarly, in England, medical assessments frequently still play a major part in procedures relating to assessment and educational placements.

Mass, compulsory primary education was introduced in France in 1882 and later extended to the secondary stage. The special institutions which were set up separately from the state education system had primarily therapeutic or medical aims. This division between an education system for pupils and a separate medico-social network of structures and professions destined to contain, care for and treat 'patients' - children and young people classified as having an impairment, or being socially deficient or difficult to control - has characterized the French system for well over a century and presents a monolithic obstacle to change. This obstacle exists at a number of levels, including:

- The rigidity of the education system in terms of its organization, curriculum and ethos.
- The existence of legislation, in which policies made in one domain are contradicted by existing legislation and practices in another (e.g. policies made concerning education may be overridden by unchanged policies and structures in health and social services).
- Attitudes in which impairment-led ways of seeing are legitimized by the continued placement of many disabled children in institutions outside the education system.
- At the level of teacher professional development. Teachers working

in specialized settings, either within the education system, or outside it – receive specialist, impairment based training in 'special education' or a named impairment, while the professional development of mainstream teachers does not prepare them to teach a wide diversity of learners or to work in multi-disciplinary teams.

These socially produced 'separations' illustrate the argument contained in the social model that material, cultural and systemic conditions create inequalities and barriers to participation and are based on an individual-deficit view of difference. The social model as described by Barnes (2003) can help us to understand the contingent, socially produced nature of barriers to participation in the French context because it draws attention to:

> the economic, environmental and cultural barriers encountered by people viewed by others as having some form of impairment. These include inaccessible education, information and communication systems, working environments, inadequate disability benefits, discriminatory health and social support services, inaccessible transport, houses and public buildings and amenities, and the devaluing of disabled people through negative images in the media – films, television and newspapers (Barnes 2003: 9).

Inclusion and exclusion in education

The situation in France is illustrative of the irreconcilability of the medical and social models. It represents the antithesis of, for example, the principles of inclusive education embodied in the Salamanca Statement (1994) which proclaims:

> Schools should accommodate all children regardless of their physical, intellectual, emotional, social, linguistic or other condition (Article 3).
> Regular schools with this inclusive orientation are the most effective means of combating discriminatory attitudes, creating welcoming communities, building an inclusive society and achieving education for all (Article 2).

The exclusion of disabled children and young people from education has been the focus of legislation at different stages since the passing in June 1975 of the *Loi d'Orientation en Faveur des Personnes Handicapées* which purported to present 'handicap' – as a social disadvantage, rather than an individual deficit. During the period between 1950 and 1970 there was a proliferation in the large network of 'médico-educatif' establishments outside the education system. By 1975 there was a general awareness that this system segregated young disabled people from the rest of the community. In response to this change in attitude the *Loi d'Orientation en Faveur des Personnes Handicapées* declared the right to social integration of all children, young people and adults identified as having physical, sensory or mental disabilities. It recorded the right to education, training, work and financial support and laid down the structural and procedural changes which would enable and facilitate increased participation of children and young people in ordinary schools. The law stated that children should where possible be admitted to ordinary schools 'in spite of their handicap'. However, the large and complex network of special schools and institutions and the intractable nature of the ordinary school ethos and curriculum remained, acting as a major barrier in terms of breaking down old systems and practices.

A report on the education of disabled children and adults in France published by the Directorate of Research and Evaluation and Statistical Studies (DREES 2003), headed by representatives from the Ministries of Education and Social Affairs and Health, contains some illuminating material. One point that is made is the difficulty in obtaining accurate information concerning disabled children who live at home and do not attend schools run by the Ministry for Education. There is unease that some children may be untraceable in terms of whether they receive any formal education at all, and what this may comprise.

The statutory starting age for formal education is six. In practice, education usually enrols at three or four years of age with over 95 per cent of children attending nursery schools which are free, and an integral part of the education system. At this stage the gates open wide and many children participate in ordinary groups, but are later removed to specialist settings. Approximately 52,000 disabled children and young people are integrated on an individual basis in ordinary schools, and 50,000 attend specialist classes or units within the education system, but the vast majority of these are in the primary sector because there are very few specialist units at the secondary level. When the professionals involved consider that placement in the ordinary education system is 'not possible' children are directed towards the medical-social structures, outside the education system. It is difficult, perhaps impossible, to actually gather together information about the whereabouts of children in the system. However, according to the DREES report, 115,000 children attend medical-social institutions and only 58 per cent of these receive a full-time education.

17 per cent are integrated into ordinary schools run by the Ministry for Education on a full or part-time basis. Nearly 25 per cent of disabled children who attend settings outside the state education system, are not 'scolarisé' - that is to say, from a formal point of view they are not receiving any schooling; this percentage reaches 94 per cent for children and young people who have what are described as multiple impairments, and 78 per cent of children deemed to have severe learning difficulties. In theory, parents have the right to insist that their child attends an ordinary school but, it appears, this is rarely evoked or exercised. A deeply embedded system of support and guidance and the omnipotent weight of professional opinion all work against the empowerment of families and children themselves in the decision-making process.

Researching structures

One of the difficulties in trying to understand a whole mass of social structures, values and practices as they work together to produce the social conditions and relations in which inclusions and exclusions occur, is the challenge of recognizing the unevenness of the terrain and the contradictions and discontinuities which arise. In my research in France between 1997-2000 into the ways in which policies are interpreted and make their way through systems, I explored policies and practices in a number of different schools and institutions in an attempt to understand the processes through which children and young people find themselves in one setting rather than another. The three settings briefly discussed below represent very different perceptions and values regarding rights, difference and disability, and show some of the possible extreme contradictions which can co-exist within one national system. Some of the material in this section is taken from my earlier research - *Spaced Out: Policy, Difference and the Challenge of Inclusion* (Armstrong 2003) where a fuller description and discussion of the settings can be found. In the account below, I have decided to use the terminology which is used in the different contexts themselves and which is recorded in the transcripts I made, although it should be borne in mind that I have translated this into English. I have put extracts taken directly from the interview material in quotation marks. The purpose of preserving the discourses used is to indicate the pervasive use of medical or pathologizing labels and their embeddedness in particular settings, as well as to show examples in which alternative values and interpretations are at work. It is particularly interesting to note the contrast in the ways children and young people are perceived in the different settings through the lens of the discourses used and the contrast between the 'medical' and the 'social'.

The 'Hôpital Sainte Thérèse', a large medical complex, is the site for the National Institute for Re-adaptation (Institut National de Réadaptation). All the children who attend the Institute at the Hôpital Sainte Thérèse have been admitted to the hospital for medical treatment. Those who are well enough and old enough are enrolled in educational programmes. The National Institute for Re-adaptation has three distinct sections, A, B and C. Service A is for children who have 'suffered some kind of brain injury as a result of accident or a stroke or after an operation for a tumour'. The orthopaedic service - Service B - is designated for children who have all kinds of problems relating to 'congenital orthopaedic pathologies requiring a programme of re-education with a great deal of physiotherapy which can only take place in a hospital'. Sector C is 'for children who have suffered neurological problems from birth, including cerebral palsy or other congenital neurological problems which are hereditary in origin and are usually very seriously handicapped - often paraplegic, or tetraplegic, without speech and with very restricted motor control'.

The school provides education for children from all three services. Approximately 160-170 children and young people are patients at the National Institute for Re-adaptation and about 140 of those are on the role in the school or attend the kindergarten. The others are not deemed well enough to receive education. While in the past, the period of care at the centre could be anything up to twelve or thirteen years, this period has been reduced to between four weeks and four years. There is residential provision for children requiring 24-hour medical care and for those whose homes are some distance away from the centre.

As far as the teaching staff at the centre are concerned, their role is primarily educational and, while differences between students are taken into account including the effects of any impairment, the curriculum and teaching are based on what goes on in ordinary state schools (in contrast to the third French setting discussed in this chapter). Teachers at the centre are fully qualified teachers and have additional specialist training. Other members of staff who work there are also highly specialized in different therapeutic disciplines.

The second setting, the 'Lycée Bresson', is a large secondary school which is part of the state education system. At the time of my visit there were 250 students at the Lycée, and over two thirds were categorised as disabled. 40 per cent of the students had 'impairments associated with cerebral palsy: other impairments were related to paralysis, brain injury, genetic factors, and a range of other conditions'. The school is lively and welcoming, throbbing with life and energy. Many students were using wheelchairs to get around; others were using technology to communicate. The outside recreation area and the inside circulation areas can be merged to form one large space through the use of enormous sliding glass walls which link 'outside' to 'inside'. The director explained the rationale for this:

> We have brought 'outside' into the building. We didn't want a situation in which everybody is crowded together unable to circulate. That's bad for everybody but there are particular problems when you have large numbers of people using wheelchairs who are trying to get to lessons or go and meet their friends. So as you see, there are no corridors - we've got these large common spaces - like avenues or freeways. As you see, we get a lot of speeding!

Although, like the National Institute for Re-adaptation, the Lycée is attached to a medical campus and there are teams of medical and therapeutic staff attached to the medical wing, the focus of the school life and ethos is not centred around the 'medical' but on the social and educational interests of the students and staff:

> This is a school like any other. Impairment is a secondary issue. In special schools all the teachers are specialized in terms of learning difficulty or specific impairment. Here, the teachers are ordinary, highly qualified teachers. There is an important 'centre de soins' (medical centre) here which is the responsibility of the Ministry for Health and Social Affairs. Teachers come here because they say they want to work here. They are not 'special' teachers and don't have any specific training. The principle is that all the young people here are students, without exception (School Director).

Although the medical centre operates quite separately from the school, there is a commitment between teaching and medical staff and students themselves to work collaboratively together to counterbalance the effects of physical impairments so that students have 'full access to the curriculum'.

There is a strong emphasis on sport and 'physical prowess' and 'grace', which are seen as belonging in different ways to all those who make up the school community. I watched students playing golf, climbing an artificial rock-face and enjoying a very fast basketball game. In each case students worked collaboratively but always with apparent determination to win. What might be regarded as 'small triumphs' in another setting, were celebrated by all participants in recognition of achievements of particular students. All sports activities were mixed gender, and members of staff could participate as well.

Another unusual feature of the Lycée is the presence of disabled teachers, one of whom explained the relationship between 'the medical' and 'the social' in ways which suggest a way forward in terms of resolving what is sometimes presented in debates around inclusion as a 'clash of interests' between the medical requirements of students and their education:

> There are some very disabled young people here, many of whom would usually attend a specialist institution outside the education system. This means that they are shut off from the ordinary community and don't have the same opportunities as everybody else. Some need a lot of medical input of various kinds, and that's available here. This means that the students have everything they need on one site. This is the reverse of the usual situation in which you have a kind of medical institution with classes attached. The emphasis here is on the education not the medical side. But without the medical centre, some of the students couldn't come here. Also, here, being disabled, requiring medical care sometimes or some kind of therapy or medication is just accepted as 'everyday'. It's not a big deal and is certainly not used as a reason for treating students differently in terms of their education and social life.

The differences between the National Institute for Re-adaptation and the *Lycée Bresson* are to be found in the reversal of emphasis in terms of the relationship between 'the medical' and 'the social', and in the way in which students are perceived and represented, and power exercised. This is evident in the kinds of discourses used in the two settings. Subtly, but powerfully, there is a real sense in the *Lycée Bresson* of a participatory and shared project in which no-one imposes 'solutions' on others, but one in which individual and collective projects are developed collaboratively and in which the voice of students are clearly heard.

The third example is a setting outside the education system. Such institutions vary a great deal in terms of the emphasis placed on *scolarisation* (schooling). In the case of one setting I visited, an *Institut Médico-Professionnel* (IMPRO) which is designated for children and young people aged between 5-19 identified as having 'psychological and psychiatric difficulties and associated learning difficulties' or as 'too delicate' or 'too vulnerable' to attend school, some young people do not receive any formal teaching in the sense of following a curriculum or having lessons with a qualified teacher. There are three primary trained teachers for 74 children and young people. Only 51 of these attend formal teaching sessions, the others work individually or in groups with psychiatrists, psychologists or with an '*educateur*' (someone trained to work particularly on the social and emotional development of children, as well as their intellectual and creative development.).

The *Institut Médico-Professionnel* is a large, rickety building which has seen grander days. Only two rooms are devoted to formal education and the teacher-in-charge has put a hand-written sign up over a door saying 'School'. Nobody attends the school on a full-time basis because they attend workshop and therapeutic activities, and receive 'treatment' of different kinds. The amount of time a child spends in school varies; some just come for two and a half hours a week, others for several full days.

Many of the pupils have attended ordinary schools in the past, sometimes for many years. Their removal is often explained on the grounds that specialist services such as psychiatry are only available in specialist institutions, so in order for a child to have intensive therapy of this kind, it is necessary for them to leave their school.

The teacher-in-charge pointed out that in 'ordinary structures' specialist help is 'not available' to children and young people with complex psychological difficulties and the emphasis placed on getting through the curriculum and reaching academic targets leads to their removal to settings outside the education system. She explained that most of the group experienced 'severe psychological difficulties'; others experienced difficulties such as 'communication problems', 'mild cerebral palsy' or 'suffered from anorexia'. Some are children or young people who have been taken into care, others have been declared 'too disruptive' to stay in ordinary schools. The teacher-in-charge described the struggles which took place between the pathologizing, deficit-driven identities ascribed to some of the children by psychologists and therapeutic staff with her own view of her students:

> There are two different ways of understanding the role of support. One is liberating and it is based on a perception of one's role which says 'This student is progressing. She's going forward because she understands what she is doing'. The other view of

support is about control and says: 'she's making progress because I am there. Her progress is because of me.'

I want to support the young people by opening out new experiences for them. That is why I have developed the integration programme with the local college and it's going well. But I've met a lot of resistance from some others, and from this psychologist in particular. When S.F., one of the young people in my class, said to us 'I want to try and be part of that,' the psychologist said to me: 'Be careful. She's very fragile. Anything might happen'. Well, I'm an institutrice, but when I hear the psychologist say 'she is fragile' that means he is saying 'she is incapable. Anything can happen! She might go completely crazy. She needs protection' and it opens up all sorts of fantastic scenarios. It's very dangerous. These two views of 'support' are totally opposed and they are played out like night and day in the institution (Armstrong 2003: 159).

This quotation illuminates the clear divide between the medicalised, pathologized gaze of some professionals towards the young people 'in their care' with the perceptions of a teacher about her students: young people going forward, with much to do and contribute – young people who must be allowed to be part of the wider community, take risks and explore boundaries, and their own possibilities. It also demonstrates how there can be profound differences between the groups and individuals working within the same setting. It shows how institutions, cultures and practices can control what people can be as well as what people can do (Reeve 2004).

Conclusion

One of the challenges of exploring different cultural settings is to try and become sensitive to one's own preconceptions and assumptions, and the kinds of conceptual frameworks we work with. In comparative work it is always tempting to iron out differences, or to make gross generalizations about countries so that we can find ways of talking about them which are economic and manageable. While it is understandable that we notice apparent extremes in terms of differences between 'other' systems and 'our own', there is a danger of latching on to these and highlighting them as 'typical' examples of, say, the ways in which exclusions take place, disregarding other aspects of that society in which, perhaps, inequalities are challenged. We may not recognize these because we are not looking for them. It is easier, for example, to say – as many have – 'France is a prime example of the medical model at work', rather than exploring counter-examples of this statement, and examining contradictions. A related challenge is that while it may be relatively easy to document the most evident structural causes of oppression and exclusion in different societies, it is extremely difficult to explore the contradictory micro-levels of social-relational interactions and position taking inside institutions.

We need to understand the complexity of working across cultures, particularly in relation to language and the danger of making assumptions based on simplistic translations which fit familiar, culturally embedded concepts and terminology. That said, and always remembering that my interpretation is as 'culturally embedded' as anybody else's, France does seem to be historically burdened with particularly deeply rooted categorical thinking at the different levels of policy making. Paradoxically, this has its roots in progressive thought and the age of enlightenment in which 'science' was seen as able to address personal and social ills, by processes of assessment, identification and intervention. Thus, earlier periods of liberal humanitarianism, republicanism and scientific work have left a gargantuan legacy of structures, values and categorical thinking, much of which is shared, at least to some extent, by other contexts, including the UK.

The social model and the medical model, when used as contrasting lenses through which to explore familiar and unfamiliar contexts, are powerful and penetrative in that they allow us to explore physical, social and bureaucratic structures and services and different discourses, policies and practices at different levels in society. Used together, they reveal the distinctiveness of the two models, but also areas and contexts where they might overlap or both be working their way through systems and practices at the same time in a process of struggle and realignment.

Bibliography

Armstrong, F. 2003: **Spaced Out: Policy, Difference and the Challenge of Inclusive Education**. London: Kluwer Academic Publications.

Armstrong, F. 1996: Special Education in France, in Moon, B. and Corbett, A. (eds), **Education Reform In Contemporary France**, London: Routledge.

Barnes, C. 2003: What a Difference a Decade Makes: reflections on doing 'emancipatory' disability research. **Disability and Society**, 18 (1), 3-17.

Boxall, K., 2002: Individual and social models of disability and the experiences of people with learning difficulties. In D. G. Race (ed.), ***Learning Disability - A Social Approach***. London: Routledge.

Direction de la recherche des Études de l'Évaluation et des Statistiques (DREES) 2003: La scolarisation des enfants et adolescents handicapées, ***Études et Résultats***, 216, 1-11.

Hughes, B. 2002: Disability and the Body. In C. Barnes, M. Oliver and L. Barton (eds), ***Disability Studies Today***. Cambridge: Polity.

Imrie, R. 2000: Disability and discourse of mobility and movement. ***Environment and Planning***, 32, 1641-56.

La Dépêche du Midi 2003: 'L'école pour tous': est-ce une réalité? 26.01.2003.

Plaisance, E. 2005: The integration of 'disabled' children in ordinary schools in France: a new challenge. In L. Barton and F. Armstrong (eds), ***Policy, Experience and Change: cross-cultural reflections on inclusive education***. London: Kluwer Academic Publications.

Priestley, M. 1999: Discourse and identity: disabled children in mainstream high schools. In M. Corker and S. French (eds), ***Disability Discourse***. Buckingham: Open University Press.

Reeve, D. 2004: Psycho-emotional Dimensions of Disability and the Social Model. In C. Barnes and G. Mercer (eds), ***Implementing the Social Model of Disability: Theory and Research***. Leeds: The Disability Press.

Thomas, C. 1999: ***Female Forms. Experiencing and Understanding Disability***. Buckingham: Open University Press.

CHAPTER 5

Disabled Peoples' International: Europe and the social model of disability

Rachel Hurst

Introduction

The term 'social model' is now freely bandied about by governments, policy-makers and all those involved in disability issues. Very few understand what they mean, but the words have become acceptable and people often feel politically correct uttering them. Others - particularly those involved in service provision - see the words as a threat. Academics wrangle over them and most disabled people who are still living lives of isolation, poverty and exclusion are so oppressed by their circumstance that they cannot grasp the implications.

For the purposes of this chapter, I use the social model of disability as the analysis of the situation of a disabled person, defining disability as the relationship between a person with impairment and the environment, including attitudes, beliefs, climate, architecture, systems and services. The social model analysis is the essential political tool of the disability rights movement. It allows activists to clarify exactly what changes and actions are necessary to ensure that disabled people's dignity, rights and freedom are guaranteed. It is important to note the difference between the social model as an analytical tool and the actions then taken for social change. In this new millennium where the words 'human rights' are heard on everybody's lips to cover any or every issue, there has been a tendency to use the term 'human rights model of disability'. This can only muddle and confuse and, inaccurately, turn human rights into an analysis of a relationship instead of what they really are: an agreed code to ensure social cohesion. There has to be clear understanding between the analytical nature of the social model and the actions needed for social change inherent in human rights (Kallen 2004). The two, properly understood and applied together, underpin the validation of disabled people as an important and discrete group of human beings.

Starting with a quick overview of the importance of the UK disability movement's adoption of the social model and then looking at the history of Disabled Peoples' International in Europe, I hope to illustrate how the social model has impacted on that history and its profound importance as an impetus to political activity, social change and the promotion of civil and human rights for and by disabled people.

UK Experience
Building on a chapter by Paul Hunt (1966) entitled *The Critical Condition*, the analysis of the experience of disability by UPIAS in the mid-1970s is well documented (UPIAS 1975). Although the term social model had already been used in relation to other groups who faced invalidation, such as women and ethnic minorities, these discussions within UPIAS first introduced the concept of the social model with regard to disability and, led by Mike Oliver (Oliver 1990), have since been further expounded and explored by numerous academics. Just as importantly, those disabled people involved in the UPIAS discussions (Ken Davis, Vic Finkelstein, Dick Leaman, among others,) then went on to be in the leadership of disability rights activism and passed their message, energy and experience on to many others at both local and national levels. Their clarity of thought in defining disability ensured that the initial constitution and manifesto of Disabled Peoples' International (DPI) set the right (and the rights) agenda. Discussions between UPIAS members and disability rights activists in North America, Ireland, Finland and Sweden also led to an understanding of Independent Living as a tool for social change.

The Birth of DPI
Why did DPI happen? It happened because disabled people grabbed an opportunity and because, among the 250 disabled people gathered at Rehabilitation International Congress of 2-3,000 non-disabled rehabilitation and charity experts in Winnipeg, Canada, in 1980, there were the thinkers from UPIAS and the independent living activists from North America. Those 250 disabled people, who came from all over the world, recognised their shared exclusion and oppression. They saw the commonality of their discrimination as a people whose humanity was removed. They saw that they should no longer be dehumanised as objects of pity and charity – as consumers of rehabilitation and medical services –

but as people who were born free and equal in rights and dignity. As a result they conceived a worldwide movement which was born a year later in 1981 in Singapore (DPI 1981). The manifesto, constitution, action plan and Congress Declaration agreed in Singapore, all focused on the 'full and equal participation of disabled people in society' and saw the implementation of rights as the solution. DPI moved the definition of disability away from the individual to limitations in society.

The European countries represented at this first congress were: Ireland, Sweden, Norway, Italy, Portugal and the UK. Liam Maguire from Ireland and Bengt Lindqvist from Sweden had been on the Steering Committee and they both went on to the first World Council as officers, with added European representation from Vic Finkelstein from the UK and Ann-Marit Saebones from Sweden. The DPI Constitution required five regional councils: Africa, Latin America, Asia/Pacific, North America and Caribbean, and Europe.

Growth of DPI European Region
Bengt Lindqvist's regional report to the DPI World Congress in 1985 (in the Bahamas) stated that contact had been made with disability organisations in 40 European countries, and they had been invited to a conference and regional assembly in June, 1985. Twenty-three countries sent representatives – from the EU and Central and Eastern Europe – but only the UK, Norway and Sweden had full membership, to be joined immediately by Cyprus and Portugal. Finland and Denmark both fulfilled the requirements of membership but wished to stay as observers. The regional council was elected and an interim working group set up, to which organisations who were not already members of DPI could be invited and who could be asked to take responsibility for further development of the European Region.

Any work carried out in Europe was completely dependent on resources from the individual members. Unlike all the other regions of DPI, there was no central funding for Europe. This omission of Europe from the DPI budget was deliberate. The DPI World Council had agreed that available resources should go to developing countries and considered that there was money available in Europe that could be obtained by the European Regional Council. It took until 1990 for members of the European region to convince the rest of DPI that though there was undoubtedly development money within Europe, very little was available to the development of disabled people's own organisations and their rights within Europe itself or within the member states.

In the 1980s, Europe - as personified by the European Economic Community - was deeply entrenched in the view of disabled people as objects of charity, rehabilitation, segregation and specialisation. The focus of European Economic Community (EEC) activity with regard to disabled people was through the Bureau for Action in Favour of Handicapped People in the Directorate of Employment, Industrial Relations and Social Affairs (DGV E3), which had two programmes: Helios 1 and Helios 2, both of which were meant to focus on the integration of disabled people in society but which were essentially an exchange of information on local models of excellence. DGV E3 had set up a form of consultation that allowed European Non-Government Organisations (NGOs) concerned with disability to join a Dialogue Group. This met two or three times a year to discuss the Helios programmes. Few of the NGOs consulted were disabled people's own organisations and most representatives were non-disabled people. DGV E3, needless to say, did not employ disabled people and its equivalent unit in the European Union (EU) still does not, to this day.

An important focus for DGV E3 during the last half of that decade was Handynet - a project on which millions of ecu were spent. Handynet was a proposal to develop a series of linked computer accessed data banks to store information aids (in the first instance) and later, other 'disability relevant' information. This project was not going to be easily available or accessible to disabled people and was another tool for rehabilitation professionals and service providers. DPI's criticism of this proposal, as expressed by their representatives at a meeting in Brussels in 1984, was that as all people were aid users, information on aids for disabled people should be integrated within a general data bank on this subject (Leaman 1984) - a social model solution.

Other events taking place during the 1980s of relevance to disabled people were the 1987 European Mid-term Evaluation of the UN Decade of Disabled People in Ljubljana, Yugoslavia, and the World Evaluation of the Decade in Stockholm, Sweden. DPI was represented and played a significant role on both occasions. The outcome of both evaluations was that very little progress had been made toward the objectives of the Decade of full and equal participation of disabled people in society and that disabled people and their organisations were not being resourced or consulted as outlined in the World Programme of Action Concerning

Disabled Persons, the UN agreed proposals for implementing the objectives of the Decade. Indeed, the evaluation showed that most countries in both Europe and the rest of the world were ignoring the World Programme of Action (UN 1987).

Also in 1987, Sweden and Italy spearheaded a proposal at the UN General Assembly for a convention on the rights of disabled people. This proposal had been supported by the UN Experts gathered for the evaluation of the Decade, in particular the DPI representatives. Unfortunately it fell at the first hurdle in New York and alternative proposals were put forward a year or two later to elaborate UN Standard Rules on the Equalisation of Opportunities for disabled persons.

Another important process was started in 1987 at the Stockholm evaluation meeting. The World Health Organization (WHO) held a separate meeting with representatives from the UN Statistical Department and DPI, who were demanding that the WHO revised their *International Classification of Impairment, Disability and Handicap* (ICIDH) (WHO 1980). DPI demonstrated to the meeting how damaging this classification had been to disabled people – primarily because a classification of people took away their identity as fellow human beings – for no other group was a classification based on their personal medical characteristics considered necessary. Also, through assessments for services and benefits, the definition of disability as a medical model only confirmed the supremacy of the medical and rehabilitation professionals as 'owners' of disability issues rather than disabled people having control over their own lives and status as participating citizens and human beings. This, fairly informal, meeting started the slow and tortuous process that eventually led to the new ICF (*International Classification of Functioning, Disability and Health*) being agreed in 2001.

It is interesting to note that the ICF, although still flawed, is now intended to classify a situation and is applicable for everyone. It defines disability as arising from an 'integrative' model – the interaction taking place between functioning and the environment (including systems, attitudes, beliefs and policies). The WHO describes disability as being a socially created problem:

> Disability is not an attribute of an individual, but rather a complex collection of conditions, many of which are created by the social environment. Hence the management of the problem requires social action, and it is the collective responsibility of society at large to make the environmental modifications

necessary for the full participation of people with disabilities in all areas of social life. The issue is therefore an attitudinal or ideological one requiring social change, which at the political level becomes a question of human rights. For this model disability is a political issue (WHO 2001).

The WHO goes on to say that the ICF is based on an integration of the two opposing models of the medical and social and uses a 'biopsychosocial' approach – to 'achieve a coherent view of different perspectives of health from a biological, individual and social perspective' (WHO 2001). Put simply (if that is possible with such a complicated procedure) – disability is defined within an integrative model (rather than a medical or social) and their approach to classification is through the three domains of body functions and structures, activities and participation and environmental factors.

If used as now devised, the ICF could be a useful tool for assessments and statistical evidence using a social model approach. However, it does still give the medical professions the opportunity to ignore environmental factors, only use it for disabled people, and just continue to repeat their prejudices of the past. It would have been preferable if DPI could have persuaded the WHO to get rid of the classification altogether but that was impossible, although they did try (WHO 2001). There were far too many medical professionals and policy-makers wanting a structure of analysis for the outcomes of disease.

Independent Living

Many of the people involved in the birth of DPI were also involved in the Independent Living Movement. Independent Living is not just a social movement with a distinct constituency and history but is inextricably entwined with the Disability Rights Movement and is more than a grass-roots effort to acquire new rights, entitlements and services.

The first documented disabled people's self-help organisation emerged in Berkeley, California (Zukas 1979). The University of California was fertile ground for civil rights activists and provided the right environment for a group of disabled students, who were using the hospital wing as their hostel, to assess their own needs and rights and to work out how they could go out into the world, get jobs and live full and active lives.

Their solution was to set up, in 1970, a Centre for Independent Living (CIL), a non-residential facility run by disabled people, providing services and programmes to allow individuals to live independently in the community. They also provided advice and information on legal and welfare rights, housing, adaptations and access. They had programmes in training, peer counselling, advocacy and independent living skills. Crucially, they also formed a strong pressure group to affect policy on disability issues at the local, state and federal levels.

CILs flourished throughout the USA and Canada and by the mid 1970s disabled individuals from the UK, Sweden, Finland and Japan had heard about or visited the Berkeley CIL and set up their own organisations in the early 1980s. These CILs were not always called that nor did they strictly follow the same formulae. But they were all run by disabled people, for disabled people's rights in their own communities and were a focus for disabled people's own response and contribution to those communities.

It must be remembered that in some European countries, notably Holland and the Nordic countries, the provision of personal assistants and some independent living initiatives had been in place since the 1950s. But none of these services were controlled by disabled people themselves - they were just recipients, without proper choice. The services were given to people with medical conditions as a rehabilitation measure and a social service in the community, not as a right to full citizenship and humanity.

During the 1980s, the Independent Living concept was picked up by many other disabled people in Europe and in 1989 a meeting was held in Strasbourg of all those interested and the disabled delegates produced a position paper on what Independent Living was and its role in promoting rights for disabled people. This was followed by a meeting of DPI (world) Independent Living Committee and Symposium on May 6, 1990 in Lahti, Finland, where the disabled delegates formulated the basic principles of independent living. Working on these basic principles the European Network on Independent Living (ENIL) was born at a meeting in October, 1992 in Berlin. ENIL occasionally manages to obtain funding for training or development projects, but it is essentially a voluntary network to exchange ideas and experiences and now has membership of the European Disability Forum in its own right. And during the 1990s, DPI Europe, in support of ENIL, was able to carry out several Independent Living programmes with funding from the European Commission (DPI 1983-1990).

Funding for DPI - Europe

At last, in late 1990, the World Council of DPI decided to allot US $40,000 to the European Region and a preliminary regional council meeting was held in Brussels that year to elect officers and agree a way forward. DPI Europe then held a meeting in November, 1991 in Paris to coincide with a Council of Europe Conference of Ministers Responsible for Policies for People with Disabilities. This had focused on Independent Living and had had good input from disabled people.

This DPI Regional Council meeting in Paris was a very productive one. Membership had increased to 14 member organisations including Bulgaria and Poland. It was decided that ENIL should become an Independent Living programme affiliated to DPI/E. It was also agreed to form a separate European Community committee within DPI/E to be formed from the national assemblies whose countries had joined the EC. The committee would be a separate entity but would work closely together with DPI/E to ensure a unified political approach. This committee could also apply for funding from the EU for projects under a new funding programme.

At the same time – the end of 1991, the European Parliament refused to pass the Helios budget. This gave DPI Europe a chance to use its lobbying skills learnt at the international level and they joined with other DPOs to demand a much more democratic consultative mechanism. The outcome was the European Disability Forum in which DPI played a significant role, ensuring that the programmes for disabled people became more centred on human rights and more open to applications from organisations such as DPI Europe.

Further meetings of DPI/Europe and DPI/EUC were held in Birmingham, UK in November 1992 in conjunction with a European Commission financed large conference and exhibition called INFORM 92. Members of other European disability organisations were also invited to a Round Table Conference to see how they could work together more effectively. Meanwhile applications had gone in to the EU for funding for projects on equalisation of opportunities and DPI/EUC were able to employ an experienced disabled person, Arthur Verney, to develop DPI/Europe. With support from a growing staff based in the offices of DAA in London and sharing expertise, DPI/E and EUC then really took off. Membership grew, action plans were agreed and all national assemblies given encouragement and financial support to be active within projects (DPI 1991-2).

At the same time as all the activity at the grass-roots and within the democratic movement, many relationships were being forged with other EU disability organisations and with the Commission. And there were major changes happening within the whole EEC. The Treaty of Maastricht focused on the European social dialogue and the Agreement on Social Policy was adopted by all member states, except the UK, in 1993.

Using experiences gained from the international movement, through events such as Independence 92 in Vancouver, Canada and the formulation of the *UN Standard Rules on Equalisation of Opportunities for Disabled People* (1993), DP/EUC sought and received considerable funding from the Commission to celebrate the first International Day of Disabled Persons. This day – December 3 – had been announced by the UN as a focus for human rights and disability, at the General Assembly in 1992 to mark the end of the Decade of Disabled Persons (Hurst 1995). DPI/EUC planned a major information campaign to raise awareness of the day with its message of human rights (not rattling charity cans at street corners!) and also arranged a Parliament of Disabled People in the official Parliament chamber of the European Union in Brussels.

Getting agreement to use the official chamber proved very difficult. Twice the College of Questors – the official arbiters of the chamber's usage – denied DPI/EUC the right of access, despite previous *ad hoc* parliaments of students and pensioners. It was only at the third time of asking and threatening direct action within the Parliament building that permission was granted. So on December 3 1992, 440 disabled people from all the EU countries met in the Parliament to debate their human rights. Egon Klepsch, the President of the Parliament opened the proceedings, which were chaired by DPI/EUC. Padraign Flynn, Commissioner for Social Affairs, Members of the European Parliament (MEPs) and Commission officials attended. They were allowed to speak very briefly and to sign an Affirmation of Commitment to disabled people's rights and the UN Standard Rules on Equalisation of Opportunities for Disabled Persons, but their real role was to listen. And listen they did and to a story they had never heard told so vividly before. Eighty of the disabled people got up and each one gave an account of the reality of their lives – they told about the abuse, neglect, segregation and isolation (DPI/E 1993).

Those stories really marked a turning point in disability and the EU. The European Parliament resolved to support the Disabled People's Parliament Resolution to support the UN Standard Rules, to research the real situation of disabled people in Europe and to find out what was happening with the rise of violence and fascism. The Intergroup on Disability of interested MEPs was strengthened and a staff person employed. The Commission also took more notice of the European Disability Forum (EDF) and raised the amount of funding available for disabled people's projects. The Treaty of Maastricht, by giving social partners, including disability organisations, a voice in introducing new basis for action also put considerable pressure on the European Commission and the other institutions to introduce the notion of non-discrimination. Disabled People's organisations - notably DPI/EUC - pushed for the adoption by the EU of the UN Standard Rules on Equalisation of Opportunities. These were adopted in 1993 and were formally endorsed by the Council in its Resolution of 20 December 1996 on Equality of Opportunity for People with Disability.

Article 13

Having affected a sea change in EU thinking on disability, DPI and the EDF then took a substantive role in lobbying with other social partners to ensure that Article 13 of the next revision - the Treaty of Amsterdam (1997) - provided for appropriate action to combat discrimination based on sex, racial or ethnic origin, religion or belief, disability, age or sexual orientation. This enables the EU to help national and local agencies to do more on the fundamentals of integration and rights, including for disabled people. Using Article 13 as a starting point, the Council adopted on 27 November 2000, a comprehensive anti-discrimination package comprising a Directive establishing a general framework for equal treatment in employment and occupation and a Community action programme to combat discrimination, 2001-2006. The Directive provides a legislative framework for legally enforceable employment rights, including provisions on a number of key issues such as protection against harassment, scope for positive action, appropriate remedies and enforcement measures. More importantly, the directive also adopts the duty of reasonable accommodation, which implies the adjustment of the workplace to meet the needs of a disabled person. It was this Directive which ensured that the UK Government altered the Disability Discrimination Act's employment section to include all employers.

In order to fulfil its commitment to Citizenship, the Commission adopted on May 12, 2000, a communication entitled *Toward a Barrier-Free Europe for Disabled People*, in which it commits itself to developing and supporting a comprehensive and integrated strategy to tackle social, architectural and design barriers that restrict access for disabled people to social and economic opportunities. The EDF is now working hard with the European Parliament to introduce a disability directive which will cover all areas, in the same way as the race directive.

Human Rights

The DPI World Council reaffirmed itself as a human rights organisation in 1992 and agreed a resolution, signed by hundreds of members, to investigate a system to obtain evidence on violations of disabled people's rights (DPI 1992). An initial feasibility study was carried out for DPI by a Canadian lawyer, Yvonne Peters (Peters 1994). The study encouraged the collection of evidence of violations from DPI organisations around the world to be put on a special database. Whilst it was seen as a good idea that DPI should take the lead in planning this and providing the information – it was felt it would be safer for some national assemblies if DPI did not actually manage the database. However, DPI Europe sought and obtained funding from the European Commission to carry out a series of projects with disabled European lawyers in assessing how the evidence should be processed and then collected by disabled volunteers throughout Europe. Several years of thought, discussion and then training resulted in Disability Awareness in Action (DAA) setting up the database in 1999 with initial information from the trained co-ordinators from DPI. The database now has evidence of violations against over two million disabled individuals (1 million plus from Europe) all of which have happened since 1990 and are fully verified. The stark realities of the evidence are that 10% of the cases are of violations to the right to life itself (that is, disabled people are killed just because they are disabled people) and over 34% are of degrading and inhuman treatment (DAA 2003).

Bioethics

Bioethics is another area in which DPI Europe has done some very good work in promoting the social model. As the DPI position paper on Bioethics and Human Rights says:
> From pre-natal screening and the selective termination of 'undesirable' pregnancies to euthanasia of disabled adults, one of the biggest threats to the rights of disabled people this Millennium lies within the field of bioethics – the ethics of advances in biological medicine and science. If disabled people's rights are to be protected, it must be in a context where we are confident that society is willing to share burdens and support

those whose needs are greater than others to ensure equality of opportunity (DPI/E, 2000).

DPI/E's aims in its Action Plan for 1999-2002 were to influence the EU, Council of Europe and national government in their way of thinking on bioethical concerns and to educate disabled people within Europe and the rest of the world on bioethics. Initial work got together disabled people from all over Europe to formulate the position paper and then to provide training so that disabled individuals could become articulate on the issue and be used as experts by their national bioethics committees.

There is no doubt that the new genetic sciences are a real threat to disabled people's humanity. The social model has flown out of the window! In genetic terms we are only seen as impaired genes and the outcomes of allowing these genes to multiply into a living person are unreasonable in terms of social support, health costs, individual pain and suffering and intolerable quality of life. This allows the massive rejection of embryos which may have impairments, late abortion on the grounds of impairment, pressure on parents to think they are producing a child whose life is not worth living - or, as one doctor said to a mother whose foetus had been diagnosed as having Down's Syndrome, 'your child will not be worth loving' - and increasing legislation in support of assisted suicide. There is neither discussion of the prejudicial and discriminatory nature of such quality of life assessments nor of the basic right to life of all human beings, regardless of impairment. There is no acceptance that the right to life of a viable foetus should take precedence over the right of a mother to choose. Nor is there admission that these late foetuses are not aborted until they have already been directly killed in the womb so that there is no danger of them living. There is little realisation that disabled people's quality of life is dependent on choice, control, proper access and support - just like everyone else. There is nothing 'special' about our needs, they are just different. By saying that the costs of our needs are too much or too difficult, society is denying that we are citizens for whom they have a responsibility. And there is little acknowledgement of the eugenic nature of these bioethical practices and the threat to our fundamental human rights.

End of DPI/E Funding

A circle seems to have formed with regard to DPI/Europe's funding. Due to the suspension of funding for all EU disability projects for a whole year, delays and audits by the Commission resulting in non-receipt or demands for repayment of final payments for projects as far back as 1999, DPI Europe had to close its books in the UK in May 2003 and was unable to continue its planned projects after 2002 or employ any staff. However, DPI Europe still has an active Executive Committee and is a member of the EDF. Its national assemblies have taken on some of the plans that were planned. For instance, the national assembly in the UK (the British Council of Disabled People) has obtained funding for training in bioethics. There is a DPI office in Hungary for Central and Eastern Europe. But there are only the small annual allocations from DPI HQ to ensure that the democratic mechanism can function.

Conclusion

Primarily through the activities of the disability movement, the social model has flourished in Europe in the last decade, combined with recognition of disability as a human rights issue. There has been real progress away from the rehabilitation, charity models, to an understanding of inclusion, choice and control for the individual. You could say that the social model rules OK. But does it? There are threats - the obvious one of bioethics, but there is the less obvious one of argument among academics of what the social model is and who owns it which allows policy-makers (for instance WHO) to ignore it and invent their own language. However, the greatest threat is to the voice of disabled people and to our status. The silencing of DPI through lack of funding, the absence of disabled people on bioethics committees and in political leadership, the growth in eugenics, all put us back into that box of 'other' and 'special' and emphasise our lack of citizenship and invalidity.

We must find new ways of working toward social change. We must form new alliances to raise the profile of disabled people. Those alliances, must, however, be alliances of equals. We must shout from the rooftops about the reality of our lives and the endless and horrific violations of our rights but we must shout equally loudly about our contributions - how Europe cannot do without us - how services and policies that include disabled people are better for everyone. And the disabled person's voice must be given its rightful status. It is a disgrace that there are no disabled people in DGV E3 - the Women's Unit would not employ a majority of men. It is a disgrace that government representatives discussing disability issues are not prominent disabled people. We need it to be fully recognised that if any piece of knowledge or happening or service or policy has a disability perspective, then disabled people must be there, giving that perspective and our time and expertise properly compensated. And the reality is that everything is about us – as it is about every single individual. Planning society does not work for anybody if the rights and needs of the individual are ignored and their participation not recognised. We each have equal worth. The social model clarifies what we are – human beings with rights. And the social model analyses the barriers to our accessing our full humanity. The social model must continue to 'rule OK' and be implemented through a human rights framework of equality, dignity and freedom.

Bibliography

DAA 2003: ***Review of Evidence contained on the DAA Human Rights Database***. London: DAART Centre.

DPI 1981: ***Proceedings of the First World Congress***. Singapore: DPI.

DPI (undated): *Minutes and reports from 1983-1999*, unpublished. London: DPI.

DPI (undated): *DPI Regional Council Meetings 1991, 1992*, unpublished. London: DPI.

DPI Europe 1993: ***Report of the First European Disabled People's Parliament***. London: DPI Europe.

DPI Europe 2000: ***Disabled People Speak on the New Genetics***. London: DPI Europe.

Hunt, P. 1966: A critical condition. In P. Hunt (ed.), ***Stigma: The Experience of Disability***. London: Geoffrey Chapman, 145-59.

Hurst, R. 1995: Choice and Empowerment – lessons from Europe. ***Disability and Society***, 10 (4), 529-34.

Kallen, E. 2004: *Social Inequality & Social Injustice: A human rights perspective*. New York: Palgrave Macmillan.

Leaman, D. 1984: *Notes of meeting with the Bureau for Action in Favour of the Handicapped*, Brussels, 9-10 October, 1984.

Oliver, M. 1990: ***The Politics of Disablement***. Basingstoke: Macmillan.

Peters, Y. 1994: ***Feasibility Study into Human Rights Abuse***. Canada: DPI.

UPIAS and the Disability Alliance 1975: ***Fundamental Principles of Disability***. London: UPIAS.

UN 1987: ***UN Global Meeting of Experts to Review the Implementation of the World Programme of Action concerning Disabled Persons at the Mid-Point of the UN Decade of Disabled Persons, Stockholm 17–22 August, 1987. Report***. Vienna: UN.

UN 1993: ***Standard rules for the equalization of opportunities for persons with disabilities*** UN General Assembly, Resolution 48/96, 20 December. New York: UN.

WHO 1980: ***International Classification of Impairments, Disabilities and Handicaps***. Geneva: World Health Organization.

WHO 2001: ***International Classification of Functioning, Disability and Health***. Geneva: WHO.

WHO 2002: *Minutes of meetings of experts in revision process 1992-2002.* Geneva: WHO.

Zukas, H. 1979: ***CIL History***. Berkeley, CA.: Berkeley CIL.

CHAPTER 6

Dismantling Barriers to Transport by Law: the European journey

Anna Lawson and Bryan Matthews

Introduction

At the heart of the social model of disability lies the notion that people with impairments are disabled by barriers to their participation in the life of mainstream society. These barriers take many forms, emerging from sources as diverse as inaccessible architecture or design, exclusionary practices or policies and negative, hostile attitudes. The barriers which people with impairments face in accessing transport play a significant role in the disabling process. Inaccessible transport not only prevents them using transport services but also excludes them from jobs, houses, goods, services and facilities to which transport provides access.

Attempts have sometimes been made to circumvent the difficulties created by inaccessible mainstream transport systems either by providing disabled people with supplementary, specialist transport services or by providing them with goods, services and facilities in their homes. However, these approaches are expensive and segregationist. They do not break down disabling barriers so as to create a public transport system accessible to all.

In Europe the last decade has witnessed some efforts to improve access to mainstream transport. Voluntary design and service codes have been developed and have been useful in fostering support for change within the transport industry. Demonstration projects have provided evidence of the benefits of accessible transport, not only to disabled people but also to those who are 'mobility impaired' for other reasons (such as parents with pushchairs). There is, however, some impatience with the pace of change achieved by these voluntary approaches and a growing belief that the force of the law should be harnessed to break down the barriers which prevent disabled people from using public transport.

In this chapter we provide a brief overview and critique of the current set of legal provisions relating to accessible transport throughout Europe. We begin with a brief insight into developments at the national level, illustrating the diversity of activity in the area. We then focus on two aspects of the pan-European dimension. First, we consider the extent to which European Union (EU) legislation requires Member States to make transport accessible to disabled people and the scope for further development in this regard. Second, we examine the extent to which disabled people may be able to challenge failures by their States to ensure that public transport is accessible to them as infringements of their human rights. Finally, we evaluate the different legal strategies which have emerged in the battle to remove disabling transport barriers.

Developments in Europe at the National Level

For most European countries, improved access to transport for disabled people is now a stated objective in the pursuance of which legislation is increasingly being introduced. Two recent reviews of actions at the national level have been undertaken. The first, emerging from the European Conference of Ministers of Transport (ECMT 2000), examines developments in national legislation to improve access to transport by disabled people. It divides these into two main categories: first, general laws on civil rights and non-discrimination and, second, specific regulations on access to means of transport. Within both categories there is a wide variation in the degree of action taken in different countries. In some, the implementation of legislation and regulations reflect a highly proactive policy in support of mobility-impaired people and, in others, very few measures have been introduced.

The second, a report presented to the Council of Europe (Steinmeyer 2003), is more broadly focused, covering all legislation relating to disabled people.

Table 1 illustrates the large number of national legislative and regulatory provisions in place throughout the EU, as well as the diversity within them. Policy is sometimes based at national level, sometimes at regional level and sometimes divided between the two. In some countries policy on disabled people is 'enshrined' in constitutions, whilst in others there is specific legislation regarding disabled people. Some countries, but by no means all, set out the rights of disabled people (including the right to mobility and the right to use different modes of transport) in accordance with principles of non-discrimination or equal treatment. Enforcement mechanisms, where they do exist, also vary widely: ranging from the withholding of operating licences, to legal actions brought by the disabled person concerned, to criminal proceedings brought by the State.

Table 1: Overview of Legislative Provisions in the EU15 countries

Country	National Regulatory Texts		Standards, Guidelines, Recommendations	Enforcement and Redress Mechanisms
	General	Specific		
Austria	1 national	Specialised transport	Recommendations for architects and transport operators	Yes, law of 1994 regarding public buildings; Road Traffic Act 159:1960
Belgium	1 national 1 regional	Air transport	Trains and metros	
Denmark		Road transport; Specialised transport; Taxis and minibuses; Air transport		
Finland	Yes	Transport terminals; Road transport; Taxis; Specialised transport	Transport terminals	Sanctions
France	Yes	Transport terminals; Buses; Taxis; Road network	Infrastructures; Bus networks; Rail networks; Specialised transport; Automatic vending machines; Airports	Sanctions which could go as far as preventing operations in case of disrespect for regulations on accessibility of terminal installations

Country	National Regulatory Texts		Standards, Guidelines, Recommendations	Enforcement and Redress Mechanisms
	General	Specific		
Germany	1 national 1 regional	Train; metro Train	DIN norms; accessibility rules	
Greece	Yes	Buses; Coaches; Ferries	Buses and coaches; Airports	Checks prior to operations and once they have begun
Ireland	Yes	Taxis		
Italy	National and regional	Specialised transport		
Netherlands		Train; metro; Road transport; and specialised transport		
Portugal	Yes	Reserved places; Specially-adapted vehicles		
Spain	2 national Several for the autonomous communities	Road transport; Air transport	UNE guidelines; Rail networks; Specialised transport; Transport by bus; Taxis	Economic sanctions which could go as far as closing down the service
Sweden	Yes	Public transport; Specialised transport;	Terminals; Bus stops and bus networks	Checks prior to operations
United Kingdom	National and regional	Trains; Thoroughfares		Sanctions

Source: ECMT 2000: 7-11

Notes:
1. This Table reflects the position in 2000. There have been a number of important subsequent developments. Steinmeyer (2003) indicates, for instance, that there is now some form of anti-discrimination legislation covering access to transport by disabled people in France, Germany, Italy, the Netherlands, Spain, the UK and Poland.
2. DIN refers to German industrial standards; and
3. UNE refers to the United Nations Economic Commission for Europe.

The ECMT (2000) identify six points which deserve careful consideration by those seeking to break down the disabling barriers in this area.

First, legislative cultures (as well as legislative provisions) in the various countries differ. Thus, differences may be found in the interpretation of similar legal provisions, in the willingness of individuals or other bodies to 'use the law' and in the attitudes adopted towards enforcement.

Second, legislation alone is insufficient to ensure meaningful access to transport for disabled people. It should be supplemented by detailed regulations and guidance, including clear communication with key actors, the provision of relevant information to, and where appropriate, the training of, those concerned.

Third, an appropriate balance must be struck between, on the one hand, legislation framed in such general terms that it leaves too much room for interpretation and, on the other, legislation framed in such specific terms that it becomes overly prescriptive. General legislation that provides for 'reasonable access' at 'acceptable cost' may result in change taking place relatively slowly, whereas specific legislative provisions may act as a block to the development of innovative access solutions. The ECMT favoured an approach in which clear access objectives were specified over one in which detailed technical requirements were prescribed.

Fourth, broad support for proposed legislation should be secured from relevant industries and other affected groups. Whilst laws might be enacted, their provisions can be blocked by technical or other obstacles if the will to implement them is missing. The ECMT cited experience in the USA from the 1970s and 1980s as demonstrating that actual litigation is often the least cost-effective means of achieving change.

Fifth, effective enforcement mechanisms must be established. While this will be relatively straightforward in the case of specific regulations or design standards, it may be more complicated, time-consuming and costly in the case of more general anti-discrimination or civil rights provisions. A mix of incentives and penalties, perhaps including linking financial aid (for example, subsidies to bus operators) to meet legal requirements, can be used to promote compliance.

Finally, the ECMT recommended that procedures be set up for reviewing the effectiveness of the legislation, both in terms of its contribution to meeting national objectives and in terms of how it compares with practice in other countries.

EU Legislation

There is currently no general EU legislation requiring Member States to prohibit discrimination against disabled people in relation to transport. In relation to employment, however, the Employment Framework Directive 2000 requires Member States to take steps to prohibit discrimination against people on a number of protected grounds, including disability. This contrasts with the situation regarding race discrimination, where the Race Directive 2000 prohibits discrimination on racial grounds both in the context of employment and in the provision of goods and services (including transport).

Despite the lack of comprehensive legislation requiring States to eliminate disability discrimination in transport, there are a number of narrowly drawn EU provisions designed to improve access to specific modes of transport. The Bus and Coach Directive 2001, for instance, requires Member States to ensure that urban buses comply with various accessibility standards. They must, for example, be fitted with a ramp or a lift as well as a kneeling system and must have wheelchair designated spaces, colour contrasting, and designated seats for persons with reduced mobility. The more recent Road Safety and Motor Vehicles Directive 2003 will require all new buses and coaches to comply with harmonised construction standards, including basic accessibility features for disabled passengers.

In relation to rail, the High Speed Trains Directive 1996 requires rolling stock and rail infrastructure to be constructed so as to facilitate access by disabled passengers. Similar requirements are now being developed for the conventional rail system. The European Commission has also proposed, as part of its plans for the development of an integrated rail system, that rail operators be encouraged to develop a voluntary charter on service quality which would include issues relevant to disabled people (European Commission 2002a).

Two directives currently have particular relevance to disabled passengers travelling on ships but their effect is very limited (Information on Disabled Passengers Directive 1998 and Accessible Information Directive 1999). There are currently moves to introduce a directive designed to implement the recommendations of the International Maritime Organisation on the design and operation of passenger ships (Draft Passenger Ships Directive). This would require ships to be constructed so as to allow disabled people to move between the main deck and the below-deck areas and would require alarm systems to be made accessible to disabled people, including those with sensory or cognitive impairments.

In relation to air travel, there are currently no EU imposed obligations to ensure accessibility. There is, however, a voluntary code drawn up jointly by the European Commission and the European Civil Aviation Conference (ECAC 2001) and implemented in 2002. Under it, signatory airlines undertake to allow disabled people to travel (except where this would not be safe or where they could not physically be accommodated), and not to pass the costs of disability-related assistance or services on to the disabled person. Signatory airports undertake to ensure that their infrastructure is accessible. The European Commission has proposed legislation to make some of these undertakings mandatory (European Commission 2002b, 2003). This was welcomed by the European Disability Forum (EDF) which has campaigned for the proposed rights to be strengthened and extended (EDF 2001, 2002).

The existing patchwork of directives on accessible transport, then, does not require Member States to implement clear, comprehensive non-discrimination measures. The focus is largely on issues of design and construction: a tendency echoed elsewhere in European policies relating to disability and transport (European Commission 1993, 2000). Aircraft have to date escaped even this form of regulation. Accessible design is clearly fundamental to the existence of a system capable of being used by all. Alone, however, it is clearly not enough. The provision of accessible information and appropriate assistance, for instance, will also be essential.

The EDF has drawn up a shadow Disability Directive which would oblige member States to take steps to prohibit disability discrimination in the provision of goods and services generally. It would require the introduction of measures designed to ensure that:

> All forms of public transport and all buildings and structures providing access to public transport, whether provided by the public or private sector, are accessible to persons with disabilities. Member States shall require that all new and, wherever possible, refitted transportation vehicles and buildings are accessible and shall set appropriate deadlines for providers of public transport with regard to achieving accessibility for existing vehicles, buildings and structures (Article 5 (2) (a)).

Thus, issues of design and construction would be covered but this directive would extend much further (Articles 2(6), 3(1) and 4). It would require all forms of public transport to be accessible to disabled people; demanding, not only that vehicles and buildings be designed appropriately, but also that information be made accessible and that reasonable accommodations be provided.

The European Commission's planned programme of work in the area of transport for this decade is set out in its White Paper *European transport policy for 2010: time to decide (European Commission 2001)*. This document contains disappointingly little of specific relevance to disabled people. Nevertheless, the relevant European Commissioner has indicated some support for the adoption of a disability-specific directive along the lines of that proposed by the EDF (Diamantopoulou 2003) but the Commission itself has, to date, remained silent. Were such a directive to be adopted, Member States would be forced to dismantle many of the disabling barriers to transport currently confronting people with impairments. For some, this would be a novel exercise. For others, which have already taken some legislative action, it would represent an obligation to reassess (and typically strengthen) that legislation. Until it is adopted, the EU legislation on accessible transport will remain patchy and incomplete.

Human Rights

The European Convention on Human Rights (ECHR)
Notwithstanding the absence of any relevant domestic anti-discrimination

law, disabled people faced with inaccessible public transport systems may be able to challenge their consequent exclusion or discomfort as an infringement of their rights under the ECHR. It has been suggested, for instance, that a public transport system requiring disabled people to travel in humiliating and undignified conditions might constitute a breach of their Article 3 right to be free from inhuman and degrading treatment (Nowak and Suntinger 1995: 119). No such challenge has yet been mounted, and success would be by no means guaranteed. The judiciary are traditionally extremely reluctant to find breaches of this Article, to which there are no qualifications or defences. This is illustrated by a recent British case, Bernard v Enfield LBC (2002), in which Article 3 was found not to have been breached even though a disabled woman had had to live for over twenty months in 'deplorable conditions' because her local Council failed to provide her with an accessible home.

Though the Article 5 right to liberty and security might seem to offer another means of challenging inaccessible transport systems, again no such case has been made and there are currently no indications that Article 5 will be developed in this way (Clements and Read 2003: ch 4). Protocol 4, which guarantees freedom of movement, provides another possible basis for inaccessible transport cases, although its potential is currently untested.

The most obvious article on which to found an inaccessible transport claim is Article 8. Though this has not yet occurred, the well-known case of Botta v Italy (1998) has obvious relevance. It is particularly interesting because it raised the question of the extent to which states should act to ensure respect for private and family life by taking positive steps to break down the social, architectural or other barriers faced by disabled people. Mr Botta, a wheelchair-user, claimed that the state's failure to enforce laws requiring private beaches in Italy to be made accessible to disabled people infringed his Article 8 right to a private life (which has been interpreted broadly to include a right to physical and psychological integrity and to the development of one's personality in one's relations with others). He argued that, in being prevented from using the beaches, he was denied a 'normal social life' and the ability 'to participate in the life of the community' (para 27). The parallels with a case in which a disabled person is unable to travel because of an inaccessible transport system are obvious.

Though Mr Botta lost his case, the reasoning of the European Court of Human Rights (ECtHR) does hold out some hope for disabled people wishing to challenge transport barriers. The Court accepted that respect for private life would sometimes require States to adopt positive measures.

More specifically, provided there was no relevant defence under Article 8, they would be required to adopt such measures where there was a 'direct and immediate link between the measures sought by an applicant and the latter's private and/or family life' (para 34). There was, however, no such direct and immediate link in Botta - the right to access beaches in a holiday destination involving 'interpersonal relations of such broad and indeterminate scope that there [could] be no conceivable direct link' (para 55).

The question, then, is how severe must the consequences of inaccessible transport be for an individual in order to establish the necessary direct and immediate link? Will it be established if the individual is unable to travel to local shops or other amenities? Will it be established if they are able to travel around their locality only at considerable risk to their safety - for example, where they would have to use pathways shared with cyclists or where bus stops or other facilities could be reached only by crossing busy roads with no audible or tactile crossings? Will the consequences of inability to use public transport ever be sufficiently severe to establish the necessary link? The post-Botta cases, though not directly concerning transport, are not encouraging.

In Zehlanova and Zehnal v the Czech Republic (2002), for instance, the link was not established by disabled people who were unable to access various buildings in their home town due to architectural barriers. Despite the fact that these buildings included the post office, the swimming pool and various medical facilities, the ECtHR was not convinced that they played a sufficient role in the everyday lives of the disabled people concerned. In Marzari v Italy (1999) and in Sentges v the Netherlands (2003), however, the ECtHR was prepared to contemplate that the required link had been established by claims for, respectively, appropriate housing and a robotic arm (which would have facilitated daily tasks such as eating and drinking). Nevertheless, both these cases failed on the grounds that requiring the State to comply with the requests of the disabled applicants would have been disproportionate and failed to accord sufficient respect to decisions about how finite resources should be allocated.

Olivier De Schutter (2003) has argued that these cases reveal reluctance on the part of the ECtHR to find that a direct and immediate link exists unless the obstacles in question relate to the immediate environment of the disabled litigant and have an effect on their everyday life which is 'permanent and important' as opposed to 'occasional or negligible'. In

Botta and Zehlanova, the two cases in which there was found to be no link, the quality of 'permanence' was missing. This does not bode well for claims based on the inaccessibility of public transport, at least where alternatives (for example, in the form of private or specialised transport) are available. Even if the direct and immediate link requirement could be satisfied, Marzari and Sentges suggest that litigants in such claims would struggle to show that it would have been a proportionate response for a State, which had offered to provide specialised, segregated services, to have made public transport accessible instead. Thus, in the context of access to transport, Article 8 might offer some prospect of success to a disabled claimant unable to access public transport to whom no alternatives were available. Such a claim, however, would seem likely to result in a State being required to provide some alternative means of transport to the particular person concerned rather than to remove the more general disabling barriers from its public transport system.

The Article 14 right to be free from discrimination in the enjoyment of one's Convention rights may also be relevant in this context. Two issues are likely to be of particular significance for disabled 'travellers' seeking to rely on this Article:

First, the alleged discrimination must affect the enjoyment of a Convention right. Thus, a claim that a State's failure to take positive steps under Article 8 to break down disabling barriers would require the existence of a direct and immediate link of the type outlined above. In the absence of any such link, an Article 14 argument will fail as it did in Botta.

Second, it would have to be shown that failing to make transport accessible to disabled people amounted to discrimination against them. Such failures are extremely unlikely to amount to direct discrimination. Concepts of indirect discrimination, however, have been slow to emerge from the Article 14 cases (McColgan 2003: 168-170) and it is still by no means certain that Article 14 will be interpreted so as to require reasonable adjustments to be made in favour of disabled people. Thlimmenos v Greece (2000) however, does provide some grounds for optimism. There, the ECtHR held that Article 14 had been breached by a state's unjustified failure (in the context of religion) to treat differently persons whose circumstances were materially different. This suggests that the failure to make relevant adjustments for disabled travellers (for example, providing them with staff assistance) may amount to discrimination for these purposes.

Disabled people, then, may attempt to use the ECHR to challenge inaccessible transport systems. Though Articles 8 and 14 both afford some hope, success would be by no means guaranteed. Even if the required 'direct and immediate link' could be established, both articles are qualified and states may well be able to argue that their policies were justified, most probably on grounds of cost. Even in the unlikely event of success, the result may well be the provision to that person of a specialised, segregated alternative means of transport rather than the wholesale dismantling of barriers to their use of public transport.

The Revised European Social Charter (ESC)
Article 15 of the revised ESC, adopted by the Committee of Ministers in April 1996, confers on disabled people a right to 'independence, social integration and participation in the life of the community'. By Article 15(3) the signatories undertake to:
> promote their full social integration and participation in the life of the community, in particular through measures, including technical aids, aiming to overcome barriers to communication and mobility and enabling access to transport, housing, cultural activities and leisure.

In Botta (para 28), the Commission on Human Rights indicated that 'the social nature' of the right to access beaches meant that it was more appropriately protected by machinery such as that provided by Article 15 of the ESC than by that of the ECHR. This observation was not expressly echoed by the ECtHR, although it did rule that the right fell outside the reach of the ECHR. The protection provided by Article 15 is, however, limited in the extreme - even for those disabled people living in countries which (unlike the UK) have signed up to the revised ESC.

The ESC imposes obligations on signatories to report on their progress in the implementation of the rights it confers. There is, however, little sanction for states who fail to comply. Since 1 July 1998, the collective complaints procedure may also be used to 'enforce' Article 15. Though this may result in a recommendation by the Council of Ministers that the offending state should bring its policies into line with the requirements of the ESC, there is again no sanction for non-compliance. There is currently no mechanism for individual enforcement of Charter rights (Novitz 2002).

Legal Strategies for Change: A Social Model Perspective
It is interesting to evaluate the different legal strategies which have emerged in the context of disability and transport against the backdrop of

the social model of disability. The social model focuses on the societal barriers which prevent people with impairments taking part in the mainstream life of their communities. It is therefore useful to consider the extent to which the different legal strategies will actually result in breaking down the disabling barriers which exist in public transport.

In the previous section we drew attention to the limited potential of European human rights legislation as a means of achieving far-reaching change in the provision of public transport. A claim under the ECHR may have some small chance of success but the outcome of that success would almost certainly not be to require States to break down the barriers to mainstream public transport which make it unusable by people with impairments. The provision of supplementary, segregated forms of transport would probably suffice. The outcome of an ESC claim is similarly uncertain and suffers from the further disadvantage of inadequate enforcement mechanisms.

Laws which require transport vehicles and infrastructure to be designed so as to maximise access, as are required by many of the current EU directives relating to disability and transport, have an obvious role to play in breaking-down some of the disabling barriers in the transport system. As mentioned above, however, such laws do not go far enough. Accessible vehicles will remain inaccessible to many disabled people (particularly those wishing to travel alone) if staff are permitted to deny entry to disabled people or simply to refuse to provide them with assistance or accessible information.

Anti-discrimination legislation has the potential to cover a wide spectrum of the barriers traditionally encountered by disabled people in accessing public transport. Yet, in many EU countries, comprehensive protection in the area of transport has not emerged even where more comprehensive protection has been afforded in other fields. In the UK, for instance, though the Disability Discrimination Act 1995 (DDA) made it unlawful for providers of transport to the public to discriminate against disabled people in accessing transport infrastructure (such as train stations and bus stops) and included various technical design standards for transport vehicles, the provision of transport services was excluded. There are, however, plans to remove this exclusion by the draft Disability Discrimination Bill 2003. It should also be noted that the EDF's shadow disability directive would require Member States to introduce anti-discrimination legislation which has a comprehensive coverage of transport.

Anti-discrimination legislation, even if comprehensive, is unlikely to prove an effective tool for the systematic breaking down of disabling barriers to transport if it relies entirely on enforcement by individual litigants. In such a system, the nature of the cases brought would inevitably be somewhat of a lottery: dependent on the type of barrier encountered by disabled travellers willing and able to endure the burden of legal proceedings. More strategic enforcement would be possible only through the work of some kind of enforcement body (such as the UK Disability Rights Commission) with a remit to support and fund individuals in cases likely to clarify or develop the law (O'Brien 2003).

Even an anti-discrimination law covering transport and supported by some kind of enforcement body may often have serious limitations as an instrument of social change. The focus is often on compensating successful individual litigants who have been discriminated against in the past rather than on changing practices and policies so as to avoid discrimination in the future (Fredman 2001a: 170-173). The prospects for social change are improved where the duties placed on service providers are of an anticipatory nature, as is the case in the UK with the duties to make reasonable adjustments under the DDA. Nevertheless, judgements have still tended to focus on compensation, rather than requiring change, where service providers have been found not to have fulfilled their anticipatory duties. If there is no obligation to consult with and involve disabled people in the design of structures, policies and systems it will inevitably prove difficult to tackle those barriers which arise from neglect or lack of understanding of their needs and frequently permeate every layer of an institution's operation (Hepple et al. 2000: para 2.19).

Some of the limitations outlined in the previous paragraph could be removed by the inclusion in anti-discrimination laws of a positive duty to promote disability equality along the lines of the UK positive duty to promote good relations between members of different ethnic groups and eliminate race discrimination created by section 71 of the Race Relations (Amendment) Act 2000. Such a duty would require organisations to consider disability equality at every stage of their design and operation. Unlike conventional forms of anti-discrimination legislation, it would require employers and service-providers to take positive steps to ensure that, wherever possible, disabling barriers were removed and, perhaps more significantly, not created at the outset. There are proposals to impose such a duty on public bodies in the UK in the draft Disability Discrimination Bill. Provided such a duty is supported by effective enforcement mechanisms, it has enormous potential to dismantle disabling barriers in the sphere of public transport and beyond (Fredman 2001b; O'Cinneide 2003). In this sense it is a legal strategy very much in line with the tenets of the social model (Oliver 1996; Quinn 1997).

Conclusion

Recent years have witnessed a significant increase in the legal requirements imposed on the transport industry in European countries to provide transport which is accessible to disabled people. Despite the apparent growth in commitment to achieving change in this area, the overall picture of legislative provision remains something of a patchwork. The national level is characterised by a wide variety of different approaches and different levels of activity. At the EU level there is a patchy coverage of transport modes (air travel remaining largely uncovered) and a patchy coverage of access issues with physical access often dominating concerns while information and customer service issues are neglected. European human rights instruments provide a possible, though somewhat uncertain, avenue of redress to disabled people in signatory States.

We have explored a number of the legal strategies which have emerged to assist disabled people wishing to challenge the inaccessibility of their public transport systems. While the human rights route may offer some redress to claimants in the most extreme of circumstances it is unlikely to lead to a general dismantling of disabling transport barriers. Traditional anti-discrimination legislation, too, is likely to have only a limited effect on the general elimination of such obstacles. The appearance of a new positive duty to promote disability equality, coupled with the duty not to discriminate, promises a more anticipatory, systematic approach to the development of a barrier-free transport system. It is to be hoped therefore, that the EU can be persuaded to adopt a disability-specific directive, such as that proposed by the EDF, and that it will include an obligation on States to impose a positive duty on public bodies to promote disability equality in the provision of transport and other services.

Law alone, however, must not be expected to achieve wholesale social change. As the ECMT stress, even the best of laws must be supplemented by clear guidance, communication, persuasion and training. Much work remains to be done both in securing appropriate legislation and in ensuring its effective implementation. Though we may have begun to make preparations for our journey towards a Europe with public transport systems accessible to disabled people, the journey itself has scarcely begun.

Bibliography

Clements, L. and Read, J. 2003: *Disabled People and European Human Rights*. Bristol: Policy Press.

De Schutter, O. 2003: Reasonable Accommodations and Positive Obligations under the European Convention on Human Rights. Paper delivered at the Disability Rights in Europe Conference, Leeds, 25-26 September.

European Conference of Ministers of Transport 2000: Legislation to improve access, Paris, OECD.

Fredman, S. 2001a: *Discrimination Law*. Oxford: Oxford University Press.

Fredman, S. 2001b: Equality: A New Generation? *Industrial Law Journal*, 30, 16.

Hepple, B. et al. 2000: *Equality: A New Framework, Report of the Independent Review of the Enforcement of UK Anti-Discrimination Legislation*. Oxford: Hart.

McColgan, A. 2003: Principles of Equality and Protection from Discrimination in International Human Rights Law. *European Human Rights Law Review*, 157.

Novitz, T. 2002: Are Social Rights Necessarily Collective Rights? A Critical Analysis of the Collective Complaints Protocol to the European Social Charter. *European Human Rights Law Review* 52.

Nowak, M. and Suntinger, W. 1995: The Rights of Disabled People not to be subjected to Torture, Inhuman and Degrading Treatment or Punishment. In T. Degener and Y. Koster-Dreese (eds), *Human Rights and Disabled Persons: Essays and Relevant Human Rights Instruments*. London: Martinus Nijhoff Publishers.

O'Brien, N. 2003: *The UK Disability Rights Commission and Strategic Law Enforcement: Transcending the Common Law Mind*. Paper delivered at the Disability Rights in Europe Conference, Leeds, 25-26 September.

O'Cinneide, C. 2003: *A New Generation of Equality Legislation? Positive Duties and Disability Rights*. Paper delivered at the Disability Rights in Europe Conference, Leeds, 25-26 September.

Oliver, M. 1996: *Understanding Disability, from Theory to Practice*. Basingstoke: Macmillan.

Quinn, G. 1997: Rethinking the Place of Difference in Civil Society - the Role of Anti-Discrimination Law in the Next Century. In R. Byrne and W. Duncan (eds), *Developments in Discrimination Law in Ireland and Europe*. Dublin: ICEL.

Reports

Diamantopoulou, Anna 2003: Statement by Employment and Social Affairs Commissioner in Rome at the closing ceremony of the European Year of People with Disabilities on Sunday 7 December 2003.

ECAC 2001: http://europa.eu.int/comm/transport/air/rights/doc/commitment_airlines_en.pdf

EDF 2001: EDF response to the European Commission White Paper 'European Transport Policy for 2010', EDF 01/11 – December 2001.

EDF 2002: DOC EDF 02-07 – October 2002.

European Commission 1993: The Community Action Programme for Accessible Transport, adopted in 1993, (COM (1993) 433 final).

European Commission 2000: 'Towards a Barrier Free Europe for People with Disabilities' a communication from the Commission, 12 May 2000 (COM (2000) 284 final).

European Commission 2002a: COM(2002)18 final. Available at: http://europa.eu.int/comm/transport/rail/newpack/np_en.htm

European Commission 2002b: 'Proposal for a Regulation establishing common rules for compensation and assistance to air passengers' (COM(2001)784 FINAL), adopted on 7 January 2002. Available at http://www.europa.eu.int/eur-lex/en/com/availability/en_availability_2001_16.html

European Commission 2003: Consultation Paper on airline contracts with passengers, 3 July 2003. Available at: http://europa.eu.int/comm/transport/themes/air/english/at_en.html

European Conference of Ministers of Transport 2000: Legislation to Improve Access. Report prepared by the Committee of Deputies Group on transport for people with mobility handicaps, Paris, OECD.

Steinmeyer, H. D, (ed.) 2003: Legislation to counter discrimination against persons with disabilities, Brussels, the Council of Europe.

Legislation

Accessible Information Directive 1999: Council Directive 99/35/EC on accessible information for visually impaired passengers.

Draft Passenger Ships Directive: Draft directive amending Directive 98/18/EC establishing safety standards for passenger ships.

Employment Framework Directive 2000: Directive 2000/78/EC 'Establishing a general framework for equal treatment in employment and occupation'.

High Speed Trains Directive 1996: Directive 96/48/EC (23 July 1996).
Information on Disabled Passengers Directive 1998: Council Directive 98/41/EC on information for the ship masters and shore service staff on disabled passengers on board passenger ships.
Race Directive 2000: Directive 2000/43/EC.
Road Safety and Motor Vehicles Directive 2003: Directive on Road Safety and Technical Standards for Motor Vehicles 2003 (amending Directive 70/156/EEC).

Cases
Bernard v Enfield LBC 2002: EWHC 2282 Admin CO/1060/02.
Botta v Italy 1998: Application number 00021439/93 24/02/1998.
Marzari v Italy 1999: Decision of 4 May 1999. Application Number 36448/97.
Sentges v the Netherlands 2003: Decision of 8 July 2003. Application Number 27677/02.
Thlimmenos v Greece 2000: 31 EHRR 411.
Zehlanova and Zehnal v the Czech Republic 2002: Decision of 14 May 2002. Application No 38621/97.

CHAPTER 7

Disabled People and the European Union: equal citizens?

Hannah Morgan and Helen Stalford

Introduction

2003 was a significant year for disabled people in the European Union (EU). It marked the tenth anniversary of the United Nations' *Standard Rules on the Equalisation of Opportunities for Disabled People* (UN 1993) which gave international recognition for a social model or rights based approach to disability. The *Standard Rules* provided impetus for a more social model-oriented EU disability strategy, the language of which is dominated by a focus on citizenship, accessibility and barrier-removal. Furthermore, the year was designated European Year of Disabled People with the clear aim of raising awareness of disability issues in general and particularly of the environmental, social, economic, procedural and attitudinal barriers disabled people face. The intention was to generate a more concrete political commitment to promote disabled people's inclusion within mainstream European law and policy.

Central to the mainstreaming of disability issues has been a focus on the extent to which disabled Europeans can actively apply and develop their Union Citizenship. Disabled people, their organisations and allies have argued strongly that disabled people are in effect 'invisible citizens' within the EU, absent from European legislation and without adequate protection from discrimination by substantive EU law (EDF 1995). While more recent developments such as the 1997 Treaty of Amsterdam (which extended the protection of EU nationals against nationality-based discrimination to a range of other grounds, including race, sexual orientation, age, religious beliefs and disability (Article 13 EC)), mark an important advancement in the formal status of disabled citizens, concern still exists around the accessibility and scope of the rights and obligations implicit in the notion of Citizenship of the Union.

In order to frame our discussion of disabled people's status at Community level, it is important, to identify from the outset what, exactly, we mean by Citizenship of the Union, both in a formal legal as well as a practical sense.

Defining Citizenship of the European Union

Citizenship in a national context is traditionally allied with the exercise, to varying degrees, of civil, political and social rights. It also commonly denotes the legal and social relationship between individuals within a community and their relationship with the State. To what extent, therefore, does EU citizenship espouse these notions? Moreover, how many of us would really celebrate our status as a citizen of the Union? What, if anything, makes us identify and engage as individuals with EU membership? And to what extent does disability alter our conception and experience of EU membership? In responding to these questions, it is useful to consider, first of all, the formal legal definition of Union citizenship.

The concept of Citizenship of the Union attained formal constitutional status following the 1992 Treaty of Maastricht. This stated quite simply that all nationals of the current 15 Member States are to be regarded as citizens of the Union by virtue of Article 17 (formerly Article 8) of the EC Treaty. But how does the status of the EU citizen differ from the actual practise of EU citizenship – in other words, to what does this status give rise in terms of substantive rights? Very generally, the EC Treaty provides that all EU nationals 'shall enjoy the rights conferred by this Treaty and shall be subject to the duties imposed thereby' (Article 17(2)). This includes a set of (albeit modest) political rights and, more significantly, 'the right to move and reside freely within the territory of the Member States' (Article 18 EC).

The link between active EU citizenship and the exercise of free movement between Member States is, therefore, firmly established in this provision and has been pivotal to the development of substantive rights under Community law over the past thirty years, opening up access to a range of welfare and employment-related rights for those who migrate to other Member States (D'Oliveira 1995; Ackers 1998; Shaw 1998). This led one commentator to suggest that free movement is 'the central element around which our other rights crystallise' (D'Oliveira 1995:65).

The symbiotic relationship between EU citizenship and the free movement provisions implies that our rights as citizens of the Union are only really meaningful in the context of intra-union mobility making it for many European citizens a 'hollow concept'. As Ackers and Dwyer assert:

> in the absence of mobility, Citizenship of the Union contributes little to the social status and day-to-day experience of Community nationals (2002:3).

This conception of EU citizenship is particularly exclusive of those with neither the means nor the inclination to move to another Member State, for example, because of disabling barriers. Even if an individual does wish to move, they must satisfy certain criteria in order to qualify under the free movement provisions and obtain access to the panoply of social rights in another Member State. These criteria can be summarised as follows: you have to be an EU national and you have to be economically active (i.e. in work) or economically self-sufficient (that is, not dependent on welfare benefits). If you are neither of these, you can migrate as a dependent family member (that is, as the spouse, child or parent) of the migrant worker.

The limitations inherent in these criteria have, by now, been well documented, particularly in respect of their disproportionate marginalisation of women and children (Scheiwe 1994; Lundström 1996; Moebius and Szyszczak 1998; McGlynn 2000; Ackers and Stalford 2004) same-sex and cohabiting couples (Stychin 2000; Wintemute and Andenaes 2001) and third country nationals (Peers 1996). The more recent lobbying efforts of national bodies, network NGOs and Commission-affiliated organisations such as the European Disability Forum (EDF) have stimulated more critical discussion on the deficiencies of free movement legislation and wider EU-policies in respect of disabled people. However, there is relatively little academic discussion on this issue - one exception is the paper prepared by Waddington and van der Mei (1999) for the EDF - and very little literature challenging the accessibility of European Citizenship in this context.

We turn now to identify and critique the definition, scope and application of the free movement of persons provisions as the principal trigger of European social rights and, indeed, European citizenship. Specifically the paper will address the implications of the hierarchical nature of entitlement for disabled people with particular reference to debates around disability, dependency and work. This discussion will enable us to question the extent to which disabled people can enjoy active citizenship of the Union outside the context of free movement.

This concern has been recently re-articulated by the European Network on Independent Living (ENIL) (2003), the first European Congress on Independent Living held in Tenerife (2003) and the European Congress on Disability in Madrid (2003).

Disabling barriers to mobility
Waddington and van der Mei, in their discussion of the free movement provisions suggest that 'Community law does not (intentionally) seek to deny this right to people with disabilities' (1999: 8). In practice, however, the interpretation attached to concepts such as 'worker' and 'dependent family member', which are so central to accessing free movement rights, act as additional barriers to disabled people's mobility. This is quite apart from the physical barriers to migration and the impact of the disparity between disability related support available in different Member States. Let us look at these two concepts in more detail.

The concept of 'worker' under the free movement provisions
The concept of work under EU law is central to the operation and enjoyment of the free movement provisions but it is not clearly defined in any of the Treaties or secondary legislation. It has, instead, been left to the European Court of Justice (ECJ) to articulate and develop its meaning. The traditional rationale underpinning the mobility entitlement of workers was primarily economic: that they would be contributing to the development of the market economy by transporting valuable labour and skills resources between the Member States.

The essential criteria for qualifying as a Community worker under the free movement provisions have now been clearly established by the ECJ in *Lawrie-Blum* (1986) as entailing the performance of services, for or under the direction of another (separate rules govern the self-employed), in return for remuneration. While initially these criteria implied a full-time, male breadwinner who was making a discernible economic contribution to society, the ECJ has demonstrated an increasing readiness over the past twenty years to construe the term more broadly to encompass a wider range of working patterns. This has coincided with and, indeed, precipitated a gradual departure from a strict assessment of the tangible economic value of the activity towards one that is more subjective and looks at the value of the activity to the life of the individual him or herself.

As such, the ECJ has reaffirmed the right of all workers in all Member States to pursue the activity of their choice within the Community, irrespective of whether they are permanent, seasonal, temporary, part-time or full-time (*Levin* 1982), and regardless of whether they are supplementing their income by recourse to welfare benefits (*Kempf* 1986). The only limitation imposed is that the work must be 'genuine and effective' and cannot be carried out on such a small scale as to be regarded as marginal and ancillary to other activities carried out by the individual in the host state, such as studying or tourism, which are governed by different, more restrictive rules (*Raulin* 1992). One of the principal reasons behind these limitations on free movement entitlement is to protect Member States against the threat of so-called 'welfare tourism' whereby EU nationals may be motivated to move to other Member States under the pretext of carrying out 'work' but, in reality, in order to take advantage of more favourable welfare provision.

The expansion of the concept of work and worker has significant implications for disabled people, large numbers of whom are engaged in part-time, intermittent work (Sly 1996). According to recent EU figures, 15 per cent of the working age (16-64) population report disability, with 10 per cent reporting 'moderate disability' and 4.5 per cent 'severe disability' (Eurostat 2001). Within this group 46 per cent of 'moderately disabled' and 24 per cent of 'severely disabled' people are engaged in some form of work. However, as Barnes notes, disabled people's participation in the labour market tends to be characterised by their employment in 'poorly paid, low skilled, low status jobs which are both unrewarding and undemanding' (1991:65). Consequently, disabled people are more likely to experience lower levels of career advancement and under-utilisation of their skills and training when in work (Thornton and Lunt 1995:2). Thus, while the free movement provisions may open up to a greater proportion of disabled people of working age the prospect of working and living in other Member States they by no means represent a panacea for existing inequalities at national level.

The status of job-seekers
Case law also exists in relation to the status of unemployed Community migrants in pursuit of employment. In *Antonissen* (1991), for instance, the Court stated that jobseekers retain the status of worker and the right to move to another Member State to seek employment but that this right is not unlimited. For example in *Lebon* (1987) the ECJ held that 'those who move in search of employment qualify for equal treatment only as regards access to employment'. In other words, they can move to another country

in order to look for work but will not enjoy all the social and tax advantages attached to the status of worker until they have actually found work. This finding is problematic for those disabled people who require support systems (which may include statutory support or benefits) to be in place to enable them to seek and obtain employment. This dilemma is mitigated to a certain degree by the existence of EU legislation (Regulation 1408/71 supplemented by Regulation 574/72) which entitles jobseekers to maintain benefits in their country of origin for up to three months while they are abroad looking for work, although certain benefits such as the provision of equipment may be restricted. A further disincentive for potential disabled migrants is that, on returning to their 'home' Member State, they may have to undergo a new assessment before they can recover any further benefits or forms of social support.

The status of voluntary workers
Some forms of voluntary work are held to constitute 'work' under Community law. In Steymann (1988) a German national, resident in the Netherlands, was refused a residence permit by the relevant authorities on the basis that his contribution to the life of a religious community could not be regarded as 'economic' for the purposes of Community law. In return for his contribution, the community provided him with accommodation and 'pocket money'. The ECJ concluded that Steymann did, in effect, provide services of value to the religious community which would otherwise have to be performed by someone else (and presumably paid for) and, on that basis, he qualified as a worker.

The ECJ found that Steymann's contribution to the community via some plumbing work, general housework and participation in the external economic activities of the community (running a disco and laundry service) were indirectly remunerated through the provision of accommodation and modest living expenses. This decision is significant for the increasing number of disabled people engaged in user-involvement, in-service provision or in the organisation and running of user-led service providers, where they may be involved in irregular or less formalised types of consultation and training for which some sort of remuneration other than cash is made (Barnes 2003).

While decisions such as that of *Steymann* advance disabled people's opportunities and status as Community migrants, it is interesting to note that the majority of ECJ cases considering the concept of work and the definition of 'Community worker' do not explicitly refer to disability or take account of the specific barriers disabled people encounter when seeking to participate in the labour market. In one of the few cases concerning a disabled person's claim, that of *Bettray* (1989), the Court rejected the claim of a disabled German man employed in a sheltered environment to be considered as a Community worker. Bettray was employed by a special Dutch scheme which aimed to 'maintain, restore or develop the capacity for work' of those who able to undertake some form of economic activity but who are not in a position to undertake regular employment either because of disability or substance misuse. The ECJ held that such schemes could not constitute 'genuine and effective' work as the activities were tailored to fit the individual and were specifically aimed at rehabilitation and reintegration into the mainstream labour market. The ruling in *Bettray*, therefore, significantly enhances the worker status of over 300,000 disabled people in sheltered employment (Samoy 1992), because as Waddington and van dei Mei (1999) point out, contrary to the image of sheltered employment depicted in *Bettray*, the work of most sheltered workshops can be considered equally as 'genuine and effective' as that of most mainstream jobs.

While the extension of the Community concept of work and the definition of what constitutes a Community worker to include less traditional forms and patterns of work often undertaken by disabled people is to be welcomed, a sizeable proportion of disabled people are not, for various reasons, active in the labour market in any sense. In fact, according to 2001 Eurostat figures, 46 per cent of 'moderate' and 61 per cent of 'severe' disabled people are reported as being economically 'inactive'. This begs questions as to the availability of an alternative status that triggers access to the freedom of movement provisions: the status of a dependent family member.

The status of 'dependent' family members under the free movement provisions

The second group to enjoy certain rights by virtue of the free movement provisions is the families of Community migrant workers. This group encompasses many disabled family members who do not, for various reasons, undertake paid employment, such as disabled children and young people, and (increasing numbers of) older disabled people. Family members who move with a migrant worker can access the same welfare-related (including disability benefits) and other social benefits in the host state as the worker and, in that sense, derive a highly privileged status from their relationship with the worker (*Michel S* 1973). However, limitations are placed on who may claim these derived rights by the way in which Community law defines who and what constitutes 'family' and 'dependency'. Again, in much the same way as the definition of work and 'worker' has evolved, these definitions and, perhaps more noteworthy, the ideologies and presumptions underpinning them have significant implications for disabled people.

The Community definition of 'family' under the free movement provisions
Currently, Community law specifies that the only family members who are entitled to move with the migrant worker and have access to the range of social and tax benefits in another Member State are: the worker's spouse (legally married, heterosexual); their children who are under the age of 21; any other children who are over the 21 but who are dependent; and dependent relatives in the ascending line (Regulation 1612/68, Article 10). It is the interpretation attached to dependency that impacts most significantly on disabled people generally.

Defining 'dependency' under the free movement provisions
A dependent relationship is, to a large degree, presumed in relation to children under the age of 21 and to the older parents of Community workers. However, the ECJ has so far failed to provide any clear guidelines as to what exactly constitutes dependency. It mostly clearly associates the state of dependency with financial dependency. For example in the case of *Inzirillo* (1976), the ECJ ruled that the son of an Italian migrant worker was entitled to claim a French disability benefit based solely on his financial dependency on his parent. However, financial dependency is not taken to require residence with the migrant worker. The ruling in *Diatta* (1985) held that a 'dependent' family member is not required to live in the same household as the migrant worker as long as some form (however superficial) of financial dependency can be demonstrated. Ironically, the financial dependency required for a family member to claim social entitlement may be extinguished once that claim is realised, making dependency 'a matter of initial [qualifying] fact' (Ackers and Dwyer 2002:44).

More appropriate in the context of disability would be a broader interpretation of dependency by the ECJ to encompass relationships of physical and emotional support, which are often of greater significance to those concerned than financial support, as this would open up derived rights to a large number of disabled (and non-disabled) family members.

The way in which dependency is construed within this context is particularly problematic from a social model perspective. A central tenet of the disabled people's movement has been a rejection of a presumed automatic link between impairment and dependency with a focus instead on less physically based notions of independence (Morris 1993; Shakespeare 2000). This is encapsulated in the philosophy of independent living which distinguishes between the physical doing of an act for oneself (such as dressing or feeding) and exercising choice and control over how these activities are undertaken. Adopting an independent living approach to dependency involves recognising that:

> no one in a modern industrial society is completely independent, for we live in a state of mutual interdependence. The dependency of disabled people, therefore, is not a feature which marks them out as different in kind from the rest of the population but as different in degree (Oliver 1989: 83-4).

Defining 'family' (and indeed 'work') to account for the interdependence between family members (and therefore the contribution that all family members make however financially or physically dependent they may be perceived to be) would have significant implications for the accessibility of the free movement provisions. It may also have implications for the hierarchical nature of entitlement as it would be difficult to sustain a privileged position for workers if other aspects of family life were recognised as equal to the breadwinning role.

Adopting a rights-based approach to European Citizenship

While the free movement of persons provisions, and particularly the extension of the concept of worker, have achieved much in enhancing the migration potential of disabled people, it is important to note their limitations. First of all, the social and economic rights arising out of free movement are based firmly on an ethic of non-discrimination. In that sense, they do not create additional social rights but merely provide migrants with access to these rights under the same conditions as nationals in the Member State to which they migrate. Consequently, the nature and level of benefits (for example, those yielded by social welfare systems) are only as good as those already available to disabled nationals within the host state. Attaining EU migrant worker or family status does not, in that sense, address the inequalities already inherent in national laws and policies affecting disabled people.

A second limitation of the free movement provisions is their emphasis on economic contribution as a basis for entitlement. Essentially, the extent to which disabled people enjoy rights in this context bears direct relation to their level of economic activity. Feminist and, more recently, children's rights critiques of EU citizenship have in particular challenged EU law's devaluation and, thus, marginalisation of economically subordinate groups in its allocation of tangible entitlement (Ackers and Stalford 2004).

These limitations suggest that a shift towards a more coherent rights-based approach to EU citizenship could effectively address the deficiencies of free movement-based conceptions of citizenship. Indeed, citizenship is not just about securing access to social entitlement. It provides an important oratory for enhancing individuals' sense of autonomy and agency and for promoting effective participation. A broader, rights-based approach to citizenship incorporates these more ideological notions of participation, inclusion and equality while acknowledging individuals' contributions as everyday social actors (Cockburn 1998). Lister notes in this respect:

> social citizenship rights also promote the 'de-commodification of labour' by decoupling the living standards of individual citizens from their 'market value' so they are not totally dependent on selling their labour power in the market (1997: 17).

Much remains to be achieved, however, to translate these ideologies into more inclusive, tangible entitlement for disabled people. So far, the EU has stopped short of implementing any binding law on Member States in respect of disability issues, opting instead for less controversial, aspirational, non-binding (or 'soft law') initiatives aimed primarily at facilitating the professional integration of disabled people. Even Article 13 of the EC Treaty, by which the 1997 Treaty of Amsterdam extended the long-standing prohibition of discrimination on grounds of nationality to other grounds including disability, has yet to be fully exploited as a legal basis on which to address the specific needs of EU nationals with impairments. Indeed, the European Disability Forum did submit proposals in 1999 for a specific disability directive based on Article 13, similar to that already implemented in the context of race equality. This recommended imposing specific obligations on Member States to take into account the impact of all laws and policies on disabled people, not only in an employment context, but also in relation to housing, education, welfare and environmental initiatives.

It was not until the end of 2003, however, that the Commission made any real political commitment to act on the proposals put forward by the EDF and other lobbying organisations. On 30 October, it presented an Action Plan to improve and facilitate the economic and social integration of disabled people in an enlarged Europe. The first two-year phase of this six-year plan, which started in 2004, focuses on creating the conditions for disabled people to access the mainstream labour market. This is accompanied by a commitment from the Commission to issue bi-annual reports on the overall situation of disabled people in the enlarged EU as a means of identifying new priorities for subsequent phases of the Action Plan.

Notwithstanding the fact that these measures are targeted primarily at those who have the capacity to engage in full-time, paid employment, it is with some optimism that we might forecast the direction of the wider EU disability agenda, particularly in view of recent constitutional developments. Perhaps one of the most promising portents in this regard is the increasing prominence of human rights at EU law-making level, most notably through the introduction in December 2000 of the *Charter of Fundamental Rights in the European Union* (CEC 2000). This document sets out, for the first time in the European Union's history, the institutions' commitment to upholding and advancing a range of civil, political, economic and social rights in favour of all persons resident in the EU. Most of the 54 provisions contained in the Charter (which are heavily inspired by the provisions of the 1950 European Convention on Human Rights) are of direct or indirect relevance to disability with Article 26 of the Charter explicitly stating that:

> The Union recognises and respects the right of persons with disabilities to benefit from measures designed to ensure their independence, social and occupational integration and participation in the life of the community.

These measures concern education, vocational training, ergonomics, accessibility, mobility, means of transport and housing as well as access to cultural and leisure activities, giving it a much wider scope than many of the other employment-related initiatives presented previously.

The Charter is currently only of declaratory (non-binding) force, although it has been incorporated in its entirety into Part II of the draft EU Constitution currently under negotiation. The new Article 26 is now enshrined in Title III of Part II (entitled 'Equality') and is supported by other provisions such as Article 20: 'Everyone is equal before the law'; and Article 21 (1):

> Any discrimination based on any ground such as sex, race, colour, ethnic or social origin, genetic features, language, religion or belief, political or any other opinion, membership of a national minority, property, birth, disability, age or sexual orientation shall be prohibited.

These measures, which reflect the spirit of Article 13 EC, are further reiterated in Part III Title I of the draft constitution entitled 'The Policies and Functioning of the Union'. Specifically, Article 3 states that:

> In defining and implementing the policies and activities referred to in this Part, the Union shall aim to combat discrimination based on sex, racial or ethnic origin, religion or belief, disability, age or sexual orientation.

Finally, Part III, Title II acknowledges the institutions' capacity to enact binding laws with a view to combating discrimination on these grounds:

> Article 8 (1): Without prejudice to the other provisions of the Constitution and within the limits of the powers conferred by it upon the Union, a European law or framework law of the Council of Ministers may establish the measures needed to combat discrimination based on sex, racial or ethnic origin, religion or belief, disability, age or sexual orientation. The Council of Ministers shall act unanimously after obtaining the consent of the European Parliament.

While institutional activity is restricted to the areas of competence articulated by the constitution, if adopted, and implemented, these provisions will provide an important template on which to enact more tailored initiatives in favour of disabled people, thereby detaching tangible rights from the economic imperative of the free movement provisions.

Conclusion

In this chapter, we have aimed to illustrate the way in which Community definitions of the concepts of work, family and dependency have significant implications for the citizenship of disabled people. The evolution of the concept of work to include new forms and different working patterns has opened up the status of Community worker to a larger percentage of disabled people. This ignores, however, the growing tension within disability studies and the disabled people's movement about the priority afforded to inclusion in the labour market (Barnes 2004). Early social model thinking clearly linked disablement with exclusion from the labour market (Oliver 1990) and therefore argued that reintegration was a precursor to disabled people's full participation and citizenship. Alongside this the independent living movement has adopted a different focus. The movement emerged largely from attempts to replace large-scale residential institutional care with services and support required for disabled people to live independently while emphasising the importance of acknowledging individuals' interdependence.

Furthermore, focusing solely upon paid employment as the precondition for the full exercise of citizenship rights provides a narrow view of contribution. In an economy driven by consumption the consumer plays a 'productive' role. This is particularly pertinent for disabled people around whom a vast 'disability industry' has emerged employing thousands in the direct provision of care and medical support as well as indirectly through the production of aids and adaptations. Likewise, as feminist writers have suggested (Ackers 1998; Lister 2002), unpaid or informal 'care' work undertaken largely by women (including disabled women) plays an important role in both supporting the traditional notion of a single family breadwinner and of dispersing much of the societal costs associated with supporting children, disabled and older people.

Quite aside from these ideological debates, we have identified a range of additional barriers that restrict disabled people's ability to effectively exercise free movement. The disparity between social security systems and welfare provision in different Member States acts as a deterrent to mobility. Moving between Member States may result in the loss of existing benefits in the sending state and there are often qualifying periods before new claims can be made in the receiving state. Moreover, the conditions under which disabled people can export certain benefits are decidedly restrictive. Non-legal barriers include barriers to physical movement especially in terms of inaccessible public transport; in addition to well-documented discrimination in employment, housing, public support, and assistance (Waddington and van dei Mei 1999).

Thus while there may be a growing formal commitment at EU-level to extend full citizenship and its accompanying free movement rights to disabled people (on the basis of non-discrimination), considerable obstacles still exist at national level which hamper their enjoyment and for which the EU cannot currently claim legislative competency. In order to engage disabled people in a more meaningful way in the EU polity, therefore, active citizenship requires a departure from traditional free movement-based interpretations which, through their elevation of formal employment, inevitably and consistently exclude a large proportion of them.

It is in this respect that a broader rights-based approach to citizenship becomes an important means by which to extend disabled EU nationals' rights beyond the economic imperative of the free movement provisions towards a more inclusive and positive declaration of their specific needs and value. As well as seeking to promote the substance of tangible entitlement, a rights-based model of citizenship provides an important platform not only for promoting individual autonomy and agency but for exposing and crediting disabled people's contribution to society through their formal and informal, direct and indirect participation in the labour market.

The EU has certainly started to adopt a more proactive stance on disability issues in the past decade or so, manifested in a number of subtle budgetary, institutional and legislative developments. However, if European citizenship is to be regarded as more than simply a showcase for modest rights available primarily to economic actors under the free movement provisions, there is an urgent need for a more enforceable and confident declaration of disabled people's status at this level.

Bibliography (legal cases are itemised separately below)
Ackers, L. 1998: *Shifting Spaces: Women, Citizenship and Migration in the European Community*. Bristol: Policy Press.
Ackers, L. and Dwyer, P. 2002: *Senior Citizenship? Retirement Migration and Welfare in the European Union*. Bristol: Policy Press.
Ackers, L. and Stalford, H. 2004: *A Community for Children? Children, Citizenship and Internal Migration in the European Union*. Aldershot: Ashgate.
Barnes, C. 1991: *Disabled People in Britain and Discrimination: A Case for Anti-Discrimination Legislation*. London: Hurst & Co.
Barnes, C. 2003: *Disability, the organisation of work, and the need for Change*. Disability Archive UK:
www.leeds.ac.uk/disability-studies/archive.uk
Barnes, C. 2004: *'Work' is a four letter word? Disability, Work and Welfare*. Paper delivered to the Working Futures seminar, University of Sunderland, 3-5 December 2003.
Cockburn, T. 1998: Children and Citizenship in Britain. *Childhood*, 5 (1), 99-117.

CEC (Commission of the European Communities) 2000: *Charter of Fundamental Rights in the European Union*. OJ 2000 C 364/01, 18.12.2000 (concluded at the Nice Summit in December 2000)

D'Olivera, J. 1995: Union Citizenship: Pie in the Sky? In A. Rosas and E. Antola (eds), *A Citizen's Europe: In Search of a New Order*. London: Sage.

European Congress on Disability 2003: *The Madrid Declaration: Non Discrimination plus positive action results in social inclusion* Madrid: ECOD.

European Congress on Independent Living 2003: *Tenerife Declaration: Promote Independent Living - End Discrimination against Disabled People*. Tenerife: ECIL.

European Disability Forum 1995: *Disabled People's status in the European Union Treaties - Invisible Citizens*. Brussels: EDF.

European Network on Independent Living 2003: *Strasbourg Freedom Drive 2003*. Dublin: ENIL.

Eurostat 2001: *Disability and social participation in Europe*. Luxembourg: Office for the Official Publications of the European Communities.

Lister, R. 1997: *Citizenship: feminist perspectives*. London: Macmillan.

Lundström, K. 1996: Family life and the freedom of movement of workers in the European Union. *International Journal of Law, Policy and the Family*, 10, 250-280.

McGlynn, C. 2000: A Family Law for the European Union? In J. Shaw (ed.), *Social Law and Policy in an Evolving European Union*. Oxford: Hart.

Moebius, I. and Szyszczak, E. 1998: Of Raising Pigs and Children. *Yearbook of European Law*, 18, 125-156.

Morris, J. 1993: *Independent Lives: Community Care and Disabled People*. Basingstoke: Macmillan.

Oliver, M. 1989: Disability and dependency: a creation of industrialised Societies. In L. Barton (ed.), *Disability and Dependency*. London: Falmer.

Oliver, M. 1990: *The Politics of Disablement*. Basingstoke: Macmillan.

Peers, S. 1996: Towards equality: actual and potential rights of third-country nationals in the European Union. *Common Market Law Review*, 33, 7-50.

Samoy, E. 1992: *Sheltered Employment in the European Community*. Brussels: Community of the European Communities.

Scheiwe, K. 1994: EC Law's Unequal Treatment of the Family: the Case Law of the European Court of Justice on Rules Prohibiting Discrimination on the Grounds of Sex and Nationality. *Social and Legal Studies*, 3, 243-265.
Shaw, J. 1998: The interpretation of European Union Citizenship. The *Modern Law Review*, 61 (3), 293-317.
Shakespeare, T. 2000: *Help*. Birmingham: Venture Press.
Sly, F. 1996: Disability and the Labour Market. *Labour Market Trends*, September, 413-24.
Stychin, C. 2000: Consumption, Capitalism and the Citizen: Sexuality and Equality Rights Discourse in the European Union. In J. Shaw (ed.), *Social Policy in an Evolving European Union*. London: Hart.
Thornton, P. and Lunt, N. 1995: *Employment for Disabled People: Social Obligation or Individual Responsibility*. York: Social Policy Research Unit.
Waddington, L. and van der Mei, A. 1999: *Free Movement of Disabled People in the European Union: An examination of relevant Community provisions and a discussion of the barriers to free movement*. Brussels: European Disability Forum.
Wintemute, R. and Andenaes, M. (eds) 2001: *Legal recognition of same-sex partnerships: a study of national, European and international law*. Oxford: Hart.
United Nations 1993: *Standard Rules on the Equalisation of Opportunities for People with Disabilities*. New York: United Nations. Resolution 48/96 20 December 1993.

Legal cases
R v. IAT *ex parte Antonissen* Case C-292189 [1991] ECR 1-745.
Bettray v. Staatssecretaris van Justitie, Case 344/87 [1989] ECR 1621, [1991] 1 CMLR 459.
Diatta v. Land Berlin Case 267/83 [1985] ECR 567, 2 CMLR 164.
Inzirillo v. Caisse d'Allocations Familiaties de l'Arrondissement de Lyon C 63/76 [1976] ECR 2057.
Kempf v. Staatssecretaris van Justitie, Case 138/85 [1986] ECR 1741 [1987] 1 CMLR 101.
Lawrie-Blum v. Land Baden-Wüttemberg, Case 66/85 [1986] ECR 2121, [1987] 3 CMLR 389.
Centre public d'aide sociale de Courcelles v. *Lebon*, Case 316/85 [1987] ECR 2811, [1989] 1 CMLR 337.

Levin v Staatssecretaris van Justitie, Case 53/81 [1982] ECR 1035 [1982] 2 CMLR 454.

Case 76/72 ***Michel S.*** v. Fonds national de reclassement social des handicappés [1973] ECR 437.

Raulin v. Minister van Onderwijs en Wetenschappen C357/89 [1992] ECR 1-1027.

Steymann v. Staatssecretaris van Justitie Case 196/87, [1988] ECR 6159, [1989] 1 CMLR 449.

CHAPTER 8

One World, One People, One Struggle? Towards the global implementation of the social model of disability

Alison Sheldon

Introduction

The production of ideology is... in general, the production of ideas within the intellectual framework of existing social relations, in such a way as to obscure the totality of which they are a part and thereby, the possibility of changing these relations (Shaw 1975: 64).

Disability in the majority world is big business. Western controlled disability non-governmental organisations (NGOs) have spread their reach to almost every corner of the globe. Disability Studies courses in western Universities spew majority world practitioners off their production line in growing numbers. Libraries and academic journals are bursting with pronouncements on the plight of majority world disabled people - predominantly written by western and western-trained academics and practitioners. There is much of value in many of these texts (e.g. Charlton 1998; Coleridge 1993; Stone 1999). Others - whilst well intentioned - leave a bitter taste in the mouth. Myth-making is there in abundance, and the current solutions proposed to the problem of disability in the majority world seem unlikely ever to produce their stated objectives.

Since disability is 'increasingly influenced by the escalating processes of "globalization"' (Barnes and Mercer 2003: 133), its complexities cannot be fully understood except on a global scale. This is a vital challenge for disability studies. Disability researchers have been urged to examine disability in the context of the global economy, and the need for 'a contemporary political economy of disability' has been stressed - one that is informed by the global mode of production (Thomas 2004). Whilst one short chapter cannot do justice to this complex task, it can raise questions about the ideological springboard from which researchers and practitioners might best launch themselves.

This chapter then will interrogate current ideologies in academic thought concerning disability in the majority world. It will explore the common cause between disabled people globally and the people of the majority world, and suggest that the insights of the social model of disability might effectively be used to challenge the root causes of their disadvantage. It will firstly consider the creation and position of the so called 'majority world' in the global economic system; before moving on to examine social model thinking about disability in the majority world and the way in which its insights have been translated in practice. The main players who are seeking to ameliorate the effects of disability and underdevelopment in the majority world will then be identified and the role of western academics in the process of change considered. In conclusion, the need for a response to the social model's insights that is material in nature will be reiterated.

Global economics and the majority world
The world we inhabit is not an equitable one. Current trends suggest that this situation can only become more extreme. The capitalist mode of production now 'shapes social relationships over the entire planet' (Castells 1996: 471), and recent years have witnessed massive increases in both poverty and economic polarisation. As the rich get richer, the poor get poorer. Of the world's population - which is rapidly approaching 6.5 billion people, over one billion live on less than US $1 a day (UNDP 2005) and around 50 per cent survive on less than $2 a day (Castells 2001). At the turn of the millennium, 20 per cent of the world's people disposed of 86 per cent of the world's wealth, leaving the other 80 per cent of the global population struggling to survive on the remaining 14 per cent (Castells 2001). This economic polarisation is happening both within and between nations, and the people of the majority world and disabled people worldwide are feeling its effects. Those disabled people who are part of the majority world are thus 'the poorest, most isolated group in the poorest, most isolated places' (Charlton 1998: 43).

The global inequality that exists today has been illuminated through a variety of theoretical frameworks - a detailed analysis of which is beyond the scope of this chapter. However, many writers have argued convincingly that the roots of the biting poverty found in the majority world are located in the global capitalist system and its inequitable distribution of wealth. It is not natural or inevitable (Hoogvelt 1997). The development of capitalism is itself rooted in colonialism, which is thus blamed for 'almost all the imbalances that now cripple the economies, societies and politics' of the majority world (Harrison 1993: 45).

The European colonial powers wiped out indigenous industry and forced the colonies to buy their goods. They furthermore undermined the self-sufficiency of majority world countries and transformed them into a source of raw materials for western industry (Fanon 1967). These raw materials, it is argued, were taken primarily because they were necessary in order for the industrial revolution to take place (Anthony 1972). Indeed without this exploitation it is questioned whether Europe would have industrialised at all (Harrison 1993).

Clearly, 'the development of capitalism had a global dimension from the beginning' (Bernstein 2000: 44), and the system has a logic 'that tends to its expansion and internationalisation' (Panitch and Gindin 2003: 4). The European states not only established 'the legal and infrastructural frameworks for property, contract, currency, competition and wage-labour within their own borders', they also generated the process of uneven development that continues to plague the majority of the world today (Panitch and Gindin 2003: 5). While Europe prospered then, colonised parts of the world were kept in an underdeveloped state (Thirlwall 2002). Even when the colonial powers retreated from the colonies, leaving unstable states with artificial and arbitrary borders 'condemned to futile border conflicts and secessionist troubles' (Harrison 1993: 46), their control over them was little diminished. Whilst the question of colonialism should still be 'central to our thinking today' (Ahmad 2003: 52), there are now more insidious forms of global control. The International Monetary Fund (IMF) and the World Bank - western controlled and set up under the sponsorship and direction of the United States - now dictate economic policy-making in much of the world. Many of the policies that countries are forced to pursue are detrimental to the interests of the populace. In addition, those multinational corporations that operate in the majority world 'often introduce consumption patterns and techniques of production which are inappropriate... and to that extent impair welfare' (Thirlwall 2002: 3).

Arguably then, we are at a stage in the development of capitalism which is 'dominated by giant corporations, each of which controls a relatively high proportion of the local or world markets for its products' – what can be called monopoly capitalism (Bernstein 2000: 250). This seems to support Lenin's (1947) theory of imperialism – 'the process of capitalist accumulation on a world scale in the era of monopoly capitalism' (Weeks 1991: 252). Whilst Lenin was confident in his assertion that imperialism was 'the highest stage of capitalism', it is now suggested that what he was observing was 'a relatively *early* phase of capitalism' (Panitch and Gindin 2003: 6). Imperialism 're-invents itself... as the structure of global capitalism changes' (Ahmad 2003: 43), and it is argued that the world system is now dominated by one leading country 'with historically unprecedented global power' – the United States (Ahmad 2003: 43). To maintain relevance in this new world order, our analyses of disability must become less parochial. A task for disability studies scholars is thus said to be:

> to locate the tap-roots of contemporary disablism in the imperatives of the system(s) of production and exchange that exist in any region, functioning as they do under the tutelage of the World Bank, the International Monetary Fund and the US treasury (Thomas 2004: 36).

As yet, few have risen to this challenge. The social model of disability could be an invaluable tool in the process. Current trends in social model thinking, especially where the majority world is considered, may not however provide the necessary answers.

The social model and the majority world
The social model of disability has been, *is*, and will continue to be a hugely important tool. It gives insights into the mechanisms and processes that disable those with certain impairments, and hence into ways in which this disablement can be challenged and eradicated. UPIAS's (1976) seminal statement of disability's *Fundamental Principles* has spawned differing interpretations of the problem however. Increasingly, people are talking about social *models* (Finkelstein 2002; Horsler 2003; Priestley 1998). Broadly speaking, these fall between two positions – the materialist and the idealist. This crude distinction is *crucial*, especially when thinking about disability in the majority world.

The 'materialist' or 'radical' social model understands disability to be a logical outcome of the capitalist mode of production. Using the insights of this model, an important critique has been developed of the root cause of disablement – the capitalist system. Disability in its current form is said to have emerged at the time of the industrial revolution, with the growth of the commodity labour market a key factor in the process of disablement (Finkelstein 1980; Gleeson, 1997; Oliver 1990; Russell 2002). This version of the social model insists that 'the fundamental relationships of capitalist society are implicated in the social oppression of disabled people'. Logically then, 'the elimination of disablement... requires a *radical transformation*, rather than a reform of capitalism' (Gleeson 1997: 196).

These vital descriptions of the role of capitalism in disablement have as yet been largely confined to examinations of minority world states. Whilst skewed economic development is acknowledged to create *impairment* on a massive and unnecessary scale in the majority world (Elwan 1999; Stone 1999), all too often the link between disablement and the capitalist system is severed. Instead of connections being made between disability and the global economy, it is widely argued that religious ideas and traditional belief systems 'are the main determinant of what is socially acceptable in non-western contexts' (Barnes and Mercer 2003: 135). This is an idealist approach to the problem, which can never get to its roots. For effective change to occur, 'disability cannot be dematerialised and explained simply as the product of discriminatory beliefs, symbols and perceptions' (Gleeson 1997: 196).

The idealist or 'rights' interpretation of the social model, whilst generally acknowledging the realities of the materialist model, understands disability to be the irrational product of deep-rooted cultural beliefs, attitudes and prejudices. Hence the claim that:

> people with impairment are disabled, not just by material discrimination, but also by prejudice. This prejudice is not just interpersonal, it is also implicit in cultural representation, in language and in socialization (Shakespeare 1994: 296).

Such analyses have definite appeal for western researchers reporting on disability in the majority world. This has major implications, both ideologically and practically as will now be considered.

It encourages analyses that are racist in nature and hark back to our colonial past. We are told that understanding traditional beliefs about disability is fundamental for those who wish to foster effective change in the majority world (Groce 1999). However, this arguably does little more than encourage a judgmental focus on indigenous belief systems and practices. Benedicte Ingstad (1999: 757) for example examines western myth-making about the plight of the 'hidden disabled' in the majority world. She highlights that whilst there are reported cases of disabled people being hidden away and abused in the minority world, these are not used to 'create a general picture of behaviour in Europe or the USA'. Such cases are viewed as 'unfortunate exceptions', not as indicative of attitudes arising from traditional beliefs. Joseph Kisanji (1995: 54) raises similar concerns about much of the published material on majority world cultures, branding them 'anecdotal', 'impressionistic' and 'written for a western audience'. He highlights that many majority world professionals are themselves the products of 'non-indigenous western education' and thus they too may misinterpret indigenous practices.

Clearly then, 'caution needs to be exercised when reviewing findings on attitudes in non-western cultures' (Kisanji 1995: 55). Indigenous beliefs and attitudes, when described and interpreted by western/western trained researchers often illuminate more about western prejudices and belief systems than they do about the societies of which they claim to be gaining an understanding. This arguably represents a cultural racism - racism where 'the object... is no longer the individual... but a certain form of existence' (Fanon 1972: 15).

It is acknowledged that disability 'is very much a development issue shared by north and south' (Coleridge 1993: 65). However, an idealist focus on cultural differences separates disabled people one from another, suggesting that we are *not* one people, and are *not* involved in the same struggle. Furthermore, in conceptualising the world 'as divided into cultures and groups defined largely by their difference with each other' (Malik 2002: 3), not only are disabled people isolated from each other, separation is also encouraged from other oppressed groups (Horsler 2003). Thus any common cause between those who live in the majority world and disabled people globally is obscured. Ideology of course informs practice, and unless the roots of global inequality are questioned and addressed, only partial change will ever be possible. How then have minority world thinkers and practitioners risen to this challenge?

The global implementation of the social model

> ... to believe the global oppression and pauperization of billions of people does not have a direct relation with the state of the human condition, a condition involving 500 million people with disabilities and a condition dominated by the political economy of international capitalism, is a political dead end (Charlton 1998: 165).

The materialist model of disability poses intensely challenging questions, and its insights are thus increasingly dismissed as 'politically naive' (Gleeson 1997: 197). How should we go about radically transforming capitalism? Putting this model into practice then is an ambitious project that the disabled people's movement has not as yet attempted. The idealist interpretation of the social model asks simpler questions and thus suggests more obvious 'practical' solutions. Its implementation has involved challenging prejudice through the courts, seeking equal rights and equal opportunities within the existing, inequitable system. Instead of facing up to the challenges that the materialist model implies then, short-term policy reforms and sticking-plaster solutions are sought to the problem of disability - an orientation that has been described both as a weakness *and* a strength of disability studies (Gleeson 1997). Whilst such attempts are indicative of an important concern with praxis, and have undoubtedly improved conditions for some, disability shows no signs of disappearing. The materialist social model however holds 'great potential for a more theoretically-informed praxis' (Gleeson 1997: 181) - one which will focus on the causes of disability, not just treat the symptoms. Thus far, symptoms are all that have been attended to, and any suggestion that this may be insufficient seems almost heretical. This is amply illustrated through a brief consideration of the ideology of 'rights'.

The rights and wrongs of 'rights'

The term 'human rights'... is used as a collective noun as if 'human rights' was a given, uncontested principle or part of the order of things, standing above and apart from ordinary life but always present. Such discourses are oppressive because they close down questions, arguments and critical examination, rather than opening them up (Armstrong and Barton 1999: 214).

Whilst the contemporary ideology of rights is largely a product of the widespread outrage at 20th century genocide in Europe, the notion of rights is not new (Young and Quibell, 2000). Early ideas of 'natural rights' - rights bestowed on the human species by God or nature - have mutated into the notion of human rights, as outlined in the 1948 United Nations (UN) *Declaration of Human Rights*. These rights are held by individuals simply by virtue of being human and are - in theory - 'enshrined in the protective guardianship invested in bodies such as the United Nations or governments' (Armstrong and Barton 1999: 214).

A distinction can be drawn between human rights and civil rights - claims made within a specific state which are upheld by specific legal systems. In this country, human rights violations are generally associated with 'uncivilised' foreign states – a dangerous and racist discourse 'rooted in English colonial history' (Armstrong and Barton 1999: 215). Civil rights however have been demanded by various disenfranchised groups at home – disabled people included. The notion of 'rights' has definite popular appeal, and a rights-based approach to disability is generally assumed to be a 'good thing' (Armstrong and Barton 1999). Rights are preferable to 'charity', and to the professionally-dominated focus on disabled people's deficiencies and 'special needs' (Drewett 1999). The rights-based strategies championed by many within the disabled people's movement are also said to have had a positive effect on practice, diverting it 'from a medical approach to a socio-political, or civil rights framework' (Young and Quibell 2000: 748).

'Rights' have indisputably been an important campaigning tool for the movement – as evidenced by successful calls for civil rights legislation in the UK and elsewhere. In the wake of disabled people's activism, and international initiatives like the UN's *Standard Rules on the Equalisation of Opportunities for Disabled Persons*, more and more states are now adopting anti-discrimination legislation. Whilst the effectiveness of such legislation is a matter for debate, at the very least, rights are acknowledged to have a vitally 'important symbolic value' (Drewett 1999: 127). We are warned then that we should tread with caution when employing arguments which undermine the 'valuable work' carried out by rights activists (Brown 1999: 121). Whilst the intention is not to undermine what disabled people and their allies have achieved, it seems clear that 'rights' alone will not eradicate disability on a global scale. Neither will documents like the UN's *Standard Rules* succeed in 'equalising opportunities' for the majority of the world's dispossessed and impoverished disabled people. There is perhaps something a little simplistic about 'the entire conceptual structure that underlies the oratory on human rights' (Sen 2000: 227); and civil rights, 'although necessary to counter discrimination, may not be radical (get to the root) enough to change our predicament' (Russell 1998: 127).

Various writers have questioned 'the dominant ideology of a rights-based approach to bring about social change for disabled people' (Handley 2000: 324). The goal of the approach is a fairly limited one – that of 'making sure that each disenfranchised group has the rights of white middle-class males' (Davis 2001: 535). Furthermore, 'rights' present an individualistic, legalistic approach to tackling disability, and are notoriously difficult to enforce. Most importantly, because of their essentially reformist nature, through demands for rights, we can never attack the root cause of disability, only its symptoms. Whilst the social model of disability embraces the notion of rights then, it is stressed that it is not 'dependent on rights - it is not a rights model' (Finkelstein 2002: 15).

Rights are a product of western liberal individualism. Hence in the UK, it is argued that the recent focus on disabled people's civil rights has helped justify a shift from 'policies of social obligation' to those 'rooted in individualism' (Thornton and Lund 1995: 1-2). Civil rights legislation represents 'a legalistic approach to emancipation' (Finkelstein 2002: 14), and hence acknowledges only those individuals 'who make a claim against the collectivity' (Robertson 1997: 431). Furthermore, such claims can be made only 'after the horse has bolted'. As such, rights are described as:

a 'band-aid' solution, which, far from stopping the injury in the first place, are often unable to even find the wound (Young and Quibell 2000: 751)

At an international level, organisations such as the UN are firmly committed to the ideology of rights, producing a number of rights guidelines, which, in theory, offer much to disabled people worldwide. However, the onus is on individual states to implement these guidelines, a particular problem in poorer countries where 'governments have very limited resources to bring about radical changes in the lives of disabled people' (Barnes and Mercer 2003: 145). South Africa, for example, ratified the UN *Convention on the Rights of the Child* in 1995. Implementation of the Convention is subject to available resources however, and '"lack of resources" has become the rationale for ignoring, or failing to implement, policies for disabled children' (Tomlinson and Abdi 2003: 54).

Rights then are all very well on paper, but 'what is a "right" when it means nothing legally?' (Young and Quibell 2000: 752). Others question the universality of rights, suggesting that the western focus on rights 'rooted in the ideology of individualism' often runs counter to 'cultural and social norms' in other parts of the world (Lang 1998: 9). Perhaps though, the most significant critique of the idealist interpretation of the social model is that in breaking 'the theoretical link between disability and capitalism' (Horsler 2003: 39), it can offer only reformist solutions - solutions that 'can only ever ameliorate the effects of a disabling society yet leave capitalism as a system untouched' (Horsler 2003: 54).

Whilst a focus on rights might improve the situation for some more fortunate individuals, the liberal rights model 'serves to forestall criticism of relationships of power at the centre of the exclusion... and inequality that disabled persons face' (Russell 2002: 121). There is a strong argument then that liberation for disabled people cannot be achieved through 'rights' alone, but only by 'questioning the very basis of the rules of the market' (Russell and Malhotra 2002: 5). What is needed then is a radical social model of disability which 'has to do with the creation of a society which enables us to be 'human' - not just access our 'rights' within an existing competitive market society' (Finkelstein 2002: 14). Since both the oppression of the majority world, and the oppression of disabled people are intimately related to the current global mode of production these arguments cannot be dismissed as naïve. If common cause is to be found between the people of the majority world and disabled people globally, this area *must* receive more attention both from theorists, activists and other 'agents of change'. It is to these agents of change that we will now turn our attention.

Nothing about us without us?
Global capitalism is on the whole regarded in a positive light by the world's decision makers. At the same time though, a need is perceived for non-market intervention 'to "ameliorate" its "disordered faults"' (Thomas 2000: 45). The responsibility for non-market intervention in 'development' was initially exercised by states within their own borders, 'or by colonial states on behalf of the colonized' (Thomas 2000: 41). The state however is now only one of various agencies playing such a role. The term 'trusteeship' is often used to describe the situation where 'one agency is "entrusted" with acting on behalf of another, to try and ensure their "development" - whether or not they have asked to be developed' (Thomas 2000: 41). Many agencies claim trusteeship over both the people of the majority world and disabled people globally - local, national and international NGOs, the United Nations and its agencies, and other international (yet western controlled) organisations such as the World Bank and the IMF.

The notion of trusteeship is highly problematic, and it is increasingly asked what right such agencies have to speak for anyone. Some have rejected the notion of trusteeship altogether. Oppressed people it is argued should become their own trustees and be enabled to solve their own problems however they see fit (Thomas 2000) - a sentiment encapsulated in Disabled People's International's eloquent slogan "nothing about us without us". Furthermore, a distinction can be made between trustees who work alongside capitalism (such as the World Bank) and those who work against it. Social movements like the disabled people's movement are seen to be working 'against' capitalism (Thomas 2000), and as such may offer the most fruitful way forward. However, disabled people's organisations often lack the necessary resources to move forward (Hurst 1999) - especially with the increased emphasis on aid conditionality (Tomaševski 1993).

If indeed we need revolutionary change, 'disabled people in isolation' are not going to lead that revolution (Brenda Ellis cited in Horsler 2003: 27). For the international disabled people's movement to grow and prosper, it must make links with other oppressed people who are engaged in the same struggle (Charlton 1998). The people of the majority world could be valuable allies in this process. The development of a global political economy of disability would make the commonalities between such seemingly disparate groups more transparent and such alliances more feasible. It is here that academics in the minority world could make a significant contribution to the struggle.

There are obvious concerns that western academics are prescribing solutions on behalf of others and thus claiming trusteeship for themselves. However, the aim of majority world writers like Frantz Fanon and C.L.R. James was not simply to reject western ideas 'but to reclaim them for all of humanity' (Malik 2002: 2). Others however have suggested that academics can do little to further the interests of 'the victims of underdevelopment', and that the most their studies can do to 'try not to obscure the structures of exploitation and oppression which underdevelopment produces, and which in turn sustain it' (Leys 1975: 275).

This is exactly what much theorising about disability in the majority world has done. Whilst it may not change the world in the short term, the adoption of the materialist version of the social model, and the development of a global political economy of disability would certainly be a step in the right direction. It seems vital then for disability studies to hang on to this radical version of the social model in order to suggest meaningful strategies and solutions to the interconnected global problems of disability and uneven development.

It is important to remember that capitalism is not an 'eternal period'. It is a mode of production that belongs to a specific period in human history. Hence, just as feudalism was superseded by capitalism 'capitalism will be superseded by a higher form of organization of production and distribution' (Navarro 1984: 45). It is suggested that contemporary factors such as increasing technological progress and social polarisation may well constitute, 'Marx's formula for revolution' (Hirschl 1997: 172). Perhaps then, academics can ally themselves with the world's poor in speeding this radical change in the mode of production and in envisaging the system that could take its place. As Marta Russell reminds us, capitalism is not god-given. Instead 'the socio/economic inequalities it generates are created by men and can be changed by the people' (1998: 142).

Conclusion

The entire world is now part of the same system of domination and oppression and disabled people everywhere are united by their shared oppression within that world system. The people of the majority world are similarly disadvantaged by imperialist capitalism, and thus have much in common with the world's disabled population. However, despite the fact that disability and uneven development are intimately related to the capitalist world system, materialist explanations of disability are rarely sought in relation to the majority world. Instead colonialist notions of the majority world as savage, primitive and hostile to those with impairments are widely propagated, and 'rights' are championed as a suitable means of securing justice for disabled people on a global scale. This situation must be redressed if academia is to contribute anything to the struggle of the poor and the disadvantaged both here and abroad.

It is clear that the practical solution to the deprivation of majority world people and the oppression of disabled people is the same. Perhaps, this solution can be implemented using the insights of the social model of disability. Systemic problems require 'systemic solutions' (Charlton 1998: 165). Hence, if the social model is ever to be effectively implemented on a global scale, we must hang on tightly to its 'radical' formulation. We need a response to the social model's insights that is both material in nature, and informed by those with a direct interest in the liberation struggle. Successful action to eliminate both disability and underdevelopment will not disregard the roots from which both spring and any ideology that serves to obscure these roots must be vigorously questioned. Idealist interpretations of the social model of disability cannot lead us to what must be our ultimate goal - the creation of a world where disability and uneven development are of merely historical interest and books such as this would no longer need to be written.

Bibliography

Ahmad, A. 2003: Imperialism of our time. In L. Panitch and C. Leys (eds), *The New Imperial Challenge: Socialist Register 2004*. London: Merlin Press.

Anthony, E. 1972: Introduction. In W. King and E. Anthony (eds), *Black Poets and Prophets: The theory, practice and aesthetics of the Pan-Africanist revolution*. New York: Mentor.

Armstrong, F. and Barton, L. 1999: 'Is there anyone there concerned with human rights?' Cross-cutural connections, disability and the struggle for change in England. In F. Armstrong and L. Barton (eds), *Disability, Human Rights and Education: Cross-cultural perspectives*. Buckingham: Open University Press.

Barnes, C. and Mercer, G. 2003: *Disability*. Cambridge: Polity.

Bernstein, H. 2000: Colonialism, capitalism, development. In T. Allen and A. Thomas (eds), *Poverty and Development into the 21st Century*. Milton Keynes: The Open University in association with Oxford University Press.

Brown, C. 1999: Universal human rights: a critique. In T. Dunne and N. J. Wheeler (eds), *Human Rights in Global Politics*. Cambridge: Cambridge University Press.

Castells, M. 1996: *The Rise of the Network Society*. Oxford: Blackwell.

Castells, M. 2001: *The Internet Galaxy: Reflections on the Internet, business and society*. Oxford: Oxford University Press.

Charlton, J. I. 1998: *Nothing About Us Without Us: Disability Oppression and Empowerment*. Berkeley: University of California Press.

Coleridge, P. 1993: *Disability, Liberation and Development*. Oxford: Oxfam in association with Action on Disability and Development.

Davis, L. J. 2001: Identity politics, disability, and culture. In G. L. Albrecht et al. (eds), *Handbook of Disability Studies*. London: Sage.

Drewett, A. Y. 1999: Social rights and disability: the language of 'rights' in community care policies. *Disability and Society*, 14 (1), 115-128.

Elwan, A. 1999: *Poverty and Disability: A survey of the literature*. Accessed at: http://siteresources.worldbank.org/DISABILITY/Resources/Poverty/Poverty and Disability A Survey of the Literature.pdf

Fanon, F. 1967: *The Wretched of the Earth*. London: Penguin.

Fanon, F. 1972 (first published 1964): Racism and culture. In W. King and E. Anthony (eds), *Black Poets and Prophets: The theory, practice and aesthetics of the Pan-Africanist revolution*. New York: Mentor.

Finkelstein, V. 1980: *Attitudes and Disabled People*. New York: World Rehabilitation Fund.

Finkelstein, V. 2002: The social model of disability repossessed. *Coalition*, February, 10-16.

Gleeson, B. J. 1997: Disability Studies: a historical materialist view. *Disability and Society*, 12 (2), 179-202.

Groce, N. 1999: Framing disability issues in local concepts and beliefs. *Asia Pacific Disability Rehabilitation Journal*, 10 (1). (Available at: www.dinf.nejp/doc/english/asia/resource/apdrj/z13jo0303, 24/2/2005.

Handley, P. 2000: Trouble in paradise - a disabled person's right to the satisfaction of a self-defined need: some conceptual and practical problems. *Disability and Society*, 16 (2), 313-325.

Harrison, P. 1993: *Inside the Third World: The anatomy of poverty*. Harmondsworth: Penguin.

Hirschl, T. A. 1997: Structural unemployment and the qualitative transformation of capitalism. In J. Davis et al. (eds), *Cutting Edge: Technology, Information, Capitalism and Social Revolution*. London: Verso.

Hoogvelt, A. 1997: *Globalisation and the Postcolonial World: The new political economy of development*. Basingstoke: Macmillan.

Horsler, J. 2003: Bridging the Divide, Unpublished MA Thesis, University of Leeds. Accessed at http://www.leeds.ac.uk/disability-studies/archiveuk/, 13/03/04.

Hurst, R. 1999: Disabled people's organisations and development: strategies for change, in: E. Stone (ed.), *Disability and Development: Learning from action and research on disability in the majority world*, Leeds: The Disability Press.

Ingstad, B. 1999: The myth of disability in developing nations. *Lancet*, 354, 757-758.

Kisanji, J. 1995: Attitudes and beliefs about disability in Tanzania. In B. O'Toole and R. McConkey (eds), *Innovations in Developing Countries for People with Disabilities*. Chorley: Liseaux Hall.

Lang, R. 1998: A critique of the disability movement. *Asia Pacific Disability Rehabilitation Journal*, 9 (1), 1-12.

Lenin, V. I. 1947: *Imperialism, the Highest Stage of Capitalism*. Moscow: Progress Publishers. (First published 1917).

Leys, C. 1975: *Underdevelopment in Kenya: The Political Economy of Neo-Colonialism, 1964-1971*. London: Heinemann Educational Books.

Malik, K. 2002: All cultures are not equal. First Published: 28 May 2002, in "spiked!". Accessed at http://www.marxists.org/subject/africa/malik/not-equal.htm, 13/03/04.

Navarro, V. 1984: The political economy of government cuts for the elderly. In M. Minkler and C. L. Estes (eds), *Readings in the Political Economy of Aging*. Amityville, New York: Baywood Publishing Company.

Oliver, M. 1990: *The Politics of Disablement*. London: Macmillan.

Panitch, L. and Gindin, S. 2003: Global capitalism and American empire. In L. Panitch and C. Leys (eds), *The New Imperial Challenge: Socialist Register 2004*. London: Merlin Press.

Priestley, M. 1998: Constructions and creations: idealism, materialism and disability theory. *Disability and Society*, 13 (1), 75-94.

Robertson, A. 1997: Beyond apocalyptic demography: towards a moral economy of interdependence. *Ageing and Society*, 17, 425-446.

Russell, M. 1998: *Beyond Ramps: Disability at the end of the social contract*. Monroe, Maine: Common Courage Press.

Russell, M. 2002: What disability civil rights cannot do: employment and political economy. *Disability and Society*, 17 (2): 117-135.

Russell, M. and Malhotra, R. 2002: The political economy of disablement: advances and contradictions. *Socialist Register*, Accessed at http://www.yorku.ca.socreg/RusMal.htm, 13/03/04.

Sen, A. 2000: *Development as Freedom*. New York: Anchor.

Shakespeare, T. 1994: Cultural representation of disabled people: dustbins for disavowal? *Disability and Society*, 9 (3), 283-299.

Shaw, M. 1975: *Marxism and Social Theory: The roots of social knowledge*, London: Pluto Press.

Stone, E. 1999: Disability and development in the majority world. In E. Stone (ed.), *Disability and Development: Learning from Action and Research on Disability in the Majority World*. Leeds: The Disability Press.

Thirlwall, A. P. 2002: Development as economic growth. In V. Desai and R. B. Potter (eds), *The Companion to Development Studies*. London: Arnold.

Thomas, A. 2000: Meanings and views of development. In T. Allen and A. Thomas (eds), *Poverty and Development into the 21st Century*. Milton Keynes: The Open University in association with Oxford University Press.

Thomas, C. 2004: Developing the social relational in the social model of disability: a theoretical agenda. In C. Barnes and G. Mercer (eds), *Implementing the social model of disability: Theory and research*. Leeds: The Disability Press.

Thornton, P. and Lund, N. 1995: *Employment for Disabled People: Social Obligation or Individual Responsibility*? York: Social Policy Research Unit.

Tomaševski, K. 1993: *Development Aid and Human Rights Revisited*. London: Pinter Publishers.

Tomlinson, S. and Abdi, O. A. 2003: Disability in Somaliland. *Disability and Society*, 18 (7), 911-920.

UNDP 2005: Millennium Development Goals. Accessed at: http://www.undp.org/mdg/, 11/02/05.

UPIAS 1976: *Fundamental Principles of Disability*. London: Union of the Physically Impaired against Segregation.

Weeks, J. 1991: Imperialism and world market. In T. Bottomore (ed.), *A Dictionary of Marxist Thought* (Second Edition). Oxford: Blackwell.

Young, D. A. and Quibell, R. 2000: Why rights are never enough: rights, intellectual disability and understanding. *Disability and Society*, 15 (5), 747-764.

CHAPTER 9

Finally Included on the Development Agenda? A review of official disability and development policies

Bill Albert

States, both industrialised and developing, have the responsibility to co-operate in and take measures for the improvement of the living conditions of persons with disabilities in developing countries.
1. Measures to achieve the equalisation of opportunities of persons with disabilities, including refugees with disabilities, should be integrated into general development programmes.
2. Such measures must be integrated into all forms of technical and economic co-operation, bilateral and multilateral, governmental and non-governmental. States should bring up disability issues in discussions on such co-operation with their counterparts.
3. When planning and reviewing programmes of technical and economic co-operation, special attention should be given to the effects of such programmes on the situation of persons with disabilities. It is of the utmost importance that persons with disabilities and their organisations are consulted on any development projects designed for persons with disabilities. They should be directly involved in the development, implementation and evaluation of such projects (*Standard Rules on the Equalization of Opportunities for Persons with Disabilities*. United Nations 1993: Rule 21).

Introduction
In a rather perverse way the promulgation of the *Millennium Development* Goals (World Bank Group website) because they did not specifically

mention disability with respect to the key aim of poverty reduction, may have served as a catalyst, encouraging many people and organisations to affirm or reaffirm the links between disability and poverty. Of course, such concerns, together with the argument that disability is essentially a human rights issue, have been around for a considerable time. These form the bedrock principles of the international disability movement. Furthermore, the adoption by the United Nations of the *Standard Rules on the Equalization of Opportunities for Persons with Disabilities* (UN 1993) marked an important milestone in the official international recognition of the need to address the social and economic exclusion of disabled people. It is against this background, as well as because of the continued lobbying by the disability movement, that we can address some of the factors which account for why disability has moved up the development agenda.

A prominent example of this was given by James D. Wolfensohn (2002) director of the World Bank:

> Addressing disability is a significant part of reducing poverty. Bringing disabled people out of the corners and back alleys of society, and empowering them to thrive in the bustling center of national life, will do much to improve the lives of many from among the poorest of the poor around the world (p. A25).

A year later the European Commission (EC) produced a *Guidance Note on Disability and Development*, in which they stated that:

> In the last few decades, disabled people's organisations around the world have promoted a human rights approach and an environmental approach to disability issues. These approaches are both based on a social model of disability....
>
> If the interests of disabled people are not recognised then the key goal of poverty reduction in developing countries will not be achieved. Nor will the human rights of people with disabilities or their participation in society be promoted. If sustainable poverty reduction is to be achieved, disability needs to be addressed by sensitising people active in development work funded by the EU to these issues (European Commission 2003: 2).

These statements are broadly representative of declarations from many other major international and national bodies concerned with development. However, despite this, in terms of having any impact on the lives of disabled people in developing countries, it is more important to consider if these pronouncements, or indeed the basic tenets of the

Standard Rules, are reflected in the official policies (defined as norms expected to be incorporated into an agency's strategy and practice) adopted by the leading development agencies. Of course, determining this is only a first step because policies are often either not put into practice or if they are their implementation is ineffective. Practice is touched on in this chapter mainly for illustrative purposes and to draw provisional conclusions about the impact of policy. To research this question in the depth it requires would be a formidable undertaking. Our primary focus here is on official policies, as this offers a first step to understanding how, and in some cases if, the relationship between disability and development is understood by the principal national and international aid agencies. It must also be said that official policy is often difficult to capture as it is constantly changing.

Finding out precisely what official policies were was difficult. Furthermore, while some organisations had disability policies, it was clear on further investigation that these had either never been implemented or had evaporated on their way down the line to the project level. Another difficulty was that many agencies have produced documents on disability and development, the status of which was unclear. For example, in 2000 the Department for International Development (DfID) published an issues paper, Disability, Poverty and Development. This was not a policy statement, never had any impact on the organisation, and indeed seems to have become better known outside than inside the DfID (Thomas 2004). However, in their 2003 report, Label Us Able, produced by STAKES for the Finnish Ministry of Foreign Affairs, it is stated that that the DfID's issue paper has been 'official policy since 1999' (p.22) Therefore, the existence of documents referred to as policies are not necessarily evidence of official policy, let alone action on disability and development. (For more detailed information on these development agency disability policies see paper by Albert at: http://www.disabilitykar.net/resources/karprogreports.html.)

Defining Disability

A clear definition of disability would seem to be central to designing a disability policy or strategy. If disability is seen essentially as a health issue the solutions will be quite different from an understanding of disability that highlights human rights, discrimination and exclusion. It was, therefore, quite surprising to find so little serious attention paid to this question. When an attempt was made at a definition, in most instances, as in the case of the DfID outline below, it represented a compromise between different, and quite opposed, ways of understanding disability. In most cases even a composite definition was not given and it was necessary to impute a working concept of disability.

The traditional understanding of disability is that it is what is 'wrong' with someone. According to this formulation disability equals impairment, being unable to walk, being deaf or blind, having a mental disorder, or a condition such as Down's syndrome. While those who adopt this view (the individual or medical model of disability) may agree that there are unfortunate social consequences which arise from being disabled, the essential nature of the problem is medical, begins with individual deficit and the primary solutions are, therefore, cure, care and/or rehabilitation.

Since the 1970s, the international disabled people's movement has challenged this understanding, arguing that it is not physical or mental conditions which are disabling but social, attitudinal and physical barriers preventing equal participation in community life. Disability, according to this conception (generally referred to as the social model of disability), is the result of discrimination and social exclusion. It is a human rights issue which demands a socio-political rather than a health-based focus (Albert et al. 2002), although this has been disputed by Vic Finkelstein (2001), one of the early pioneers of the social barriers approach.

Only the European Union Guidance Note, quoted above, mentions the social model of disability. In all the other official documents either a medical model may be assumed or a definition is adopted which tries to combine both models. The clearest example of the latter is found in DfID's (2000: 8) issues paper which considers both models and then decides it is preferable to go for 'an integrated approach using best practice in both social and medical terms'. On the main web page of their disability website, *World Bank* observes:

> Defining what is meant by disability is sometimes a complex process, as disability is more than a description of a specific health issue; rather it is affected by people's cultures, social institutions, and physical environments. The current international guide is the World Health Organization's discussion and classification within ICF: *International Classification of Functioning, Disability and Health*. ICF presents a framework which encompasses the complex multifaceted interaction between health conditions and personal and environmental factors that determine the extent of disablement in any given situation.

The Asian Development Bank (ADB 1999) adopted a similar position, opting for the World Health Organization (WHO 1980) definition. More recently, in a draft of a handbook addressing disability and poverty they seem to sign up for the revised ICF. It is perhaps to be expected that these major international bodies choose to follow the definitional guidelines established by such an influential sister organization.

The new ICF seems set to become the gold standard for defining disability. However, even though disability ('disablement' is the word used in the ICF) is now seen as arising from the negative impact of the environment in its broadest sense, the minute classifications of health and functioning remain central. Many critics have argued that the ICF represents medical model thinking clothed in watered down social model language (Bury 2000; Pfeiffer 2000; Miles 2001). As with the DfID definition, it starts with the individual, rather than society, and tries to find a compromise between the two ways of understanding disability:

> Whist the ICF asserts that individuals are but one element in the analysis of disability, the 'biopsychosocial' approach is not that far removed from its forerunner in that it retains the individual as the starting point for the analysis of 'bodily function and activity'. The concept of participation is included but underdeveloped in the scheme and is still linked to individual circumstances rather than tied firmly to social and political inclusion (Barnes 2003: 9).

Of course, ICF comes from the WHO, so it is hardly a surprise that health is the primary concern. But the extension of this concern to a conception of disability as a socio-political construct may not be particularly helpful for the practical business of designing development policies and practices which break with traditional medical assumptions, seek to promote human rights and bring disabled people into the mainstream of society.

Rachel Hurst, an experienced disability activist who took part in redrafting the ICIDH, has no illusions about the difficult compromises that had to be made, but claims:

> ICIDH2, with all its many faults and its misuse of disability language, can, I believe, now be used as an international example of how the environmental impacts are the key to understanding the nature of disability/disablement and how solutions must come through social change (Hurst 2000: 1086).

Whatever the possible benefits with respect to planning for health provision and whatever the ICF says about the need to see disability in terms of environmental factors, because of its genesis in the medical world, its emphasis on classification of function and its staggering complexity, it is doubtful whether it will overturn deeply-held medical assumptions about the nature of disability. Because such assumptions tend to inform action, there is the strong possibility that, no matter what is said, in practice international development agencies will default at all levels to a health-centred understanding of disability. The only way this will be avoided is by an ongoing, critical awareness of the contradictions inherent in the ICF together with a vigorous commitment to human rights supported by clear practical guidance for implementation.

Approaches adopted towards disability issues
Despite a lack of a clear definition, the use of the ICF or a medical model understanding of disability, in the cases where there have been policy statements, the majority advocate a human rights approach. This might indicate that how disability is understood is of little concrete importance, but the overall failure to implement human rights policies and/or mainstream disability in development may suggest just the opposite. This is not, however, to argue that adopting the social model will in itself be the key to more effective engagement with disability issues.

The increasing focus on a human rights agenda follows decades of lobbying by disabled people, the lead given by the United Nations, particularly since the promulgation of the *Standard Rules* in 1993, and the more recent negotiations on an International *Convention on the Promotion of the Rights and Dignity of Persons with Disabilities* (UN ESCAPP/CDPF 2003). It is, therefore, to be expected that various UN agencies have a stated commitment to a human rights approach. Such a commitment is also prominent in the policy statements of Scandinavian countries, suggesting at least an implicit acceptance of some key arguments derived from the social model of disability.

The Scandinavian DPOs and their countries have played a leading role in putting human rights at the heart of disability and development. In 1991 the Nordic DPOs agreed to lobby their governments for increased action on disability and development. In 1996 the Finnish government made a formal Decision-in-Principle to include 'the status of disabled people as a concern in the context of poverty reduction and human rights' (STAKES 2003: 28). Four years later in Copenhagen, the Nordic ministers for development co-operation declared:

Recognise and promote the UN *Standard Rules* as guidelines for all bilateral and multilateral development work and to assure, that special measures are taken to create accessibility and participation in development society for persons with disabilities in order to strengthen their possibilities to exercise their human rights (Copenhagen Conference 2000: 5).

While this commitment continues to be reflected in some of the Nordic countries' disability policies, there has been criticism that with the exception of Norway, overall there has been a failure to establish national strategies for the inclusion of the disability dimension in development. Indeed, in Denmark there has been a decision not to make mainstreaming of disability a priority (Ulland 2003). Even in those countries with positive sounding policies what the human rights approach means in practice remains at best ambiguous.

Elsewhere, although a number of other European countries have indicated that they are considering disability and development policies, only Italy has one. The Italian guidelines are comprehensive, if at times somewhat eclectic. They begin with strong statements on the centrality of human rights and then detail how disability needs to be twin tracked - both mainstreamed into overall policy and supported through disability specific projects.

The USAID policy seems set more in the traditional anti-discrimination mode which characterises the Americans with Disabilities Act and other civil rights legislation in the US. The 1997 policy document states:

> To avoid discrimination against people with disabilities in programs which USAID funds and to stimulate an engagement of host country counterparts, governments, implementing organizations and other donors in promoting a climate of non-discrimination against and equal opportunity for people with disabilities (USAID 1997: unpaged).

The definition of disability is, however, strictly medical.

> For purposes of this policy, a disability is defined as a physical or mental impairment that affects a major life function, consistent with the definition of the Rehabilitation Act (USAID 1997: unpaged).

This is similar to the UK Disability Discrimination Act 1995, which defines disability medically, while setting out social-model-like provisions about non-discrimination.

Policies into Practice

Good disability policies are important, but little more than empty rhetoric unless they are effectively implemented. Unfortunately, with few exceptions, this is generally the case. One of the clearest examples is that of USAID which since 1996 has been trying to develop a more inclusive approach to disability issues. In its 1998 report on policy implementation it explained the key reasons behind the new policy initiative:

> It was recognized that the needs of PWDs (*people with disabilities*) are the same as the needs of other constituencies with whom USAID works. Segregation of PWDs in USAID activities would tend to increase discrimination among our ranks and in the countries we serve. Consistent with our participation efforts, the Team recognized that to be effective, programs must be constructed to include PWDs at all stages of implementation (USAID 1998: unpaged).

To carry out this programme they established a central disability team and moved to ensure that each USAID mission devised a disability plan and established links with local DPOs. The policy was backed up by plans for disability equality training for the organisation, although no extra funding was appropriated. While all this sounded promising, by 2000, and the second implementation report, although some positive results were evident, the overall evaluation was notably candid and downbeat:

> Efforts at promoting the USAID Disability Policy have been disjointed and minimally effective. Strong words at the highest levels dissipate rapidly. Opportunities for personal contact with PWDs, while fruitful, have not been deemed a priority, while a reward structure does not exist to promote adherence to this policy. While the Disability Policy and the World Program of Action call for inclusion rather than distinct disability programming, feedback to Team members strongly suggests that in this time of conflicting priorities, specific funding must be attached to this target (USAID 2000: unpaged).

A third report in 2002 was considerably more optimistic (USAID 2003). In that year, disability reports were received by 48 USAID missions, as opposed to only 28 two years before. While just 11 said they had drawn up specific disability plans, 34 reported they were working actively with local disability organizations. A most positive feature of the report was that democracy and governance accounted for the largest single number of projects (19). Nonetheless, important problems remain. Specific disability projects, many in traditional social welfare areas, rather than mainstreaming, seem to account for most missions' efforts. Unlike the disability movements in the Scandinavian countries, disabled people's organizations in the USA have had little input into USAID policy. A report from the National Council on Disability in the following year was even more critical, noting that besides being underfunded:

> The USAID Disability Policy includes no specific objectives or timetables, creates no new initiatives to reach out to people with disabilities, and does not require U.S. Missions abroad to change their practices (National Council on Disability 2003).

Another national agency which has carried out an evaluation is the Finnish Ministry of Foreign Affairs. In absolute terms their spending on disability is small averaging (1991-2001) just 6.2 million euros, although this did represent a respectable 5 per cent of their aid budget. As with other Scandinavian countries their disability and development policies have in general been advanced compared with the rest of the world. Nonetheless, the report found that:

> Most of the assistance via NGOs has been effective and has made an impact on the planned target groups, for example, training of the deaf and blind in specialised institutions has received a lot of funding. However, the impact on some individuals has been limited and it has had less influence on communities and countries. This is because most of the assistance has been disability-specific (targeted at the people with disabilities) and has been based on the dominant social welfare approach (STAKES 2003: 80).

There were also criticisms that disability had not been mainstreamed into development, that there had not been enough attention paid to adjusting policy in line with the shift from a social welfare to a human rights approach and that the overall policy had to be overhauled to take into account the new international aid instruments for the poorest countries, such as SWAps (Sector Wide Approaches) and PRSPs (Poverty Reduction Strategy Papers).

Norway too has an excellent disability in development policy and in 2002 produced a detailed guideline for its implementation (NORAD 2002), but two years later a commissioned study concluded that:

> A main finding of the review is that the guidelines were not known among the target group; not by the Norwegian

Embassies nor by Norwegian NGOs or international NGOs that receive most support from NORAD/MFA (Ministry of Foreign Affairs) (Hertzberg and Ingstad 2004: 9).

An important issue raised by all three examples, and one which seems to apply to almost every agency, is the failure, despite stated intentions in some cases, to mainstream disability into development policy. Although far more detailed research would be needed to confirm this, if the Finnish, Norwegian and US experiences are even close to representative (Denmark 2000), in the vast majority of cases when there is a disability focus it continues to be on the traditional areas of health or special education, relatively small scale projects funded through NGOs, and almost all undertaken with a social-welfare mindset (even if human rights language is used) rather than a meaningful human rights framework. If true, this means that, with very notable exceptions - mainly capacity-building projects run by NGOs - disability issues remain trapped within a special-needs ghetto, the language of human rights remains empty rhetoric and the needs of disabled people for equality, dignity, social inclusion and poverty alleviation remain unfulfilled.

Such a pessimistic analysis seems more likely if we consider what has happened with PRSPs, which since 1999 have become the main multilateral instruments (mandated by the World Bank and IMF) for providing debt relief and, therefore, development aid, to the poorest countries. According to an International Labour Organisation (ILO) Report which reviewed 29 Interim PRSPs for Africa:

> ... apart from some notable exceptions - persons with disabilities have again been either 'forgotten' or treated in a way that does not correspond to their aspirations to socio-economic integration. Up to now, persons with disabilities have not been involved in an opportunity to be included in the most important poverty reduction initiative of recent years (ILO 2002: unpaged).

A sampling of the World Bank website confirms that in almost all PRSPs there is either no mention of disability, if it is mentioned the reference is to 'the disabled' within a list of vulnerable groups and/or to either social welfare or health. Perhaps this should not come as a surprise when overall PRSP implementation has been seriously flawed, particularly in terms of human rights (UN 2001), and poverty reduction has been minimal (Oxfam 2004). Furthermore, gender, a much more prominent cross-cutting issue than disability, has also not been well served by PRSPs:

On gender equity, almost all PRSPs have been very weak, with minimal attention paid to the issue. World Bank and IMF Joint Staff Assessments of PRSPs singularly fail to address gender equity. Oxfam and its partners believe that gendered poverty strategies are the only ones that will actually succeed in reducing poverty, and that the IMF and World Bank could do much more to ensure that the next round of PRSPs routinely and comprehensively addresses the issue (Oxfam 2004: unpaged).

The failings of PRSPs to include disability are echoed in a 2002 baseline assessment of the World Bank's activities relating to disability which concluded that:

Based on the sampling from this study, few of the current activities of the World Bank include disability in any meaningful way (Stienstra et al. 2002: unpaged).

When they went on to look at five key criteria for assessing inclusion – lending, knowledge, mandate, resources and accountability, all were found significantly deficient. Their comments on lending are particularly interesting. They observe:

According to the survey results of Bank projects, a majority of respondents thought their projects addressed disability. However, almost all responses suggested that disabled people might benefit, rather than that they were included explicitly. Only one project had specific disability components and none mainstreamed disability into the project (Stienstra et. al. 2002: unpaged).

It is probably too early to judge the World Bank's efforts, as these were given a new impetus only in 2002 by the appointment of Judith Heumann as their first Adviser on Disability and Development. In the intervening period (to 2004) there have been lots of upbeat statements, but on the ground little seems to have changed. For example, at a recent meeting hosted by the World Bank, 'International Dialogue on Disability and Development', in Helsinki the participants were extremely critical of the lack of action and concluded:

that the disability and development landscape has been characterized by small, fragmented, unsustainable projects; a disconnect between disability and mainstream development efforts; a 'flavor of the month' approach to country focus; preoccupation with prevention, to the exclusion of rehabilitation and inclusion; 'exclusion by design' in mainstream projects; and poor coordination, evaluation and knowledge-sharing (Disability World 2003: unpaged).

The Bank has launched a consultation process to develop a Global Partnership for Disability and Development, but while this is a positive step, the preamble to the draft 'Concept Paper' shows just how far there is to go before any meaningful changes can be expected.

Poverty alleviation in developing countries and genuine progress toward achievement of the Millennium Development Goals requires that disabled people be explicitly taken into account in national and international economic development efforts. The social and environmental obstacles that marginalize and impoverish disabled people cannot be dissolved by any one kind of entity or organization, but only through the collaborative efforts of diverse stakeholders, including governments of developing and developed countries, multilateral development agencies, members of the United Nations family of agencies, foundations, national and international NGOs, and the private sector.

Yet the idea of mainstreaming disability into the economic development agenda is a novel concept to many foreign assistance providers, developing country governments, and even NGOs. There is sometimes a disconnection between the people who are knowledgeable about international economic development and foreign assistance on the one hand and disability on the other (World Bank 2004: unpaged).

Conclusion

Is disability really on the official development agenda? If by this we mean are some of the main players talking about the issues, then the answers would be 'some of them' and 'sort of'. If, however, we are concerned about real changes being put in motion, even with a small percentage of the degree of the commitment given to gender, another major cross-cutting issue in development, the most optimistic answer would be 'not yet'. In fact, disability still does not figure as an official cross-cutting issue for any national development agency (Yeo and Moore 2003). The experience of gender indicates how far there is to go, for despite the strong policy commitment of almost all development agencies on gender, a great deal remains to be done and this commitment has not been followed through in the poorest countries with respect to the new international aid instruments.

While the World Bank, major UN-related agencies, the US, and most Scandinavian countries have made positive statements on disability, up to now these remain little more than statements. In most cases their policies have not been implemented and it seems they are struggling to find practical means to deliver their promises. Most of the evidence and comments, even from major agencies like the World Bank, seem to confirm this. The European Union has promulgated excellent guidelines for disability and development, but most of the major European countries have not even progressed to the stage of formulating policies.

Of course, there have been many disability-focused development projects, and some of these have undoubtedly delivered positive results for disabled people. The reports from the USAID missions seem to be particularly encouraging in this regard. However, reports from the USA and the UK (Thomas 2004) and from Finland (STAKES 2003) suggest that most of these projects remain locked within a traditional social welfare paradigm with limited value for mainstreaming disability in development and delivering a wider human rights agenda. In cases where the disability agenda is farmed out to NGOs, as in the UK, despite the excellent results achieved (Action on Disability and Development 2002), this may have simply confirmed the 'special' nature of disability and to that extent made effective mainstreaming within the DfID more problematic.

What is called for from international aid agencies, besides a far stronger and far clearer commitment, is a genuine understanding that disability is a social issue which cannot be addressed without bringing disabled people's organisations, both in the South and in the North, into the heart of the process, as has been done in the latter case in Finland, Norway and Sweden. There has been a strong emphasis on inclusion of disabled people in the South in USAID policy where:

> it is clear that "best practice" occurs when USAID and disability voices are combined in developing solutions (USAID 2003: unpaged).

Disability needs to be mainstreamed, promoted explicitly and officially as a cross-cutting issue as has gender. In fact, as a start it would be useful to consider disability within the same general parameters that have been set out for gender (Derbyshire 2002). Above all, we must not let good intentions or fine sounding declarations about human rights substitute for action which addresses the social exclusion, grinding poverty and human rights' abuses which continues to blight the lives of disabled people throughout the world.

In summary, development agencies need the following:
- a precise, high profile and robust policy on disability;
- a time-bound strategy for its implementation specifying 'who, what, when and how';
- tracking indicators and the linking of disability policy to other monitoring and evaluation procedures;
- a clearer understanding of the social model of disability and how this relates to effective human rights policy and practice;
- a stronger commitment to involve DPOs from both North and South at every level of development work;
- the mainstreaming of disability explicitly as a cross-cutting issue on a par with gender;
- to learn disability-relevant lessons from their experience of work on gender.

Acknowledgements

This is a revised and updated version of a paper first produced for the Knowledge and Research Programme funded by DfID. Initial research on policies was carried out by Michael Turner. We would like to acknowledge the assistance of the many people from the national and international agencies who replied to our queries, as well as Sue Stubbs, Herman Janssens and Gabriele Weigt. For helpful comments on the paper, thanks to Roger Drew, Philippa Thomas, Martin Long, Louise Wapling, Mark Raijmakers and Rachel Hurst.

Bibliography

Action on Disability and Development 2002: ***Annual Review 2002***. Frome, Somerset: ADD.

ADB 1999: *Disability and Development*. Report of the Workshop Organized by the Asian Development Bank and the Disabled Peoples International, Co-financed by the Government of Finland. 13-14 October. Manila, Philippines.
http://www.adb.org/Documents/Conference/Disability/default.asp

Albert, B., McBride, R. and Seddon, D. 2002: ***Perspectives on Disability, Poverty and Technology***. A Report to Healthlink Worldwide and GIC Ltd, September, 14-18, 22-24.
http://www.disabilitykar.net/karreport/spring2004/disabilityissue.html

Barnes, C. 2003: Rehabilitation for Disabled People: A 'sick' Joke? ***Scandinavian Journal for Disability Research***, 5 (1), 7-24.

Bury, M. 2000: A comment on the ICIDH2. *Disability & Society*, 15 (7), 1073-1077.

Copenhagen Conference 2000: *Final Report from Copenhagen Conference*. Inclusion of the Disability Dimension in Nordic Development Cooperation. November.
http://www.disability.dk/site/viewdoc.php?doc_id=195

Denmark (Ministry of Foreign Affairs) 2000: **From Charity towards Inclusion: the Way Forward for Disability Support through Danish NGOs. A Study of Danish NGO Support to Disability Organisations in Developing Countries**. Copenhagen: Ministry of Foreign Affairs.
http://www.disability.dk/site/viewdoc.php?doc_id=932

Derbyshire, H. 2002: **Gender Manual: A Practical Guide for Development Policy Makers and Practitioners**. London: Department for International Development.
http://www.jsiuk.com/docs/gender_manual.pdf.

DflD 2000: **Disability, Poverty and Development**. London: Department for International Development.
http://www.iddc.org.uk/info/dfid_policy.pdf

Disability World 2003: June-August. http://www.disabilityworld.org/

European Commission 2003: *A Guidance Note on Disability and Development for EU Delegations and Services*. March.
http://europa.eu.int/comm/development/body/theme/hum-03_guidance_note_disability_EN.pdf.

Finkelstein, V. 2001: The Social Model of Disability Repossessed. Manchester Coalition of Disabled People.
http://www.leeds.ac.uk/disability-studies/archiveuk/archframe.htm.

Hertzberg, A. and Ingstad, B. 2004: *In Development? Report from a Follow-up study December 2003 - January 2004 of the Norwegian Action Plan for Inclusion of People with Disabilities in Development Cooperation*. Unpublished. Oslo.

Hurst, R. 2000: To Revise or Not to Revise. *Disability & Society*, 15 (7), 1083-1087.

ILO 2002: *Disability and Poverty Reduction Strategies. How to ensure the access of persons with disabilities to decent and productive work as part of the PRSP process*? Discussion Paper, November. International Labour Organisation.
http://www.ilo.org/public/english/employment/skills/disability/download/discpaper.pdf

Miles, M. 2001: ICIDH Meets Postmodernism, or Incredulity toward Meta-Terminology. *Disability World*, No. 7, March-April.
http://www.disabilityworld.org/03-04_01/resources/icidh.html

Ministero degli Affari Esteri 2004: Direzione Generale per la Cooperazione allo Sviluppo, Italian Cooperation Guidelines Concerning the Disabled.
http://www.dcdd.nl/default.asp?action=article&id=1771
National Council on Disability 2003: September.
http://www.ncd.gov/newsroom/publications/2003/foreign03.htm
NORAD 2002: *The Inclusion of Disability in Norwegian Development Co-Operation Planning and monitoring for the inclusion of disability issues in mainstream development activities.*
http://www.norad.no/norsk/files/InklusionOfDisability.doc
Oxfam 2004: '*Donorship' to Ownership*? Moving Toward PSRP Round Two, Oxfam Briefing Paper, January. Oxford: Oxfam.
Pfeiffer, D. 2000: The Devils are in the Details: the ICIDH2 and the disability movement. *Disability & Society*, 15 (7), 1079-1082.
Stienstra, D., Fricke, Y., D'Aubin, A. et al. 2002: *Inclusion and Disability in World Bank Activities*. Canadian Centre on Disability Studies, June.
http://www.disabilitystudies.ca/baselinehtml.html
STAKES 2003: *Label Us Able*. Helsinki: Ministry of Foreign Affairs, Finland. http://global.finland.fi/evaluations/labelable.pdf.
Thomas, P. 2004: *DFID & Disability A Mapping of the Department for International Development & Disability Issues*. June. (available at http://www.disabilitykar.net/resources/newresources.html)
Ulland, K. H. 2003: *People with Disability in the Development Aid Policy of Scandinavian Countries*, Conference: Development needs participation – Nothing about us without us: People with Disability as Partners in Development Cooperation. Berlin, 14 November.
UN 1993: *Standard Rules on the Equalization of Opportunities for Persons with Disabilities*. New York: United Nations.
UN 2001: *The Highly Indebted Poor Countries (HIPC) Initiative: a human rights assessment of the Poverty Reduction Strategy (PRSP)* Economic and Social Council, Commission on Human Rights, E/CN.4/2001/56, January.
http://www.unhchr.ch/huridocda/huridoca.nsf/(Symbol)/E.CN.4 2001.56.EN?Opendocument
UN ESCAP/CDPF 2003: *Regional Meeting on a Convention on the Promotion of the Rights and Dignity of Persons with Disabilities*. November. Beijing, China.
http://www.worldenable.net/beijing2003/

USAID 1997: ***USAID Policy on Disability***. September.
http://www.usaid.gov/about/disability/policies.html
USAID 1998: ***First Annual Report on Implementation of the USAID Disability Policy***. December.
http://www.usaid.gov/about/disability/policies.html
USAID 2000: ***Second Annual Report on Implementation of the USAID Disability Policy***. February.
http://www.usaid.gov/about/disability/policies.html
USAID 2003: ***Third Annual Report on Implementation of the USAID Disability Policy***. May.
http://www.usaid.gov/about/disability/policies.html
WHO 1980: ***International Classification of Impairments, Disabilities and Handicaps***. Geneva: World Health Organization.
Wolfensohn, J. D. 2002: Poor, Disabled and Shut Out. Washington Post, Dec. 3, Page A25
World Bank 2004: *Global Partnership for Disability and Development*. Draft Concept Paper, 4 September.
World Bank Group website:
http://www.developmentgoals.org/About_the_goals.htm
Yeo, R. and Moore, K. 2003: Including Disabled People in Poverty Reduction Work: 'Nothing About Us, Without Us'. ***World Development***, 31 (3), 571-590.

CHAPTER 10

Definitions of Disability and Disability Policy in Egypt

Heba Hagrass

Introduction

In this chapter, I will show, using Egypt as a case study, how definitions of disability in developing countries are still dominated by a broadly individualistic medical approach. Yet despite this dominance, there is little consistency in usage, particularly in official data. This has resulted in a rather limited knowledge of the numbers of disabled people in Egyptian society. This lack of clarity inevitably influences the work of politicians and policy makers when they are formulating laws and policies directed at services and support for disabled people.

The significance of exploring recent policy developments in Egypt is that it is one of the first countries in the Middle East to address the support needs of its disabled citizens. As a result, its experience is considered highly significant in neighbouring countries, if not developing countries more generally. I will begin with an examination of the major causes of impairment and disability in an Egyptian context. Attention in the following sections will centre on, first, the various interpretations of disability in Egypt and, second, how they are reflected in Government legislation and policy.

Major causes of impairment and disability in Egypt

In Egypt, there are two major causes of impairments - economic and social. As a developing country Egypt suffers from widespread poverty. This is associated with unsanitary living conditions, lack of access to safe drinking water, and inadequate means of garbage disposal. All these factors are the cause of communicable diseases leading to various impairments (Qandil 1989: Teçke et al. 1994). More specifically, these diseases place a strain on

the physical and mental growth of children, which may lead to permanent impairments (El Safty 1994; Fahmy 2000). As stated by Boylan:
> No vaccine exists that can immunize against hunger or malnutrition. No substitute exists for safe drinking-water, which is currently not available to 50 per cent of the world's population (1991: 21)

Another major cause of impairment in Egypt is malnutrition. Because of the poor economic income generated in rural and lower-class urban areas, malnutrition is very common. It affects mostly women and children, which puts them at a great disadvantage to fall victims of impairment. Vitamin A deficiency, which causes a very high rate of blindness, is mainly caused by malnutrition (Nosseir 1989; Fahmy 2000). Malnutrition is also very common among pregnant women, and this has a potential effect on the unborn child. It may lead to low birth weight, which affects the physical and mental development of the child and may lead to a form of cognitive impairment or 'mental retardation' (Nosseir 1989). Also, iron deficiency, which causes anaemia, and iodine deficiency, can cause loss of hearing (Scheper-Hughes 1984; El Safty 1994; Fahmy 2000).

Social causes are also implicated in high levels of impairment. One is endogamous marriage. Although there is some debate over the accuracy of the figures it has been suggested that they account for 67 per cent of the total number of people with impairments (El Banna 1989). People usually prefer to marry cousins for a variety of economic, social and cultural reasons. This type of marriage arrangement is very popular among the well-to-do as well as among the poor. However, hereditary factors can result in all types of impairments - sensory, mental and physical. When first cousins marry, these genetic disorders can easily affect their children. In the National Research Centre in Egypt, clinical and genetic examinations were carried out on 100 cases of children with 'intellectual impairments'. The findings showed that 90 per cent were genetically affected by intermarriage among relatives - with 50 per cent involving cousin marriages (Nosseir 1989).

High fertility rates also contribute to the impairment of women and children. In traditional societies like Egypt, families tend to encourage women's early marriage, often in their teenage years. Despite the success of family planning campaigns the prevailing beliefs are that contraceptives damage health or are unacceptable on religious grounds. Thus many women have a long experience of child-bearing. Having children at an early age and repeating the process throughout the fertility period causes these women to be physically and mentally exhausted. Their general state of health becomes weak which makes them prone to illness and impairment (Hagrass 1994). In addition, children born by younger and older women have various impairments including low birth weight, lower growth rates and other physical and cognitive conditions. Pregnancy after the age of 37, for example, puts the mother at a very high risk of giving birth to a child with Down's syndrome. These practices further contribute to the malnutrition of the child and subsequently their likelihood of experiencing impairment (El Safty 1994). Another widespread social practice is circumcision. In Egypt, although female circumcision is forbidden by law, it is still practised. Again, this results in various kinds of impairment (Ras-Work 1991; Abdel-Salam 1998).

Nosseir (1989) argues that the frequency of impairment is notably higher among illiterate women and their children rather than among those who have had only a basic education. In Egypt, families tend to prioritise education for their male children and only if their financial means are above average do they extend such opportunities to their female offspring. This is quite evident in the national statistics which show that illiteracy among women age 15 and over range from as low as 40 per cent to 97 per cent. Also, it has been shown that there is a very high correlation between women's educational attainment and their level of fertility. This is why recent research suggests that the best health investment that could be done in developing countries is the education of girls (Boylan 1991).

Ageing is another societal problem which may result in impairment. Although Egyptian society is generally characterised by its young population, people in the older age groups are still supported and cared for by their family. As there are no financial or other forms of help provided by the Egyptian Government, the responsibility for supporting older people, whether impaired or not, inevitably falls to younger family members, and, as in the UK, women have most of the caring responsibilities (Boylan 1991). The high cost of medication also poses a major problem for families with very limited resources living in poorly resourced rural and urban areas. Furthermore, violence and war in developing countries such as Egypt are a major cause of impairments. The use of modern military technology such as land mines, for example, has resulted in the injury of many women and children. Those who survive are often left with permanent physical and/or psychological conditions (Nosseir 1990).

Academic definitions of disability in Egypt

In view of the apparent commonality of impairment in Egypt it is important to consider the meaning of disability within an Egyptian context. This review will initially centre on those definitions favoured by Egyptian scholars and policy makers that, in various ways, have impacted on national statistics, laws, and policy formulation. Hence it is important to examine two key considerations that flow from these interpretations. First, it is necessary to explore the explicit and implicit meanings of the terms themselves as well as their meaning within legislation. Second, as the meanings of particular words and phrases change over time, it is useful to consider when they came into use and also their longevity. This is essential in order to reflect effectively on their impact and usefulness in a period when ideas about disability are changing due to the assertion by disabled people and their organisations that disability is a social problem and a human rights issue.

At this point it is important to note that several of the texts quoted are written in Arabic and translated into English by the author. Osman et al. (1969: 183) define the disabled person as:

> Any individual who differs from normal individuals in physical, mental or social aspects to the extent that requires special rehabilitation action to make him/her reach maximum abilities and potentials.

Clearly, as the words 'physical' and 'mental' are used quite explicitly, it may be argued that this definition is limited in scope in that it does not include people with sensory or hidden impairments. Moreover, by referring to people who are 'different from the normal' Osman et al. imply that people with 'physical' or 'mental' impairments are actually 'abnormal'. Here, the meaning of normalcy seems to be shaped by an individualistic medical perspective of biological functioning and limitations. It may be argued too that with the insertion of the phrase 'social aspects', this definition extends to prisoners and delinquents since these groups are usually perceived as in need of rehabilitation services. Significantly, there is no reference whatsoever to any environmental, cultural or social influences on the process of disablement.

Another definition is given by Abdel Nour who defines the disabled person as:

The citizen that one or more disabling barriers have resided in, which weakened his/her ability and made him/her in serious need for outside help or institutional support based on scientific and technological basis to render him/her to normal level or as close as possible to normal level (Abdel Nour 1973:157).

As in Osman et al. (1969), the author identifies disability as coming from within the person (personal tragedy) and not from outside (Oliver 1990, 1995; Morris 1991; Lunt and Thornton 1994; Davis 1996; Hagrass 1998; Sapey 2000). Furthermore, when he mentions that the disabled person is the one who 'needs outside help' he is alluding to other members of the population. This sidesteps the fact that everyone needs outside help to survive.

In common with many interpretations these two definitions do not appear to distinguish between impairment and disability or the biological and the social. Impairment and disability are treated as if they were the same thing. As in conventional western thinking individually based functional limitations are presented as the cause of disability. It is quite evident that there is no clear-cut line between impairment and the person. The two are one. Both definitions implicitly if not explicitly imply that that some form of medical/rehabilitative interventions is the only way to resolve the problem of disability, and that the disabled person must strive to achieve normality.

The assumption of abnormality or 'otherness' in these interpretations can be very stigmatizing for people with impairments. This is especially the case for those who are struggling for self-fulfilment in their everyday life by furthering their education or looking for work; activities which are often denied disabled people due to the widely held association between impairment, disability and incompetence amongst non-disabled peers. Given recent developments within the academic arena and disability studies in particular, it may be said that these scholars have adopted a limited and outmoded approach to the disability question. Nonetheless, their work continues to have a significant influence on the writings of other writers working in the disability field, such as Fahmy (1995, 2000) and Ahmed (1997).

These academic contributions include definitions of disability from international organisations such as the World Health Organization (WHO) and the International Labour Organisation (ILO) in their literature to illustrate their awareness of developments at the international level, the influence of those mentioned above remains dominant. Their work exemplifies Mairian Corker's (1998) assertion that in most disability literature traditional individualistic approaches co-exist alongside the newer more radical ones generally associated with the social model of disability. Moreover as there is no serious consideration of the 'social consequences' of the process of disablement or 'handicap', it may be said that they are more damaging than the WHO's International Classification of Impairment, Disability and Handicap (ICIDH) (WHO 1980). It is also evident that they are unaware of the more recent socio/political approaches associated with the social model of disability.

Therefore, if disability is seen as an individual medical problem or a 'personal tragedy' (Oliver 1990), then disabled people will be treated as victims in need of pity, sympathy and charity. As a consequence, non-disabled people are frequently asked to be sympathetic toward their less fortunate peers and give to disability charities and so alleviate the need for state sponsored support. Furthermore, the perception of disability in the personal tragedy model assumes either consciously or unconsciously that disabled people should be viewed as individuals whose experience is defined by their impairments. Hence, the medicalization and individualisation of disability leads to policies that focus almost exclusively on the individual rather than on the economic, environmental and cultural problems disabled people encounter daily (Oliver 1990, 1995; Lunt and Thornton 1994; Davis 1996). All of which compounds the feelings of powerlessness felt by many people with impairments and, consequentially, inhibits, in various ways, their ability to interact on an equal basis with non-disabled people including parents, teachers, medical and rehabilitation professionals, and other members of the community (Morris 1991; Sapey 2000).

Alternative perspectives

i. Social model approaches
Since the 1970s disabled activists and their organisations, mostly in the West, have rejected the individualistic medical approach to disability as exemplified by the WHO's ICIDH. Instead, they have argued that whilst impairment is an individual biological phenomenon, disability, or the inability to do things, is the outcome of an inhospitable physical and cultural environment that prevents people with impairments from participating in their communities on an equal level with non-disabled contemporaries. An overtly political response to the problems encountered

by disabled people this perspective is now widely referred to as the 'social model of disability' (Oliver 1990; Morris 1991; 1996; Swain et al. 1993; Shakespeare et al. 1996; Barnes 2000).

Increasingly over recent years this socio-political interpretation of disablement has had an important influence on disabled people's organisations across the world. It has provided them with an effective tool with which to bring to the attention of policy and decision makers the limitations of traditional medically inspired thinking on disability. Their aim is to encourage politicians and those in power to formulate new policies and practices in order to give disabled people the same rights and opportunities as other citizens. It is also the case that these arguments have had some considerable impact on governments in developing countries like Egypt, as many now acknowledge the right of disabled people to lead a 'normal' life like others. Yet in many respects these statements seem little more than an empty reflection of those that appear in documents produced by western policy makers as there are no meaningful policies in place with which to make this a reality. Consequently, it might be argued that in Egyptian society, as in many other developing nations, there is little real evidence of the influence of the social model of disability in everyday life.

ii. Lay interpretations
The individual and medical models of disability are deeply rooted in many societies including Egypt. Here, as in many countries, disabled people are generally perceived as objects of charity (Hagrass 1998). At this point it is worth noting that I do not believe that the lay person's view of disability or their responses to individual disabled people are as one dimensional or as rigid as the literature discussed above would suggest. This assertion is based on my experience as a disabled woman living in Egypt. Whilst a charitable response to disability may be seen as problematic in rich, technically developed countries such as the UK or USA, in many nation states it is considered a morally acceptable and proper response to an often assumed insurmountable social problem. Indeed, this perception is easily activated in a Muslim society where religion plays a pivotal role in people's daily lives. Indeed, non-disabled people's responses to people with impairments are influenced by a number of factors. Two important examples are religion and familial relationships. Both need to be contextualized within a society in which Government has up to now proved to be ineffective in responding effectively to the needs of disabled people.

The Islamic faith explicitly encourages Muslims to help the poor and less fortunate in society, including disabled people. In most Muslim societies giving '*zakah*', which may be understood as a form of income tax but in a religious context, is considered an obligation of duty. Moreover, many Muslims give part of their '*zakah*' to various charities, non-government organizations, and disability groups in accordance with their religious beliefs. The extended family is still prevalent throughout the Middle East, and family ties and responsibilities remain strong. The conventional division of labour in this type of family structure requires women who do not go to work to be responsible for the care and support of children and older and disabled family as and where necessary (Teçke et al.1994; Hagrass 1998). Moreover, because in countries like Egypt social policies are not well developed, or in some cases non-existent, disabled and frail older people have little alternative but to rely on their families for care and support. It is important to point out here that, although disabled activists argue that disabled people's problems should be addressed within a human rights framework I would suggest that in most cases the type of familial support described above, is given willingly and signifies a more positive aspect of inter-relations between disabled and non-disabled people that is not always reflected in the disability and policy literature.

Disability policy in Egypt

As in many countries traditional medical definitions are reflected in official statistics and survey data. However, what might be termed a more socially aware approach to the problems encountered by disabled people is clearly evident in welfare policies particularly with reference to employment issues.

In 1976 the Central Agency for Mobilisation and Statistics (CAPMAS) used a six-category 'disability' typology in its population Census to estimate the numbers of disabled people in Egypt. People were counted as disabled if they were: blind, had the use of only one eye, were 'deaf and dumb', had lost one or both upper limbs, lost one or both lower limbs, or were considered to have 'mild mental retardation'. Based on these criteria the data show that 111,324 people could be categorised as disabled out of a total population of 36,622,040; approximately three people per thousand (Fahmy 1995). Just over a decade later, a health profile of Egypt reported that the percentage of disabled people in the general population had risen to 1.52 per cent. One year later the Polio Institute declared the number of disabled people to be 11 per cent. In 1992, the *Pan Arab Project for Child*

Development suggested that disabled people numbered 1.54 per cent of the population (Shukrallah et al. 1997). The latest CAPMAS census of 1996 expanded its 'disability' categories to eleven. In addition to the above, these included people perceived as 'deaf', 'dumb', had polio, experienced 'total or partial paralysis', and/or 'other disabilities'. The survey concluded that 284,188 people out of a population of 59, 273,082, or 4.8 per thousand, should be classified as disabled (CAPMAS 1996). It is also worth noting that the CAPMAS data show that the number of disabled men far exceeds that for disabled women: 64.4 per cent and 35.6 per cent respectively. This might be due to the numerous conflicts that have plagued Arabic countries over recent years (Ahmed 1997) or that impairment amongst women is less likely to be reported (Hagrass 1998). It has also been suggested that only 20 per cent of the disabled population live in urban areas and that cities account for 80 per cent of disability related services (Nosseir 1989; El Banna 1989).

The discrepancies among estimates of the incidence of impairment may be attributed to several factors. First, the criteria upon which 'disability' may be reported are vague. Second, in most of these studies, the reporting of disability is to disabled people themselves or, in most cases, family members. Hence there is reliance on subjective understandings of what constitutes impairment or 'disability'. Finally, in each of these studies, the items pertaining to disability are usually considered of minor importance. This led to them being taken lightly or ignored (Fahmy 1995, 2000; Ahmed 1997; Shukrallah et al. 1997). As international estimates suggest that around 10 per cent of the population in most nation states may be considered 'disabled' these figures have only limited reliability (Fahmy 2000). What is certain is that the number of disabled people in Egypt is not small. Therefore, their rights should be ensured through the enactment of appropriate laws and policies.

Interestingly, since the 1950s several laws and policies concerning disabled people have been introduced in Egypt. The social welfare legislature of 1950 contained a specific chapter dealing with the 'rehabilitation of disabled persons' (Fahmy 1995; 2000). However, greater emphasis was placed on disability issues following the 1952 revolution when the Government issued several legislative measures intended to secure 'care' and security for disabled individuals. Among these were the: Labour Law, 91 (1959), Rehabilitation Law, 14 (1959), Social Welfare Law, 133 (1964) and the Health Insurance Law (1964) (Ministry of Insurance and Social Affairs 1987).

A number of points need to be considered when assessing the impact of these laws on Egyptian society. Significantly the Government Department responsible for issuing and implementing both the Labour and Rehabilitation Laws is the Ministry of Social Affairs and Manpower. Hence the responsibility for rehabilitation, training and employment is located in one government department. While there are potentially clear advantages to this approach in terms of internal communication amongst the staff concerned with various elements of policy implementation; communicating with other relevant ministries may be problematic. Further, following similar policies elsewhere in the 1950s (Lunt and Thornton 1994) the Labour Law of 1959 introduced a 2 per cent quota scheme for employers to ensure the recruitment of disabled workers to their workforce indicating Governmental recognition of the importance of employment in disabled people lives.

The Social Welfare Law 79 of 1975, and subsequent amendments, in particular, Law 25 (1977) and Law 92 (1980), are amongst those that deal specifically with disabled people's welfare rights. Their principal function is to ensure that people who acquire impairment through work related injuries or diseases receive appropriate compensation and pensions. However, payments and benefits are calculated solely on the basis of individualistic medical assessments. These assessments do not take into account the psycho-emotional consequences of the onset of disablement or the social circumstances of the individual concerned. Moreover, the Law of Civilian Employees 47 of 1978 and the Law of Public Sector Employees 48 of 1978 also include articles relating to the employment of disabled workers. These statutes were introduced to secure employment for disabled workers in state sponsored agencies and organisations. Priority is given to disabled war veterans, their children and family members if they are judged to be unfit for work.

During the 1970s the Egyptian Ministry of Social Affairs (MoSA) introduced the Rehabilitation Law 39 (1975), later amended under Law 49 (1982), in order to bring together disability policy under one statute. The new Law raised the employment quota for disabled workers, mentioned above, from 2 to 5 per cent. Whilst this may be seen as a step forward, it can also be argued that it reinforces the conventional notion that disabled people are somehow different from the rest of the community and, therefore, need 'special' provision. Even though the quota scheme ensures that there are some job opportunities for disabled workers, its application in practice is restrictive in that it tends to alienate disabled workers from non-disabled colleagues, inhibits their ability to compete in the open job market and, consequentially, does not promote equal opportunities in the workplace.

Significantly, there is no reference to disability issues in other Egyptian legislation. Consequently there is a tendency for policy makers generally to ignore disability issues; they are viewed as a rehabilitation issue and someone else's problem. For example, the employment of disabled people is covered by the Rehabilitation Law 39, but not in the Employment Law 137 (1981), apart from a brief reference to the registration form that should be completed by employers who employ disabled people (Ministry of Manpower 1981:213).

This exclusion of disability issues from other policy initiatives can be explained with reference to the underlying assumptions upon which the Rehabilitation Law is based. For example a disabled person is defined as:

> any individual who became unable to depend on him/herself in performing his/her work or another [type of] and remains in it. His/her inability to do so is the result of physical, mental, sensory or congenital impairment.

Furthermore, rehabilitation is described as:

> presenting social, psychological, medical, educational, and professional assistance to all disabled persons and their families to enable them to overcome the negative consequences resulting from impairment (Law 39, 1975: 1).

It is clear that both definitions focus exclusively on the functional limitations of the individual and their assumed lower job performance and inability to function without professional support. In the same way as the academic definitions discussed in the first section of this paper, they present only an individualistic medical portrayal of disability. A major concern is that impairment is the sole cause of the problems associated with disability and once again, there is no reference whatsoever to environmental and cultural barriers. Furthermore, in the definition of rehabilitation, impairment is the problem and rehabilitative interventions are directed exclusively toward the needs of the individual and their family.

By continually re-enforcing the orthodox essentially negative views of disability and, by implication, people with impairments, the interpretations of both disability and rehabilitation in Egyptian law inadvertently perpetuate discriminatory attitudes and prejudice toward people with impairments. Furthermore, some sections of the disabled population are treated more favourably than others. For example, Article 3 specifies that disabled citizens on a 'low income' are entitled to free rehabilitation. Those on higher incomes are not. It is worth noting that there have been no further amendments to these laws since the 1980s. As a consequence Egyptian disability policy is still encapsulated within a traditional individual, medical model of disability framework. The underlying assumption is that disabled people's experiences and life chances are determined exclusively by their impairment. At the societal level, the individualisation, medicalization and objectification of disabled people's lives remains intact. As a result the powerlessness that characterises the experience of many disabled people's lives goes unchallenged.

Conclusion
In this chapter I have endeavoured to show how the traditional individualistic medical or personal tragedy model of disability continues to dominate Egyptian disability legislation and policy. It has also been suggested that although cultural factors play an important role in social interactions between disabled and non-disabled people and, as a result, lay responses to the support of people with impairments are often less harsh than those suggested in some of the disability literature, this continued dominance has significant negative implications for disabled people's ongoing struggle for human rights and equal treatment. This is especially worrying given the growing acknowledgement at the international level that disability is both a medical and social issue that warrants nothing less than an overtly socio-political response (see, for example, *Standard Rules on the Equalization of Opportunities for Persons with Disabilities* (UN 1993)).

In an effort to resolve this unfortunate situation it is therefore imperative that the international disability movement and their allies within the academic community continue to draw attention to the policy implications of both the medical and social models of disability and, in so doing, help influence national governments, such as that of Egypt, to re-formulate disability policy within a universally acceptable human rights framework.

Bibliography

Abdel Nour, M. 1973: *Al-Kidmah Al-Ijtimaciah Al-Tebbeyah wa Al-Taahil*. Trans.: *The Socio-Medical Service and Rehabilitation*. Cairo: Maktabet Al-Kahira Al-Hadithah.

Abdel-Salam, S. 1998: *Female Sexuality and the Discourse of Power: the Case of Egypt*. Cairo: The American University in Cairo (MA thesis submitted to the sociology/anthropology department).

Ahmed, M. 1997: *Al-Khidmah Al-Ijtimaciyah fe Majal Recayat Al-Mucakin*. Trans.: *Social Service in the Area of Care for Disabled People*. Alexandria: Dar El-Mecrefah Al-Jamicayah.

Barnes, C. 2000: A Working Social Model? Disability, Work and Disability Politics in the 21st century. *Critical Social Policy*, 4, 441-457.

Boylan, E. (ed.) 1991: *Women and Disability*. London: Zed Books Ltd.

Central Agency for Mobilisation and Statistics (CAPMAS) 1996: *The Distribution of the Disabled Persons in Egypt According to Age Categories, Disability, and Gender in the Republic Governorates According to the Final Results of Population Count 1996*. Arab Republic of Egypt: General Agency and Statistics. (In Arabic).

Corker, M. 1998: Disability Discourse in a Postmodern World. In T. Shakespeare (ed.), *The Disability Reader: Social Science Perspectives*. London and New York: Continuum.

Davis, K. 1996: Disability and Legislation: Rights and Equality. In G. Hales (ed.), *Beyond Disability: Towards an Enabling Society*. UK: The Open University Press.

El Banna, A. 1989: The Situation of the Disabled in Egypt. Paper presented at the 'Capabilities and Needs of Disabled Persons', ESCWA Conference, Amman, Jordan.

El-Safty, M. 1994: Women and Disability: the Role of the Family. Paper presented at 'The Role of the Family in Integrating Disabled Women into Society', ESCWA Conference, Amman, Jordan.

Fahmy, M. 1995: *Al-Selouk Al-Ijtemaci Lil Mucakin*. Translated as: *The Social Behaviour of the Disabled*. Alexandria: Dar El-Mecrefah Al-Jamicayah.

Fahmy, M. 2000: *Wakic Recayat Al- Mucakin fe Al-Wattan Al-Carabi*. Translated as.: *The Situation of the Care for the Disabled Persons in the Arab Homeland*. Alexandria: Al-Maktab Al-Jameci Al-Hadith.

Hagrass, H. 1994: Women with Disability in Egypt. Paper presented at 'The Role of the Family in Integrating Disabled Women into Society', ESCWA Conference, Amman, Jordan.

Hagrass, H. 1998: *Gender, Disability and Marriage*, MA thesis presented to the American University in Cairo.

Lunt, N. and Thornton, P. 1994: Disability and Employment: Towards an Understanding of Discourse and Policy. ***Disability and Society***, 9 (2), 223-238.

Ministry of Manpower 1981: (23rd edition). ***Law 137 of 1981 for Issuing Employment Law According to the latest Amendments***. Cairo: Al-Amireya Printing. (In Arabic).

Ministry of Insurance and Social Affairs 1987: ***Law 39 of 1975 for the Rehabilitation of the Disabled***. Cairo: Al-Amireya Printing. (In Arabic).

Morris, J. 1991: ***Pride against Prejudice: Transforming Attitudes to Disability***. London: The Women's Press Ltd.

Morris, J. (ed.) 1996: ***Encounters with Strangers: Feminism and Disability***. London: The Women's Press Ltd.

Nosseir, N. 1989: Women and Disability. Paper presented at the 'Capabilities and Needs of Disabled Persons' ESCWA Conference, Amman, Jordan.

Nosseir, N. 1990: Disabled Females: Egypt. Paper presented at the United Nations 'Seminar on Disabled Women', Vienna, Austria.

Oliver, M. 1990: ***The Politics of Disablement***. London: Macmillan.

Oliver, M. 1995: Disability, Empowerment and their Inclusive Society. In G. Zarb (ed.), ***Removing Disabling Barriers***. London: Policy Studies Institute.

Osman, A. et al. 1969: ***Al-Recayah Al-Ejtemaciyah Lil Mucakin***. Translated as: ***Social Care for Disabled Persons***. Cairo: The Egyptian Anglo Library.

Qandil, A. 1989: Social Aspects of the Disabled in the Western Asia Region and the Importance of their Modification. Paper presented at the 'Capabilities and Needs of Disabled Persons', ESCWA Conference, Amman, Jordan.

Ras-Work, B. 1991: Traditional Practices that Inflict Disability. In E. Boylan (ed.), ***Women and Disability***. London: Zed Books Ltd.

Sapey, B. 2000: Disablement in the Informational Age. ***Disability and Society***, 15 (4), 619-636.

Scheper-Hughes, N. 1984: The Mindful Body: a Prolegomenon to Future Work in Medical Anthropology. ***Medical Anthropological Quarterly***, 1, n.s. 6-41.

Shakespeare, T., Gillespies-Sells, K. and Davies, D. 1996: *The Sexual Politics of Disability: Untold Desires*. London and New York: Cassell.

Shukrallah, A., Mostafa, H. and Magdi, S. 1997: The Current State of the Disability Question in Egypt: Preliminary National Study. Presented to North-South Inserm Network.

Swain, J., Finkelstein, V., French, S. with Oliver, M. (eds) 1993: *Disabling Barriers Enabling Environments*. London: Sage Publications.

Teçke, B., Oldham, L. with Shorter, F.C. 1994: *A Place to Live: Families and Child Health in a Cairo Neighborhood*. Cairo: AUC Press.

WHO 1980: *International Classification of Impairments, Disabilities and Handicaps*, Geneva: World Health Organization.

UN 1993: *Standard Rules on the Equalization of Opportunities for Persons with Disabilities*. New York: United Nations.

CHAPTER 11

An Evaluation of the Impact of Medical Services Provided by General Hospitals Compared with Services Aligned to a Social Model Perspective at a Spinal Cord Injury Centre in Bangladesh

A. K. M. Momin

This chapter explores the differences arising from two distinctive approaches to supporting people with spinal cord lesion (SCL): first, those services offered by general hospitals that operate exclusively within a medical model; and second, the services provided by the Centre for the Rehabilitation of the Paralysed (CRP), which draw on a social model perspective. It will be argued that the exclusive reliance on a medical model that underpins general hospital provision too often results in health and rehabilitation problems and inadequate support services for people with SCL. In contrast, the combination of social and medical services at CRP delivered a range of support that produced better outcomes for people with SCL. On this evidence, the approach taken by CRP should be more widely adopted by government and non-government organisations in developing services for people with SCL.

Study Context
Bangladesh is one of the poorest countries in the world, with an estimated 45 per cent of the population living below the poverty line (ILO 2001). Poverty is defined here in terms of an individual's calorie intake, health care, educational opportunities, safe drinking water, sanitation and shelter. Approximately 60 per cent of the population does not have access to modern primary health care services beyond immunisation and family

planning (Abedin 1997, 2000), while only 25 per cent of pregnant women receive antenatal care, and a mere 14 per cent of births are attended by someone with formal training (World Bank 1999). Furthermore, only 44 per cent of the population uses a sanitary method of sewage disposal (BBS 1997). The life expectancy at birth is 60 years (BBS 2001a). However, sons are often preferred to daughters (Rahman and Davanzo 1993) and as a result, female children may be discriminated against in terms of the provision of food (Chen et al. 1981 cited in World Bank 1999) and medical and health care (Hossain and Glass 1988). Overall, 65 per cent of the adult population in Bangladesh is illiterate, but this figure rises to 78 per cent among females (World Bank 1993). The per capita income is US $386 (Abedin 2000). Agriculture generates about one-third of the Gross Domestic Product (GDP), and provides employment for over 60 per cent of the labour force (NFOWD 1999).

In Bangladesh there is no specialist government hospital for the treatment and rehabilitation of people with SCL. Instead, there is a single non-government organisation (NGO), CRP, which has been working in this field for the last 25 years. Without a comprehensive government programme, the vast majority of people with SCL have not received any services and little attention has been given to how they cope in their respective communities. The incidence of people with SCL in Bangladesh has been estimated as six persons per million (Hoque 2002), although this is not a comprehensive study as many people with SCL do not survive after their injury, or do not (or cannot) access medical care. The World Health Organization (WHO) (1997) has suggested a much higher figure, between 20-40 persons per million, although it has been estimated that in Sri Lanka the equivalent rate is as high as 66.7 persons per million (Motivation 1999).

Conceptualising disability

The government of Bangladesh regards 'disability', including people with SCL, as solely a medical problem. In contrast, many people with SCL feel their condition is a curse from God because of their misdeeds, feelings that are reinforced by the negative attitudes of society towards disabled people (Momin 2003). This means that when people with SCL return to their communities they are not able to participate in everyday activities due to social and environmental barriers, ranging from overt discrimination to the lack of physical access in their locality.

Unlike some other 'low resource' countries Bangladesh has been slow to adopt a rights-based approach to providing services for disabled people.

There has been a widespread lack of community awareness of disability issues, although as a result of the United Nations (UN) initiative, the Bangladeshi government has begun to rethink its approach. It has agreed to implement the United Nations' *22 Standard Rules on Equalisation of Opportunities for Persons with Disabilities* (UN 1993) and incorporated these within a national policy for the welfare of disabled people. However, there has been little action to advance the integration of people with SCL into community life. One of the reasons for this failure is the continuing perception that disability can only be tackled by medical and allied treatment services. Hence the importance of exploring a social model approach which highlights the attitudinal, institutional, and environmental discrimination against disabled people.

Though there are many issues surrounding the application of a social model approach in a non-western country (Stone 1999), it is useful to remember that the social model is an holistic approach that focuses on the entire disability experience. While it may be possible to distinguish between medical and social issues in the well-resourced countries of Europe and North America, it is not so easy in poor countries like Bangladesh where medical and rehabilitation services are extremely scarce. Again, a social model approach does not reject the significance of appropriate medical and rehabilitative interventions (Oliver 2004). Indeed, their denial is a political and human rights issue (Hurst 2001; WHO 2001). Hence, the value of a social model analysis of the support available to people with SCL in poor countries like Bangladesh.

Services for people with SCL in Bangladesh
Both specialised spinal cord lesion centres and general hospitals in Bangladesh provide services for people with SCL, although the level of medical care, rehabilitation and support services is generally regarded as inadequate and below the standards of similar services in India (Sinha 2000). Many people after sustaining a spinal injury are not immediately diagnosed or are mis-diagnosed, and a person acquiring a spinal cord injury will often be kept at home and seek support from a traditional healer. As a result, many people with SCL experience medical complications such as urine infections and bedsores.

As their condition deteriorates some are taken to *upazilla* or district hospitals. Those who are taken to the nearest *upazilla* health complex (a 31-50 bed government hospital staffed by, on average, eight qualified physicians) or to a nearby clinic, typically find that these institutions provide them with little more than an initial assessment and basic treatment. Indeed, it may already be too late to save their lives. In other cases, the receiving hospital will refer the patient to a specialised hospital or medical college hospital or to CRP for further treatment (although there are no specialised government hospitals for the treatment and rehabilitation of people with SCL). However, transfer to a general hospital is dependent on the availability of beds and appropriate medical expertise in dealing with SCL. Given the widespread shortage of specialist skills at general hospitals, once their medical condition is stabilised, people with SCL are usually discharged even though therapeutic and support services in the community are inadequate.

Almost all people with SCL return to their own homes after being discharged, with only a few staying in specialist homes or rehabilitation centres for a short time. CRP receives 88 per cent of its users either as referrals from general hospitals, or when patients themselves decide to leave hospital in search of better care (CRP 2002). No matter what the source of the referral, many SCL patients experience severe pressure sores and other major complications. A significant number of those who do not receive specialist care die within two years, while most of those who do survive are dependent on their families for their personal care.

There is no standardised system of service provision in general hospitals in Bangladesh for people with SCL. Data collected as part of my study showed that on average people stay at these hospitals for 8 weeks after injury and then go back to their communities. Although hospital providers often declare an intention to 'cure' their patients, very few receive any treatment from therapists during their hospitalisation. Nor is there provision for any dialogue between patients and service providers. Therefore, when people with SCL are discharged from general hospitals, there is little or no follow-up treatment or advice, despite its obvious importance to their well-being. In comparison, India has significantly more hospital facilities for people with spinal cord injuries that include an established protocol of treatment (acute care) and rehabilitation (physical, emotional, social and economic) through to discharge into the community (Sinha 2000; Momin 2003).

In Bangladesh, general hospitals and clinics offer very little in the way of health education training programmes for people with SCL or their family members. The majority of people with SCL do not receive any mobility aids, even when such aids are essential. Very few are involved in self-care activities, continuing education or employment following their hospitalisation. As a result they are often trapped within their homes with only their family to help them. Some hope that they will be 'cured' one day and return to a normal life, but when this does not happen they often lose confidence in themselves, and become fully dependent on their families for survival. This is a too-frequent outcome for ex-general hospital users because no training is provided to help them or their families adjust to their new life situation.

In contrast, CRP has developed a standard and comprehensive system to provide services for people with SCL, based on its existing resources. It has made a vital contribution to the rehabilitation of paralysed people, and the quality and importance of its work is widely recognised both in Bangladesh and elsewhere in South Asia. CRP has developed an approach that provides treatment and rehabilitation to the 'whole' person. It also campaigns for preventive measures and the avoidance of SCL through meetings, seminars, the electronic media and feature films.

Figure 1 summarises this process. In general, a person with SCL stays on average 16 weeks in the hospital under the care of a multidisciplinary team. During this time comprehensive medical intervention and physical rehabilitation support is provided. Once the medical condition is stabilised, attention is directed to the care of the skin, the bladder and the bowels, and the prevention of complications such as pressure sores, urinary infections and muscle contractions. This is done through the delivery of health education training to users and their carers/family members. Half-hourly turning and lifting takes place to prevent pressure sores, and intermittent catheterisation and bladder washouts are conducted as required.

At the same time the physical and social rehabilitation process is provided through the involvement of physiotherapists, occupational therapists and social workers. Health education and activities for daily living training are provided by ex-users who are mainly wheelchair users. Mobility aids are distributed along with instruction on their use and maintenance. If required, training of carers or family members also takes place. 'Active rehab' courses are provided to users to develop their self-confidence in the use of the wheelchair, within and outside the home environment. In addition, users are encouraged to share their ideas with the service providers (doctors, nurses, therapists and social workers).

The next stage is to refer users to a halfway house, where they usually stay for four to eight weeks while undertaking vocational training. The halfway house is modelled on a traditional Bangladeshi 'bari' (house). Its purpose is to build confidence in the person with SCL and their family

168　　　AN EVALUATION OF THE IMPACT OF MEDICAL SERVICES
　　　　PROVIDED BY GENERAL HOSPITALS

Figure 1: CRP service provision

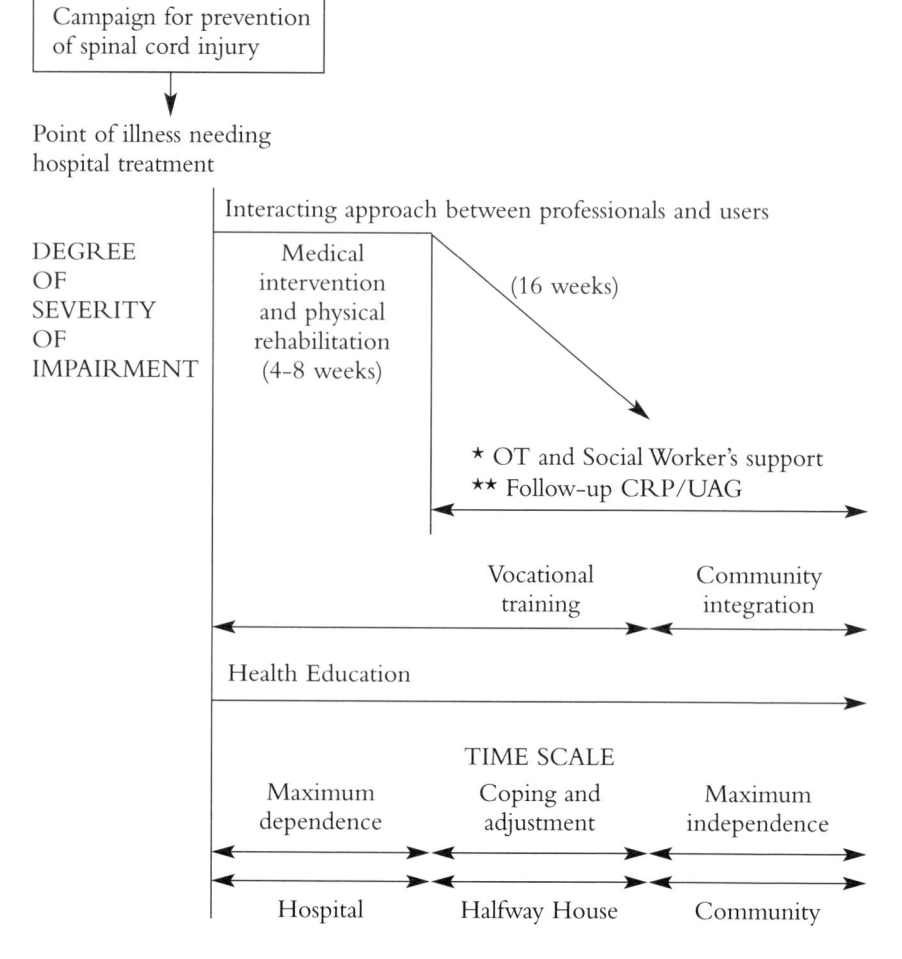

```
┌─────────────────────────┐
│ Campaign for prevention │
│ of spinal cord injury   │
└──────────┬──────────────┘
           ▼
Point of illness needing
hospital treatment
                  │ Interacting approach between professionals and users
DEGREE            │   Medical
OF                │   intervention       (16 weeks)
SEVERITY          │   and physical
OF                │   rehabilitation
IMPAIRMENT        │   (4-8 weeks)
                  │                    ▼
                  │              * OT and Social Worker's support
                  │             ** Follow-up CRP/UAG
                  │
                  │              Vocational        Community
                  │              training          integration
                  │
                  │   Health Education
                  │
                  │                 TIME SCALE
                  │   Maximum       Coping and       Maximum
                  │   dependence    adjustment       independence
                  │
                  │   Hospital      Halfway House    Community
```

Key: ★ Occupational Therapy;
      ★★ *Upazilla Action Group*, a forum for disabled people promoting community based rehabilitation

Source: Adapted from Finkelstein (1989: 8).

members so that when they return home they can manage themselves without support from professionals. There is no electricity supply and oil lamps are used for lighting the room, and no water supply so that a hand tube-well is used to provide water. In addition, there is no gas supply and firewood is used for cooking. There is a small vegetable plot, flower garden, and a small poultry/goat house. Users are responsible, on a rotational basis, for undertaking important activities such as cooking and looking after the poultry.

Family members are encouraged to accompany people with SCL during their stay at the halfway house to familiarise them with the new environmental demands. All the facilities are accessible to wheelchair users who are encouraged to look after themselves and carry out their own activities of daily living. No personal assistance or nursing care is provided; instead, a member of the user's family is encouraged to give support. CRP's role is to facilitate a level of 'independent living' for users with the support of their family. If the individual is a tetraplegic, then a family member is supported to provide care, often by an ex-service wheelchair user. Furthermore, occupational therapy is available to the user when required. When people with SCL are in the halfway house, a CRP social worker visits their home to advise family members if any adaptations or modifications are required and to see if any professional advice is needed about what to do once the person with SCL returns. At the same time staff from the social welfare department discuss their plans for becoming self-reliant including, if required, specific work training.

After leaving the halfway house, people with SCL go back to their own communities. A social worker or a Community Based Rehabilitation (CBR) worker carries out a follow-up visit to a user's home to check if any physical, social, emotional or economic support is required in the community. The users will often be supported by members of the Upazilla Action Group Committee, so they are briefed about its functions and forms of assistance while they are at the Centre. Once back in the community, they are given an opportunity to share their experience with people with similar impairments, while CRP social workers or CBR workers make home visits to support them. The whole approach is designed to facilitate people with SCL in achieving a self-supported life.

In accordance with CRP's positive discrimination policy, women are given higher priority than men during service provision. In this way an attempt is made to redress the situation whereby women are deprived of available services by the traditional domination of males in Bangladeshi society. CRP aims to offer the fullest support to people with SC in order to assist their reintegration into community life.

Research study
The research findings reported here are based on fieldwork conducted as part of a PhD project undertaken by the author. The project adopted a

participatory approach based on the philosophy of emancipatory research (Oliver 1992; Barnes and Mercer 1997). People with spinal cord lesion played a key role in the research design, and it was considered vital that their views should be presented as accurately as possible.

In total, 64 individuals were recruited for face-to-face, semi-structured interviews. Half the sample came from CRP, selected through stratified random sampling, and the other half comprised general hospital patients identified by a process of quota sampling. The participants were aged between 10 and 59 years, and all had received services between 1994 and 1999. Data were analysed using the Statistical Package for the Social Sciences (SPSS). A detailed comparison was made of the views of CRP and general hospital users, and a chi-square test (with a 5 per cent level of significance) undertaken to assess the statistical significance of selected variables. In addition, more qualitative data have been used to present participants' views. All interviewees have been given pseudonyms to ensure their anonymity.

Health problems

Health problems for people with SCL are generated from poor medical treatment, nursing care and therapeutic services, received either at the institutional or community level. Eighteen common secondary problems related to medical services were identified from the review of the literature (e.g. Johnson et al. 1998). The interviews with users confirmed thirteen of these: superficial, deep and infected pressure sores, infections of respiratory tract, urinary tract or wound, bowel complications, regular and/or chronic pain in shoulder or abdomen; painful spasms, depression, relationship problems with partners, families or friends and psychological health.

Chi-square analysis was carried out to determine whether there was a significant difference between the percentage of CRP respondents and other respondents reporting secondary health problems. As illustrated in Table 1, the difference was significant ($p<.05$) for 11 of the 13 symptoms, with a lower percentage of CRP users reporting secondary problems. It is suggested that the care and service provided by CRP accounts for this pattern. The differences experienced by respondents are illustrated by comments from individual interviews. Thus, Rashida, a woman who received services in a general hospital and was suffering from pressure sores, said:

I developed my pressure sores at the hospital. No one told me why it happens or what to do about it. When they saw my physical condition was deteriorating they released me, saying it was not worth treating.

Rashida's comments reflect the experiences of the majority of general hospital users (72 per cent) who had developed their pressure sores when in hospital, and had not received advice about their prevention or treatment. Nafiza, a female CRP user who had earlier developed pressure sores at the general hospital, reported that:

When doctors at the general hospital saw that they were unable to manage the 'patients' in their own hospitals during the last stage, when their physical condition became unmanageable, then they referred them to CRP.

Table 1: Comparison health problems as between CRP users and general hospital users

Health problem	CRP % (Number)	General hospital % (Number)	Total % (Number)	Statistical Significance
Superficial pressure sores	16 (05)	59 (19)	38 (24)	p<.000
Deep pressure sores	19 (06)	50 (16)	34 (22)	p<.008
Infected pressure sores	03 (01)	44 (14)	23 (15)	p<.000
Respiratory tract infection	16 (05)	47 (15)	31 (20)	p<.007
Urinary tract infection	13 (04)	63 (20)	38 (24)	p<.000
Bowel complications	16 (05)	44 (14)	30 (19)	p<.000
Regular shoulder pain	47 (15)	69 (22)	58 (37)	p<.076
Regular abdominal pain	09 (03)	53 (17)	31 (20)	p<.000
Wound infection	03 (01)	44 (14)	23 (15)	p<.000
Painful spasm	44 (14)	59 (19)	53 (34)	p<.211
Depression	22 (07)	59 (19)	41 (26)	p<.002
Relationship with partner	09 (03)	28 (09)	19 (12)	p<.014
Relationship problems with family/friends	16 (05)	38 (12)	27 (17)	p<.048

This reflects the experience of 88 per cent of CRP users who were initially admitted to general hospitals. Moreover, there was a statistically significant relationship reported between 'severity of injury' and reports of 'superficial pressure sores' ($p<.000$), 'deep pressure sores' ($p<.001$), 'infected pressure sores' ($p<.004$), 'bowel complications' ($p<.000$), 'abdominal pain' ($p<.002$) and 'depression' ($p<.005$). Although respiratory tract infection itself does not demonstrate a statistical relationship to severity of injury, individuals have a greater chance of contracting respiratory tract infections if their injury prevents them from supporting themselves in a vertical position. As a rule, patients confined to their beds will be more prone to respiratory tract infection, as will those in poor health. There were no significant differences in the experiences of health problems of men and women.

Problems relating to rehabilitation services

Rehabilitation covers three different areas: physical, social and economic. Physical rehabilitation includes health education provided to users and their family members for prevention of further complications from spinal cord injury, such as pressure sores and urine infection. It has been found that of those participants and their family members who had received health education, very few reported health problems after being discharged from the hospital. Social rehabilitation was carried out through home visits to provide support to people with SCL in order to integrate them into family life, social activities, health care and education. Economic rehabilitation was provided through vocational training. When people with SCL are unable to return to their previous occupations, they require new skills to be able to take part in economic activities. CRP provides such rehabilitation, unlike most other SCL treatment centres.

Health education training for users

Health education training on the nature of SCL and the ways of managing and caring for associated health problems is crucial for people with SCL if they are to be kept fit, self-supportive and independent.

A statistically significant difference separated health education training between CRP users and general hospital users ($p<.000$). CRP encourages all its users, when they are ready, to join health education training so that they have appropriate basic self-care knowledge before they are discharged. This service is provided at CRP through peer group support with former users taking part in demonstrations and training. Many respondents commented that they learn most when they can exchange experience with other people with SCL.

The general hospitals offered health education, but only 9 per cent actually received this service. Moreover, the training was partial and dependent on a user's determination to be shown some of the techniques of personal care during their hospital stay. Many general hospital users said they had some idea about self-care but this was mostly restricted to taking medicines and continuing exercise. This proved inadequate in community situations where the majority experienced pressure sores, urinary tract infections and bowel problems. Needless to say, such conditions made it difficult to continue with their everyday lives.

As an illustration, one general hospital user with a severe impairment, Akbar, reported that he had not received any training in bladder control and experienced severe infection:

> I have no control of my bladder. I was asked to attend fortnightly checks at the doctor's clinic at …. hospital, which I did for the first few months. I no longer attend and still have persistent leaking of urine.

Akbar's wife complained that she had to take her husband to a doctor's clinic. Neither she nor her husband knew about the use of a catheter.

In contrast, the great majority of participants who received services from CRP said that they were able to control secondary complications such as pressure sores, urine infection and bowel complications. As Rajib, who was severely impaired, noted:

> I have no bowel complications when I am regular but otherwise complications arise. I have learned at CRP how to manage my bowel and it is important that I follow CRP's advice to keep me fit.

No association was found between 'health education' and 'severity of injury' or 'gender'. This may be because all CRP users receive health education training.

Health education for family members

Family members of all CRP users were given health education training, unlike family members of general hospital users. Those people who attended CRP sessions were usually women, although males included the husband of a paraplegic user and some fathers and brothers of individuals with SCL. Health education training begins at CRP from the day the patient is transferred to the halfway hostel. There are two health educators, one male and one female, who are ex-patients of CRP and wheelchair users. Their job is to deliver health education so that family members can help prevent medical complications. This training is provided in an informal setting, with practical demonstrations of lifting from the wheelchair to prevent bedsores, dressing of bedsores, use of the toilet and catheter, cleaning catheters, bowel training and the maintenance of technical aids and equipment.

Home visits
Home visits by social workers, rehabilitation workers, therapists and nurses proved to be very effective, especially given the absence of community nursing or other such services. CRP's policy is to visit all users once a year in their homes, and keep in touch with users every four months through a newsletter and a questionnaire to ascertain their physical, social, emotional and economic condition. Subsequent feedback is given by CRP staff, through home visits and associated support, or if necessary by re-admitting users. Conversely, general hospitals do not provide a home visit programme, and their staff do not know how their patients cope once discharged.

Users who are experiencing problems with adjusting to their new life in the community are visited by CRP staff more frequently. The majority of those receiving multiple visits were people with complete tetraplegia and paraplegia. It was felt by CRP users that home visits were successful in empowering those who were socially deprived or emotionally depressed. They have the added function of recognising service users as human beings and worthy of respect and support. No association was found between a home or follow-up visit and gender. Again this may be explained with reference to CRP's equal opportunities policy.

Vocational training
Vocational training offers an option to those who cannot return to their previous jobs with the opportunity to acquire new knowledge and skills. Fifty per cent of CRP users with tetraplegia, and 63 per cent of people with paraplegia received such training. For example, Hafiz, who was severely impaired, said:

> When I was in …. hospital I felt that I was powerless and would soon die. Fortunately I was able to go to CRP where I accessed medical and rehabilitation services. As my physical impairment did not allow me to return to my previous occupation I also received vocational training in poultry keeping. I now have 300 ducks and am able to earn enough to maintain my family.

Hafiz's experience illustrates the usefulness of vocational training. CRP users who were unable to go back to their previous occupations received vocational training from CRP and as a consequence were able to maintain a self-supported lifestyle. Fifty per cent of CRP users, mostly mildly impaired, both men and women, felt no need for any vocational training, either because they were able to continue their previous occupations or because they found new occupations not requiring any training. Of those receiving vocational training, the great majority had either a severe or moderate impairment.

A few individuals receiving CRP services did not avail themselves of vocational training in the hope that they would be able to continue with their education or previous job, but others felt vocational training could help them to get paid work or run a business. One user commented that CRP should offer tailor-made training so that there would be no uncertainty about work. Another felt that because of his lack of confidence and insecurity about obtaining work, he did not wish to join the vocational training programme. General hospital patients generally regarded medical treatment as the priority, and few received vocational training, although several recognised the significance of becoming more self-reliant. There was no association between 'vocational training' and 'severity of injury' among CRP users, and no relationship between 'vocational training' and 'gender' – perhaps because a higher number of female users of CRP in the sample received vocational training.

Reported problems relating to support services

In this study, support services include provision of technical aids and appliances. The term aids covers mobility aids such as wheelchairs (fixed or folding, motorised or manual), trollies, crutches and walking frames. No participants had motorised wheelchairs, although CRP users had the choice of a fixed or folding manual wheelchair, whereas some general hospital were only offered a fixed wheelchair. In interview, one CRP user and two general hospital users made occasional use of crutches, but this lasted no more than six months. According to participants, when they left the hospital, doctors/therapists advised them to use crutches because of weakness in the lower limbs but over a period of time the lower limbs strengthened and crutches were discarded. Another three general hospital users reported that although it might have helped their movement, it was not suggested that they use crutches. Mannan, with a mild impairment, commented:

I took treatment from various hospitals. No one advised me to use a walking stick or crutches. After I received services at CRP I came to know the benefit of the use of crutches. Prior to that, I was homebound.

Table 2: Use of mobility aids (CRP and General Hospital users)

Mobility aids	Service providers		
	CRP % (Number)	General Hospital % (Number)	Total % (Number)
Don't require mobility aids	50 (16)	41 (13)	45 (29)
Required but didn't have mobility aids	06 (02)	53 (17)	30 (19)
Have mobility aids	44 (14)	06 (02)	25 (16)
Total	100 (32)	100 (32)	100 (64)

A statistically significant relationship was found between 'service provider' and 'user of mobility aids' ($p<.000$), and also between 'severity of injury' and 'use of mobility aids' ($p<.000$) (Table 2). A major weakness of general hospitals was that 50 per cent of people with tetraplegia and 31 per cent of people with paraplegia did not receive any mobility aids, which may be one of the reasons most of them depended on family members to carry them around. Fifty-three per cent of the general hospital users who were not using mobility aids believed that one day they could go back to their normal lives. In addition, their family members were reluctant to procure mobility aids even when they could afford to buy them. In contrast, only 6 percent of CRP users who said they needed them lacked mobility aids. One user's family believed that he would walk again, while another user felt that a wheelchair would make it more difficult to move around inside her house.

There was no statistically significant relationship between the 'user of mobility aids' and 'gender' – again perhaps because of CRP's priority support to female users. With one exception, all who required mobility aids received them. Moreover, CRP provides a free wheelchair to women if they are too poor to purchase one. It also has an on-site workshop that builds mobility aids for users. This is particularly important because there are very few places in Bangladesh where mobility aids are available. 'Appliances' include collars and splints, which directly or indirectly help in personal care. For example, a finger splint may enable someone to grasp a pen for writing or typing, and at least six CRP participants were using splints, compared with none in the general hospital group.

Conclusion
The research fieldwork confirms that people with SCL are seldom a priority in Bangladesh. They do not receive adequate medical and support services in government hospitals which remain dominated by a medical approach. Present provision in the government and private sectors does not help people with SCL to survive or to become re-integrated into society. As a result many hospital patients lead an isolated life and experience higher levels of morbidity and a greater likelihood of premature death.

Conversely, the research demonstrates that people who go to CRP have fewer pressure sores, chest infections and less constipation than those who have sought help elsewhere. It also demonstrates that they suffer less pain and depression and experience a satisfactory level of support services, leading to better health. CRP services promote self-reliance rather than dependence on health and social services, with consequential cost savings. Nationwide availability of specialist CRP centres could revolutionise the health care outcomes and quality of life of people with SCL in Bangladesh – as has happened in Sri Lanka (Chappell 2001).

It is therefore recommended that the Government should re-think its exclusive support for medical and support services and establish a spinal unit modelled on CRP in each division of Bangladesh. This would help prevent people with SCL experiencing increasing morbidity and premature death. Greater collaboration between CRP and the general hospitals is necessary for the early transfer of people with SCL to CRP or similar spinal unit centres. It has been observed that those participants referred to CRP at an early stage required less time at the Centre than those admitted at a later stage. Moreover, the majority of clients admitted to CRP were referred from general hospitals with severe pressure sores. In the absence of standard protocols for treatment and rehabilitation of people with SCL they are often given the wrong diagnosis or inappropriate treatment which results in more suffering and may lead to death. Thus, protocols should be formulated to guide service development nationally in order to meet the continuing needs of people with SCL.

The Government has a long way to go to ensure that disabled people have access to high quality medical, rehabilitation and support services and facilities as a basic right, freely available to all people with impairment, regardless of the severity of injury, age, gender, race and sexual orientation.

Bibliography

Abedin, M. N. 1997: *Health and Population Sector: An Overview and Vision.* Paper prepared for the Logical Framework Workshop for the Fifth Health and Population Programme (HAPP-5), 23-25 February 1997. Dhaka: Ministry of Health and Family Welfare.

Abedin, M. N. 2000: Poverty in Disability: The Case in Bangladesh. *The Daily Star.* 24 May.

Barnes, C. and Mercer, G. (eds) 1997: *Doing Disability Research.* Leeds: The Disability Press.

BBS 1997: *Progothir Pathey: Achieving the Goals for Children in Bangladesh.* Dhaka: Ministry of Planning, Bangladesh.

BBS 2001a: *1999 Statistical Year Book of Bangladesh.* Dhaka: Statistics Division, Ministry of Planning, Bangladesh.

BBS 2001b: *Census Report.* Dhaka: Ministry of Planning, Bangladesh.

Chappell, P. 2001: *Quality of Life Following Spinal Cord Injury: 20-40 Year Old Males in Sri Lanka.* MSc Dissertation, Unpublished. Community Disability Studies, Institute of Child Health, University of London.

CRP 2002: *Towards Equality.* Annual Report 2001-2002. Dhaka: Centre for the Rehabilitation of the Paralysed: Savar, Bangladesh.

Hoque, M. F. 2002: *Management of Spinal Cord Disorders in Bangladesh.* Second National Physiotherapy Seminar-2002, Evidence Based Practice in Physiotherapy. Dhaka: CRP.

Hossain, M. M. and Glass, R. 1988: Parental son preference in seeking medical care for children less than five years of age in a rural community in Bangladesh. *American Journal of Public Health*, 78: 1349-1350.

Hurst, R. 2001: The International Classification of Functioning, Disability and Health, *Disability Tribune*, September, 11-12.

ILO 2000: Informal sector: Who are they? (Available at: www.ilo.org/public/English/bureau/stat/res/accinj.html) 15.6.2002.

ILO 2001: *Bangladesh: Country situation* (Available at: www.ilo.org/public/english/employment/skills/informal/who.htm) 15.6.2002

Johnson, R. L. et al. 1998: Secondary complications following spinal cord injury in a population based sample. *Spinal Cord*, 36: 45-50.

Momin, A. K. M. 2003: *The levels of integration of people with spinal cord lesion in Bangladesh*, PhD Thesis, Unpublished. School of Sociology and Social Policy, University of Leeds.

Motivation. 1999: National Plan for Spinal Cord Injury Rehabilitation in Sri Lanka. *Concept Paper*, Unpublished.

NFOWD 1999: *Light on the Horizon, Annual Activity Report 1996-1999*. Dhaka: National Forum for Organizations Working with the Disabled.

NISC 2002: *NSIC GAP Analysis. Final Draft*. March. Stoke Mandeville: National Spinal Injuries Centre.

Oliver, M. 2004: The Social Model of Disability in Action; If I Had a Hammer, in C. Barnes and G. Mercer eds. *Implementing the Social Model of Disability: theory and research*, Leeds: The Disability Press.

Oliver, M. 1992: Changing the Social Relations of Research Production? *Disability, Handicap and Society*, 7 (2), 101-114.

Rahman, M. and Davanjo, J. 1993: Gender preference in birth spacing in Matlab, Bangladesh. *Demography*, 30: 315-332.

Sinha, K.C. 2000: *Manual for the Patna Model of Care of Spinal Cord Injury Patients*. Jakkanpurok: Society for the Prevention, Awareness and Rehabilitation of Spinal Handicapped.

Stone, E. (ed.) 1999: *Disability and Development*. Leeds: The Disability Press.

UN 1993: *Standard rules for the equalization of opportunities for persons with disabilities* UN general assembly in resolution 48/96 of 20 December 1993. New York: UN.

WHO 1997: *World Health Report*. Geneva: World Health Organization.

WHO 2001: *Rethinking Care from Disabled People's Perspectives*. Geneva: World Health Organization.

World Bank 1993: *World Development Report: Investing in Health*. Oxford: Oxford University Press.

World Bank 1999: *Quest for a healthy Bangladesh: A vision for the twenty-first century*. Dhaka: The University Press Limited.

CHAPTER 12

'Food' or 'Thought'?
The social model and the majority world

Tara Flood

The social model is under attack not just from disabled and non-disabled academics, but also from disabled people around the world who have reached the conclusion that the social model has no relevance to real life. However this clearly demonstrates confusion as to the intention of the social model. People appear to see it as a problem solver and something that will both put food on the table and tarmac on the road - in actual fact it is none of these things. Neither is the social model, as it is often suggested, the only conclusion one should come to when trying to understand disability. Rather, as I understand it, the social model is a way of characterizing or interpreting the relationship between a disablist society and people with impairments.

The social model was and still is a statement of disabled people's exclusion from full participation in a society where the non-disabled majority view impairment as different, inferior, and something, most certainly, to be eliminated. Applying a social model understanding to explain the exclusion of a particular group of individuals is not a new idea. It has been used by many grassroots organisations around the world to explain their experience of poverty, injustice or exclusion from the political agenda. Why it was particularly important to place disability within a 'social model' context was to remove disabled people from the de-humanising effects of the traditional and invalidating medical and charity models.

For centuries disabled people have been seen as everything from the embodiment of sin to super-heroes triumphing over the 'tragedy' of our impaired situations. We have never been seen as equal members of the human race and more often than not every effort is made to exclude us from social, economic, educational and political opportunities. Society is organised in such a way as to limit our participation and to measure the value and status of each of its members by economic and normalized standards. It is no wonder disabled people are positioned somewhere on the outermost fringes.

Social model thinking was first used to explain the situation of disabled people, by Paul Hunt (1966). His ideas were developed some ten years later by UPIAS (Union of the Physically Impaired Against Segregation) (1976). But it was not until 1983 that the disabled academic, Mike Oliver, described the ideas that lay behind the UPIAS definition as the 'social model of disability'. For disabled people in the UK the social model was the key to our politicisation. It allowed a common space from which to develop politicised actions and theories to explain our experience of exclusion, discrimination and oppression. Even now, for many disabled people, discovering the social model can feel like a liberating factor. I did not find out about the social model until my early thirties, but I remember distinctly that it was like a light switching on - no more accepting society's lies about the tragedy of my life - bring on political activism!

The beginnings of an international movement of disabled people
Internationally, discussions and interpretations about disabled people's experience of exclusion started to take shape during the 1960s and 1970s with the rise of the Independent Living movement in the US and in European countries such as Sweden. Disabled people were tired and frustrated by the 'specialness' of service provision and considered their access to essential services controlled by non-disabled people as the key to their oppression. Service provision, until this point, was deeply medicalised and often institution-based. Disabled people were viewed as passive recipients of state funded care with little or no opportunity for flexibility or influence. The philosophy of independent living was, and is, about the empowerment of the individual through the taking of choice and control in their life. It is about recognising that the disabled individual's rights as a human being are equal to those of the non-disabled majority. Most importantly it is about social action and social change - a recognition of our rights as human beings as the route for the implementation of that social action and social change.

Is the social model international?

Is the social model as relevant to disabled people in the South as it is for those of us who live in the North? Is it imperialistic of those of us living in the North to impose social model thinking on disabled people in the South (Stone 1999) and does the concept of disabilism transfer across countries and continents? The truth is that the social model is as relevant to disabled people in London as it is to disabled people living in Lusaka. Why? Because it focuses on the commonality of our exclusion, rather than the traditional approach of seeing impairment as the problem, or the result of 'sin'. What may be different are the cultural and attitudinal barriers, systems and structures that are designed to keep disabled people out. Some societies are more accepting of disabled individuals, whereas others are deeply repressive and many more are indifferent to their disabled citizens. For many countries in the majority world, cultural influences are much greater than the medical influences of the North. Therefore Disabled People's Organisations (DPOs) must battle against traditional myths that state disabled people are everything from the embodiment of hereditary evil to the cure for HIV/AIDS.

The social model and international agencies

International agencies that do disability-related work, such as the WHO (World Health Organization) have done very little to change the traditional perception of disability which sees disability and impairment as a health and welfare issue. It's only in the last three years, and after ten years of discussion, that the WHO have revised the ICIDH (International Classification on Impairments, Disabilities and Handicaps) to include the disabling impact of the environment on people with impairments. The new ICIDH or ICF (International Classification for Functioning, Disability and Health) is far from perfect, but it is a move in the right direction (Hurst 2000). It will of course take years for the new classification to be implemented at all levels and for a culture shift away from a medicalised approach to disability, to recognition of the negative impact of an inaccessible environment. Unfortunately the situation around an international change in attitude has not been helped by the recent adoption of a health measurement called DALYS (Disability Adjusted Life Years) by bodies such as the World Bank (Russell 2003). DALYS focus on a 'cost benefit' analysis on impairment. Such measurement only serves to reinforce the negative assumptions made about our lives.

Conservative estimates indicate that there are approximately 600 million disabled people, the majority of whom live in countries in the majority world (UN 1990). Taking this into account, it is extremely hard to understand why it is that disabled people are absent from the text of international human rights instruments. In fact the only United Nations (UN) Convention to mention disability at all is the Convention on the Rights of the Child. Disabled people are conspicuous by our absence from the other conventions and indeed the Universal Declaration of Human Rights elaborated in 1948 confines disabled people within the category of 'and others'.

However in 1980, after years of lobbying by disabled people, the UN General Assembly declared 1981 International Year of Disabled Persons. During 1981 a resolution was passed that 1982 to 1993 would be a UN Decade of Disabled Persons that would deliver on the World Programme of Action Concerning Disabled Persons. For the first time the UN demonstrated a commitment to take steps to addressing the worldwide situation of disabled people or the 'silent emergency' as described by UN Secretary General, Perez de Cuellar.

By 1993 *The Standard Rules on Equality of Opportunities for Persons with Disabilities* had been adopted by the UN, in response to calls for a thematic legally binding human rights convention, from the international disabled people's movement. At the time the Standard Rules felt like a real breakthrough because disabled people thought that they were a framework that would create an implicit moral and political commitment from each member state to adopt measures to assure equality of opportunities. Unfortunately some 10 years down the line, the Standard Rules, because they have no basis in international human rights law have resulted in, at best, patchy implementation.

The social model and the international movement of disabled people
The social model is a catalyst - a driver for social action and social change and for disabled people coming together to form their own organisations - working together to identify the barriers to their full and equal participation - and the creation of an action plan for social change.

For disabled people living in countries in the majority world, their first contact with the reality of these new ideas was in 1980 at a Rehabilitation International (RI) conference in Winnipeg, Canada, to formulate an action plan for the 'International Year of the Disabled' in the following year. The 250 disabled people from 40 different countries who were invited, soon realised that there would be no opportunity to be part of discussions, so chose to boycott the conference and hold their own discussions. Disabled Peoples' International (DPI) was born, in 1981, out of this frustration and its founders sent a clear message to bodies such as RI that never again would it be acceptable for discussions about disabled people to take place without our full and equal participation. Some international organisations of disabled persons already existed at this point, but they had been set up to work on impairment specific issues and were individually campaigning to get disability rights onto the international agenda. None as yet had consultative status with international bodies such as the UN.

At its first congress in 1981, founder members of DPI set out a Manifesto for change which called on:

> disabled people all over the world to unite in organisations of their own and to join DPI in a common struggle for full participation and equality with our fellow citizens (DPI 1981).

DPI's Manifesto set out a set of Basic Rights which included key demands for a right to independent living, a right to economic security and a right to influence. Disabled people were no longer prepared to accept non-disabled experts speaking for them and for the continued exclusion of disabled people from debates and discussions about our lives. DPI through its membership was committed to disabled people being 'where the power is and where important political decisions are made' (Malinga 2002). And so the slogan 'Nothing about us - without us' was born.

This ethos was the message that delegates took back to their own countries. They did not use social model language but the essence was the same - social action and social change. For many countries, particularly those in Africa and Asia, grassroots organisations have been battling, for years, against the ghosts of a colonial past and more recently, the western world agendas of the development agencies. Above all, for disabled people in these countries, the greatest battle has always been about day-to-day survival.

Ironically for many disabled people, in the South one of the greatest barriers to their empowerment, and ultimately their survival is the very aid agencies that secure millions from funders to support development work. Traditionally, development and aid has been seen as the attempt by those who have, to give to those who have not. Aid and development agencies have, historically, given money, time and expertise based on their experience in more 'developed' countries. Although there is now a better understanding by those involved, that they should bring their expertise to good use in locally appropriate ways, and that development must be led by the people themselves, as far as disability is concerned, it is usually the case that traditional habits die hard.

Disability projects are still, in the main, paternalistic, medically based, exclusive and controlled by non-disabled people. In many cases agencies are still working with organisations that treat disabled people as passive receivers of charitable services, rather than working directly with, and being led by disabled people. As Joshua Malinga (past President of DPI) has said:

> when you (funding agencies) come to us please make sure you consult with us and find out exactly what our needs are and provide permanent solutions and not palliatives (Malinga 1981).

Some development and aid agencies have, in a very cynical move, taken on the language of disability rights and the social model, but continue to consider non-disabled people as experts when it comes to disabled people and our issues. Unfortunately for groups of disabled people based in rural communities in majority world countries, challenging such practices is almost impossible. After all these agencies are often gatekeepers to capacity-building opportunities and vital sources of funding.

There is some good collaborative work being done with the support of development and aid agencies and some are genuinely wanting to work within a social model paradigm - 'mainstreaming' is the new buzz word in development. But for some agencies, such as United Nations' Children's Fund (UNICEF), mainstreaming disability issues has effectively meant that disability issues fall off the international rights agenda. In fact some are more interested in prevention and rehabilitation than human and civil rights. In the case of UNICEF there is no longer anyone who has the sole responsibility for ensuring disabled children remain a priority issue. No surprise then that disabled children continue to remain invisible in policy documents and strategy papers looking at the situation of children generally.

To mainstream disability, development and aid agencies must ensure that they take a holistic approach to issues such as poverty reduction. Agencies must ensure that the monitoring and evaluation of projects are based on an assessment of environmental impacts and the barriers overcome, as well as on individual progress. Without taking a holistic approach to this process, the emphasis will continue to remain on changing individuals rather than changing society as a whole.

The social model in action

The social model of disability, as I have already said, is facing its own battle for survival. Since Oliver (1983) first coined the phrase back in the early eighties the social action to create social change element of the social model has been somewhat overshadowed by circular academic debate about its irrelevance to particular groups of disabled people or debates about the social model's 'failure' to recognise the impact of impairment related issues. As Oliver says:

> we have spent too much time talking about the social model.... and not devoted enough attention to actually implementing or attempting to implement it in practice (Oliver 2004).

Across the world I think there is a very different story going on. The best way to illustrate this is by giving some examples where disabled people living in majority world countries have identified the barriers to their participation and what action they have taken to effectively create social change.

I have recently returned from Mexico where I visited a project called Projimo, a rural Community-based rehabilitation (CBR) programme run by disabled people. The Projimo project was started in the early 1980s, in response to the lack of healthcare support for disabled children in a remote village in the Sierra Madre mountains. Initial support and advice came from David Werner, a disabled American from California, who had been involved in the independent living movement. News of the project soon spread and disabled adults and children began to arrive from every part of Mexico. Many of the disabled people who initially came to Projimo for CBR have ended up staying to help others. Since then Projimo has changed and developed the services and support it provides. They currently make a wide range of mobility devices such as wheelchairs, tricycles, artificial legs and accessible toys and aids for disabled children. It has now moved to a small village called Coyotitan and the disabled people living and working in Projimo are an integral part of village life.

I am delighted to say that my visit to Projimo was everything I expected and more. Its strength is that it is run entirely by disabled people, but more than this, it is a community of about thirty people, disabled and non-disabled, people raising families, people of all ages, visitors staying there for CBR and then sometimes people like me, desperately trying to learn Spanish. The main part of their work is taken up with hand-made cost-effective solutions to the mobility needs of disabled children and adults who arrive on Projimo's proverbial 'doorstep' with nowhere else to go.

The more subtle stuff goes on virtually unnoticed. I met a fantastic young boy, Moises, who has been at Projimo for rehabilitation for about a year. Moises is seven, and attends the village school. He has incredible confidence in his future potential quite clearly gleaned from his time spent with other disabled people. This is also the case for families of disabled children visiting the project and for the local community, whose children play with the disabled children at Projimo because that is where the swings are!

However Projimo is not perfect. How could it be, it is run by human beings. For example the group of disabled people who live and work there are mostly people with physical impairments. Projimo is run by a core of strong and capable disabled women and there is the risk, as has happened elsewhere, that those whose voices are not as strong, or perhaps those who have greater personal assistance needs, are not heard. However, it was incredible to see, in a country were there is very little welfare support or social provision, a group of disabled people getting on and doing it for themselves — working and supporting themselves and others. Projimo gives a clear message that disabled people are our own experts and can and should have choice and control. This has also been the message throughout each of the books published by Projimo's founder, David Werner (1998). When I met David he told me that they did not want people to copy the work being done at Projimo but to use the ethos of 'Nothing About Us Without Us' when thinking about their own situation.

Projimo is in essence the social model in action and in a world where 98% of disabled people living in developing countries have no access to any form of rehabilitation, Projimo is an outstanding example of disabled people taking control. I have no doubt that my suggestion that a rehabilitation programme could ever be considered a good example of the social model in action, will be criticised by some people reading this chapter. I would argue that again those taking this stance are confused about the original intention of defining disability within a social context. In my reading, the social model supports any self-help activity controlled and supported by disabled people which shifts the cause of disability away from the individual and places it within the exclusionary nature of a disablist society. The social model does not deny the need for appropriate medical interventions (Campbell and Oliver 1996) but the key is what constitutes 'appropriate' — for example, who is controlling the intervention? Back in 1981, disabled people, who started Projimo, identified the main barriers to their participation as the lack of healthcare and assistive devices.

They then turned their interpretation of their particular situation into practice by making what was needed themselves and providing the necessary and 'appropriate' services themselves.

Another example of the social model in action is the SHAP (Self-help Association of Paraplegics) in Soweto in South Africa (Fletcher and Hurst 1995). This project was started by Friday Mandla Mavuso, who after becoming disabled during the struggles against apartheid, discovered that the lot of a disabled person was not good, with very little chance of surviving in such an inaccessible and hostile environment. Friday got together with other disabled people and devised a self-help business development project with the aim of creating employment for disabled people. After initial start-up funding, the SHAP project found markets for their products and began building on their original idea of taking action for themselves. Twenty years on SHAP, to all intents and purposes a Centre for Independent Living, still provides employment opportunities and all managerial positions are held by disabled people, but now SHAP is also involved in community initiatives to improve access to health, education, public transport and housing. They have also found the time to set up a choir of local disabled people which has made a number of successful records.

Through DAA's recent 'Rights for Disabled Children' project we have found some good and positive examples where disabled children are using social model understanding to push for their greater inclusion. One such example is the work being done by the Cambodian Disabled Peoples' organisation which supports the inclusion of deaf children into mainstream education. Until CDPO's Deaf Development programme (DDP) (Lansdown 2001), those deaf children who did have the opportunity to go to school were given no support to enable them to follow lessons. Mainstream schools did not recognise sign language and so the children were excluded from learning and often became targets for bullying. Many deaf children and adults were already using their own home-grown sign language but nothing had been done to actively teach signing, or to work on recognising sign language at a national level.

After a number of meetings, set up by CDPO, where deaf people of all ages who did sign met others who didn't, the use of sign language started to spread. The DDP has started to train deaf people as sign language teachers. The CDPO also organised a programme where deaf children met and talked with deaf adults who served as role models. Now the DDP has developed to the point where the deaf children are included in mainstream education so they are able to learn alongside their non-disabled peers and where sign language is incorporated into the teaching programme.

The last example I am going to give you of what I believe is the social model in action relates again to education. I think that if only 2 per cent of disabled children living in countries in the majority world attend school, then lack of access to education is undoubtedly one of the greatest barriers. The Divine Light Trust, in India, started out, in the 1950s, as a school for visually impaired children. However, after it had been open for a number of years (35 to be precise), the school's Director discovered that only about 5 per cent of visually impaired children throughout India had access to education. It was decided that something radical needed to happen for this to change.

The Divine Light Trust school turned itself into a resource centre training teachers in mainstream education to enable disabled children with visual impairments to be fully included into their neighbourhood schools. The outcome, of course, is not just that now many more children have access to educational opportunities, but also such an approach makes segregated education provision redundant.

At the heart of the social model is the understanding that until disabled people are part of the fabric of society then we will continue to be excluded and treated as 'other'. I have talked about some of the work being done in Mexico, South Africa, India and Cambodia but the fact is groups of disabled people across the majority world are using social model thinking in their daily lives.

Quite exceptionally, two countries, South Africa and Uganda have achieved the social model within their political systems, and in the case of South Africa, have actually articulated it in a White Paper on Disability. (Office of the Deputy President 1997). The South African Government's Integrated National Disability Strategy White Paper 'provides a vision and coherent value structure for driving disability issues in government and society' (Matsebula 2003). It is interesting to note that both these political approaches have arisen as a result of their emergence from apartheid, oppression, violence and conflict and an understanding that disabled people are a specific group which has faced social inequality and injustice.

In South Africa, the Office on the Status of Disabled People is in the President's office, is run by disabled people, has executive powers over other departments, including monitoring their use of the statutory 10 per cent of their budgets on disability. Regional sub-offices also only employ disabled people. Disabled people are appointed to leading political jobs and are members of parliament and regional and local authorities.

In Uganda, the Movement Government, under President Museveni, has assured for disabled people, 5 seats in parliament, one ministerial post and 6,000 local council positions from village to district level. All are elected into their positions by the disabled community. The disabled politicians at all levels have played a significant role in influencing all other public policies, including ensuring that Uganda's recent 'Education for All' legislation stipulates that for the four free places provided by the state for each family, priority must be given to any disabled children. But as Macline Twimyuke, the Executive Director of the National Union of Disabled Persons in Uganda, has rightly said:

> Although Uganda boasts the largest number of political representatives of disabled people in government structures in the world, we (disabled people) cannot afford to be complacent. If there is a change of government these advances could be swept away (Twimyuke 2001).

Inevitably, in both these countries, this high level of status of disabled people has not meant an end to poverty and exclusion, any more than it has for the poor non-disabled people. But the understanding of the social model is both articulated in political agreements and implemented in the political systems. This is a far cry from the status of disabled people in other countries around the world!

Lessons from majority world interpretations of the social model

For me, what is clear from the examples I have given is that disabled people in countries in the majority world are taking *social action for social change*. They are getting on with it themselves, either because no one else can or will, or because disabled people have disengaged from those agencies and charities which have traditionally provided western-driven aid, which is both irrelevant and paternalistic. There are very few countries in the majority world where there is any kind of state or social support. The onus is on individuals to identify self-help solutions – the alternative is starvation. For those of us who live in countries where there is some level of welfare support, we are not going to starve, but welfare is itself a barrier to our participation.

Conclusion

The truth of the matter is that despite the social action examples I have identified in this chapter, for many disabled people around the world, their situation and status whether it be at the grassroots or at a national level remains at a de-humanising low. Disabled people remain the poorest of the poor whatever the economic state of the country. Disabled people in every country around the world are still being excluded, abused and killed because of the continued lack of value given to our lives and lack of recognition of our humanity. And for many disabled people facing such a fate, a social model explanation for their experience seems irrelevant because it is not the quick fix solution many desperately want. The evidence from Disability Awareness in Action's Human Rights Violations database shows that nearly half a million disabled people have had their human rights violated - 10 per cent of this number have been denied the 'Right to Life' - 31 per cent experienced cruel and degrading treatment (Light 2003). This clearly shows that we are still a long way from a world free of disablism.

The social model has illustrated clearly that solutions to our exclusion, our oppression lie in human rights, equality and justice and the celebration of diversity. The social model is not just an academic tool, it is a lived experience as can be seen from the work being done by the disabled people living in Projimo, Africa, Asia and in many other parts of the majority world. So in conclusion the social model is still absolutely relevant as an explanation of our experience as disabled people whether we live in the developed or majority world. The barriers may be different but the solutions are the same - social action creating social change.

Bibliography

Campbell, J. and Oliver, M. 1996: *Disability Politics: Understanding our Past, Changing our Future*. London: Routledge.

DPI 1981: *Proceedings of the First World Congress*. Sweden: Disabled Peoples' International.

Fletcher, A. and Hurst, R. 1995: *Overcoming Obstacles to the Integration of Disabled People*. London: Disability Awareness in Action.

Hunt, P. 1966: A critical condition. In P. Hunt (ed.), *Stigma: The Experience of Disability*. London: Geoffrey Chapman, 145-59.

Hurst, R. 2000: To Revise or Not to Revise? *Disability & Society*, 15 (7), 1083-1087.

Lansdown, G. 2001: *It is our World Too! - a report on the lives of disabled children*. London: Disability Awareness in Action.

Light, R. 2003: *Review of Evidence contained on the DAA Human Rights Database*. London: Disability Awareness in Action & DAART Centre.

Malinga, J. 1981: Zimbabwe Independence and DPI. ***Proceedings of the First World Congress***. Sweden: Disabled Peoples' International.

Malinga, J. 2002: *The Disability Movement is at a Crossroads*. A speech at the DPI World Congress. Sapporo, Japan.

Matsebula, S. 2003: *Lessons learned from the Office on the Status of Disabled People in the Presidency* - a speech at the 'Left off the Agenda - Mainstreaming Disability in Development' Conference 11/12 November. London.

Office of the Deputy President 1997: ***Integrated National Disability Strategy White Paper***. South Africa: Office of the Deputy President, Government of South Africa.

Oliver, M. 1983: ***Social Work with Disabled People***. Basingstoke: Macmillan.

Oliver, M. 2004: The Social Model in Action: if I had a hammer. Barnes, C. and Mercer, G. (eds), ***Implementing the Social Model of Disability: Theory and Research***. Leeds: The Disability Press.

Russell, M. 2003: ***Nothing About Us Without Us: Human Rights and Disability***. Znet Commentaries. http://www.zmag.org

Stone, E. (ed.) 1999: ***Disability and Development in the Majority World***. Leeds: The Disability Press.

Twimyuke, M. 2001: *The need for a United Nations Convention on Disability* - a speech at the Disability Rights: A Global Concern Conference. 21 June 2001. London

United Nations. 1990: ***Disability Statistics Compendium***. New York: United Nations Statistics Office.

UPIAS 1976: ***Fundamental Principles of Disability***. London: Union of the Physically Impaired Against Segregation.

Werner, D. 1998: ***Nothing About Us Without Us: Developing Innovative Technologies For, By and With Disabled People***. Palo Alto: Healthwrights.

CHAPTER 13

Disability and Rehabilitation: Reflections on working for the World Health Organization

Enrico Pupulin

Introduction

As a trained medical doctor I have been involved with disabled people and their families throughout my working life. Much of my work experience has been in the poorly resourced 'developing' nations of the majority world; first, as a voluntary worker in Africa and later as Chief Medical Officer of the World Health Organization's (WHO) Disability and Rehabilitation (DAR) Team. Although my medical training impelled me, almost exclusively, toward individually based solutions to the problems encountered by disabled people and their families, these experiences led me to think that a wider, more holistic approach was needed commensurate with the notion of Community Based Rehabilitation (CBR). Notwithstanding that CBR may be criticised on several different levels (Stone 1999; Ingstad 2001; Barnes and Mercer 2003), it is, for me, an approach that is very similar to that advocated by disability activists such as Vic Finkelstein (1998) and sometimes referred to as the social model of disability. It is also a strategy that was advocated and adopted by the WHO's DAR following my appointment in 1990. To explain the reasoning behind this claim I shall provide a brief overview of the experiences that have influenced my views on CBR.

Learning about CBR

After my initial training in the medical profession I decided to specialise in paediatrics. Because of my interest in children's health, especially in poor nations, I decided to work in Africa. I spent more than five years as a voluntary worker in Uganda and Kenya. In order to gain a greater insight into the difficulties delivering effective health care and support in difficult circumstances, I chose to work in the 'bush' rather than in an urban environment similar to that of large cities. Through these experiences I quickly became aware that my training in western medicine had left me ill-prepared for the situation in Africa, where the resources, including hospitals, trained staff and essential drugs, necessary for the delivery of the most basic of health 'care' services are extremely scarce. These experiences taught me that apart from our involvement in emergency health situations the most important intervention that medical and rehabilitation professionals could make is to provide health education to the general population. The aim is to give them the knowledge and skills to take responsibility for the prevention and management of minor diseases.

Upon my return to Italy and practice in western medicine I specialized further in children's neuropsychiatry. After a short while I was appointed as head of a children's rehabilitation department based in a hospital in which many multi-disciplinary teams were operating. It soon became evident that inter-professional rivalries within these groups were preventing them from functioning effectively. This was because individual doctors and rehabilitation professionals in the team tended to prioritise their own particular interests and involvement with patients, and they were not sharing information with colleagues. Also, as the multi-disciplinary team was staffed mainly by professionals 'allied to medicine' they concentrated almost exclusively on the biomedical components of health. In so doing they overlooked the social elements of the health experience: in particular, that good health depends on the individual's sense of physical, mental and social well-being.

Through these observations I began to realise that the conventional individualistic medical approach to disability and rehabilitation could not provide disabled people with the facilities and support needed to achieve equal opportunities within their communities. Whilst retaining the role as Chief of the Interdisciplinary Team, I later accepted the role of Social Co-ordinator in the region. This gave me the opportunity to work with local municipal officials and council leaders. Through this involvement I tried to convince them that successful rehabilitation is about far more than medical interventions and treatments, and that it involves the entire community. Furthermore, they, as local leaders and policy makers, had a responsibility to ensure the well-being of all their citizens including disabled people.

Concerned that I would lose the insights and skills that I had learnt in Africa, I occasionally returned to voluntary work with an Italian non-government organisation (NGO) working with people with leprosy. After joining this organisation, I was involved in a community based support programme for people with leprosy in the slums of Bangalore in India. Here I witnessed first hand the stigma associated with leprosy and disability generally. It was also evident that the stigma associated with disability not only affects the individuals with impairment, but also their families, and. in the case of leprosy, the professionals that work with them. Taken together these first-hand experiences re-affirmed my growing conviction that in order to support disabled people in their own homes and reduce or eliminate stigma altogether it is necessary to educate the wider community that disability is almost always bound up with poverty and hardship.

While supporting the NGO the organisation became involved with the WHO's DAR programme. At a meeting at their offices in Geneva, I met the then Chief of the WHO Rehabilitation who invited me to observe and contribute to the establishment of WHO CBR schemes in developing countries on behalf the Italian NGO. The idea of launching a CBR type programme had been introduced in the early 1980s. It was aimed mainly at developing countries and was the first attempt to create a world-wide model that could be applied across very different cultures (Ingstad 2001). Subsequently, governments were encouraged to co-operate with the WHO and NGOs to plan for the setting up of CBR projects within the context of primary health care (PHC).

For the WHO primary health care:
> is the central focus of health reform. It places a variety of services in the community's environment. Although the services lie largely within the domain of health professionals, PHC also incorporates community participation and promotes the concept of community ownership over health (WHO 1998: 4).

During trips to Burma and Mauritius I learnt a great deal about CBR and was particularly impressed by the way in which this approach attempted to bring together the medical and social aspects of the rehabilitation process.
> The major objectives of CBR are to ensure that persons with disabilities are able to maximise their physical and mental abilities, have access to regular services and opportunities, and achieve full social integration within their communities and societies (WHO 1998: 4).

Before implementing CBR in developing countries I felt it would be both beneficial and instructive to introduce a similar strategy to the area in Italy where I was still employed as the Social Co-ordinator. The reasoning behind this course of action stems from my sincere conviction that it is not proper to implement a CBR type approach in countries with few medical and rehabilitative services if it is not equally applicable to other social and environmental contexts. With hindsight, it was not an easy task to introduce CBR in Italy. This was mainly because the majority of the professionals involved held the view that CBR was ideally suited to the needs of those working in the developing world, but it was not applicable to the situation in developed nations and, therefore, not for them. Despite these reservations we devised and established a small CBR scheme as a pilot project. In a relatively short space of time the sceptics quickly realised that the constructive involvement of family members, neighbours and teachers in the rehabilitation process helped produce more positive results.

In 1990, I was appointed Chief Medical Officer for DAR at the WHO. I was impressed by the CBR programme already in place and made plans to develop it further. Drawing on previous experience a key aim was to equip volunteers and family members with the knowledge and skills to provide rehabilitation services and support to people with impairments living in rural areas where there are no specialists. In the initial stages of the programme several pilot projects were set up in which voluntary workers were trained by international rehabilitation consultants.

However, although these projects were supported by donor organisations, it was not possible to implement this strategy in large rural areas due to a chronic shortage of funds. Further, disabled people's organisations were cynical about the benefits of CBR. They considered it an inappropriate strategy because the services were provided by family members and volunteers rather than by professionals and specialists and, therefore, lacked the quality of provision and support that was assumed to be available to other sections of the community. In response we tried to consider how primary health care professionals could provide rehabilitation as specified in the WHO's (1978) Declaration of Alma-Ata. Certainly we believed that in all countries, even the poorest, disabled people should have access to similar services and support that is available to all citizens, regardless of the degree or nature of impairment and, also, that they be served by the same health care system.

Implementing CBR

As already noted, a significant justification for the implementation of the CBR programme was the successful integration of disabled people into the community. But from the outset one of the main problems encountered when implementing CBR through existing governmental health care systems was the severe shortage of trained rehabilitation specialists in poor nations. Moreover, most of these worked in the large cities or the nation's capital while in rural areas medical services are usually provided by nurses. In order to overcome this problem we devised a two-way communication system whereby relevant information could be transferred from primary health care workers in rural areas to rehabilitation specialists working in cities and back again. In this way workers in the field could access specialist knowledge.

Several countries including Mongolia, Vietnam and Indonesia agreed to support pilot projects. These early schemes provided the kind of information needed for effective implementation. For example, established practice was for technical aids and assistive devices to be stored and distributed from a central location: usually in a large city. It was evident from the experiences of people working at a pilot scheme that the management and delivery of such items as prosthetics was significantly improved through the involvement of community based primary health care workers. It was also apparent that before the effective transfer of knowledge was possible, if was necessary to identify the different organisational levels involved in the national health care system. In general, three levels were identified; community, district and regional/central levels. It was also clear that regionally based specialists could not be held responsible for training rehabilitation workers at both the district and community levels as it would undermine the role of district level staff and their relationship with community based workers. To resolve the problem it was necessary to develop a cascade approach to training. Regional staff train district staff who, in turn, are responsible for training community workers. Also, to ensure that the flow of knowledge is both accurate and effective, follow-up and re-training schemes were incorporated into the training programme.

The WHO is concerned with the promotion and development of a holistic model of health care and support for all citizens. In reality though, its involvement with Member States' Ministries of Health mean that its main activities are inevitably limited to medical considerations and physical well-being. Although many disabled people's organisations are concerned about the lack of adequate medical services in developing countries, their main concern tends to relate to disabled people's social well-being and their exclusion from educational and economic activities. Whilst these considerations are outside DAR's brief and are covered by various United Nations (UN) agencies, where possible we decided to adopt a multi-sectoral approach.

This approach was adopted in various countries including Guyana, Cambodia and Eritrea. It involved co-ordinating policy initiatives at the national level that involved several government departments including health, social welfare, education and labour. However, we encountered several problems. First, whilst many health departments have staff working at the regional and community levels they are concerned solely with primary health care and are not equipped to adopt a multi-agency approach to health and rehabilitation. Similarly whilst education departments have teachers in most villages they too are not trained for community development work, Further some government agencies although enthusiastic about disabled people's economic and social inclusion were, in most cases, very centralised and had very limited resources beyond the nation's capital.

In order to exchange expertise and avoid duplication DAR collaborated with other relevant UN agencies such as the International Labour Organisation (ILO) and United Nations, Education, Science and Culture Organisation (UNESCO). Meeting colleagues from these organisations proved to be very productive. We were able to harmonize our programmes and in order to avoid different interpretations a Joint Position Paper on CBR was edited and distributed. In this way we were able to provide a more authoritative and unified approach in discussions with representatives of national governments and various government departments.

As a result, joint multi-sectoral pilot projects were established and developed in Ghana and Namibia. These were co-ordinated by staff from the ILO and were supported by each nation's Ministry of Social Welfare. However, it soon became apparent that where one government department is viewed as responsible for a particular programme, other departments will be reluctant to get involved and, most importantly, are not prepared to commit the resources needed to put the programme into practice.

To strengthen the multi-sectoral approach and to secure the participation of disabled people's organizations in the development of and co-ordination of rehabilitation policy, many countries organised their own national CBR committees. The committees included representatives from disabled people's organisations, staff from relevant government departments, and delegates from NGOs. Unfortunately, the impact of these committees was not always as effective as had been hoped. It was concluded therefore that an international conference would be useful in order to exchange ideas and develop new ideas. This event was organised and co-ordinated with the help of the Indonesian Ministry of Health.

Several important issues were discussed. One of the most interesting outcomes concerned the location and membership of the national committees for CBR. It was suggested that in order to avoid the problems of inter-agency rivalry, and reluctance on the part of some government agencies to become involved in disability and rehabilitation issues, that future multi-sectoral initiatives must be co-ordinated at the highest level. In the case of South Africa and Mexico this meant that they were situated in the President's Office. In addition, the Committee must be chaired by someone with sufficient authority to ensure that the different stakeholders participate in an effective and appropriate manner. It was also suggested that these committees should not operate in isolation. A similar structure had to be in place at the community level. Furthermore, as with the national bodies, these groups must be chaired by a local leader, village chief, or someone with similar local standing. Community based committees should also include delegates from across the community. These might include women, children, religious leaders and representatives of other local organisations. In situations where local CBR committees needed the input of government departments and ministries in order to achieve their designated goals, they should elicit support from established regional and national administrative authorities such as the Governor's office. Such a structure was tried and tested by the WHO and International NGOs in Eritrea with the full support of the national Government.

However, there is a well-established link between disability and poverty. Indeed, the main causes of chronic illness and long-term impairment in 'majority world' countries are poverty, inadequate sanitation, poor diet and bad housing (WHO 2001a). But in developing countries poverty is a general experience and not confined to disabled people. This raises the question is it fair to ask poor communities to take responsibility for the support of disabled people?

In response, the WHO developed a programme of action to address the problems of what are often termed 'slum communities'. These are areas characterised by squalid, usually urban, environments with few or no public amenities and populated by desperately poor people living in overcrowded and often unsanitary conditions. Workshops were organised for slum dweller leaders in Manila in the Philippines, and for refugee leaders in Kampala, Uganda. The proposed CBR programme was presented by WHO workers and the discussions that followed were extremely positive. Delegates were generally agreed that not only could a well-organized CBR programme promote equal opportunities for disabled people 'but that the promotion of a caring community will reinforce community linkages and promote inter community development' (WHO 1998: 16). Participants identified a number of potential problems and proposed several recommendations on how CBR could be implemented under such difficult conditions.

A little funding was made available for initial training but community leaders were confident that they could mobilise existing community resources. It soon became clear that commonly held assumptions about people living in 'slum' conditions are often quite incorrect. A frequently held view is that such communities have scarce resources, and are in desperate need of help and interventions from external sources. But although the environment may be poor, the people who live there are often rich in human kindness and solidarity. In my experience, people in very poor communities are both keen and able to help and support the poorest among them. For example, it was proposed that to be effective, the CBR programme must address the needs of all disadvantaged groups within the community. In addition to disabled people these included women with HIV and AIDS and children who had been abandoned, or had no-one to look after them.

It was also apparent that no single CBR strategy could be implemented across all communities. Indeed, different communities within the same country often have different needs. A CBR approach has to be flexible enough to adapt to the differing needs of different communities. In order to make a positive impact, CBR must belong to the community and reflect the culture and needs of the host community and not the theories and practices of external experts, international agencies and NGOs.

Revising the Disability and Rehabilitation Team's activities
The work of DAR is bound to follow the WHO's Constitution. In this, health is defined in terms of physical, mental and social well-being. Additionally, the WHO Declaration of Alma-Ata states that primary health care should address the main health problems within the community. To

fulfil this goal preventive, curative and rehabilitative services should be provided along with general health promotion strategies. Furthermore, DAR is also committed to incorporate the approach of the United Nations (1993) Standard Rules on the Equalisation of Opportunities for Persons with Disabilities. This was introduced following the UN Decade of Disabled Persons (1982-1992) and comprised twenty-two 'rules' to facilitate full participation and equality for disabled people. These cover all aspects of daily living, including awareness raising, medical and support services, education, employment, leisure and cultural activities. DAR is concerned with the first four rules. These cover awareness raising, medical, rehabilitation and support services and are considered as preconditions for wider social participation:

> Rule 1: States should take action to raise awareness in society about persons with disabilities, their rights, their needs, their potential and their contribution,
> Rule 2: States should ensure the provision of effective medical care to persons with disabilities
> Rule 3: States should ensure the provision of rehabilitation services to persons with disabilities in order for them to reach and sustain their optimum level of independence and functioning.
> Rule 4: States should ensure the development and supply of support services for persons with disabilities, including assistive devices, to assist them to increase their level of independence in their daily living and to exercise their rights (UN 1994: unpaged).

To ensure that our projects were compatible with the Standard Rules it was agreed that we should discuss future plans with the UN Special Rapporteur on disability, Bengt Lindqvist, and his panel of experts before presenting them to the WHO Director for approval. It was a fruitful decision that gave us the opportunity to discuss in some detail the work of DAR with representatives of several leading international disabled people's organisations who were also members of the UN's panel of experts. Many suggestions were made that helped the WHO Team clarify its policy on disability and rehabilitation.

These discussions provided the stimulus for a major revision of the Team's programme. Three core initiatives were identified: *Rethinking Care from Disabled People's Perspectives*, a review of CBR, and a review of medical rehabilitation and assistive devices.

a) Rethinking Care from Disabled People's Perspectives
The first of these projects included data collection from various sources on recent developments within the general area of health and disability and concluded with a conference: 'Rethinking Care from Disabled People's Perspectives' held in Oslo in 2001. It was founded on the idea that disability and rehabilitation cannot be understood solely in terms of orthodox medical interventions and conventional notions of care. Instead, it set out to achive the following aim:

> give disabled people requiring health and social support an opportunity to contribute to the process of Rethinking Care with respect to policy regarding the development of health and social services, and, in so doing, provide new insights and knowledge for the formulation of appropriate recommendations for WHO Member States (WHO 2001a: 9).

To accomplish this aim data were collected from various sources. These included the commissioning of the discussion paper written by Vic Finkelstein (1998) *Rethinking Care in a Society Providing Equal Opportunities for All*, and a request for testimonials and additional papers from disabled people and professionals from all over the world. During the year 2000, 'Over 3500 responses were received, over 80 per cent from disabled individuals themselves and many by email' (WHO 2001a: 7). These testimonials and papers are available from the WHO as *Voices* (WHO 2001b) and *'Rethinking Care' from Different Perspectives* (WHO 2001c).

The Rethinking Care Conference brought together disabled people, parents and 'carers' of disabled individuals, professionals and policy-makers from rich and poor countrioes to reflect on and discuss relevant issues and concerns with reference to current provision within the context of the first four UN Standard Rules in order to formulate appropriate policy recommendations for WHO Member States with respect to awareness-raising, medical care, rehabilitation and support services. A conference report was later produced which contained an outline of the proceedings and recommendations.

Adopting a broadly social model approach to disability the recommendations included:

> the recognition that Member States must adopt a holistic approach that incorporates the introduction of policies to eliminate poverty and secure equal access to *all* community-based services and facilities. These include medical services, education, employment, housing, transport, and public amenities.

This must be accompanied by the introduction of comprehensive and enforceable anti-discrimination laws and policies to secure the active and meaningful involvement of disabled people and their organizations in all future policy developments.

States must adopt a truly inclusive approach to these issues that addresses equally the needs of *all* disabled people. This includes disabled women, disabled children, and people with complex and/or multiple impairments with potentially high dependency needs (WHO 2001: 4).

Delegates also made several recommendations for the implementation of policies on medical care, rehabilitation, support services and awareness-raising and stated that access to medical and related services is a basic human right and, therefore, must *not* be determined by the ability to pay. Moreover,

the responsibility for introducing and financing these developments rests with national governments. High-income states, international monetary institutions and transnational organizations should make resources available to the governments of low-income countries that do not have the means to secure these developments (WHO 2001a: 5).

b) Reviewing CBR

The second initiative involved a review of DAR's CBR strategy in collaboration with other UN organisations, WHO member States, NGOs, and disabled people's organisations. The Government of Finland agreed to host and support this review which culminated with a conference staged in Helsinki during May 2003 (WHO 2003).

From 2000 to 2002 the WHO sponsored a series of meetings on CBR. These identified four major topics for the improvement of the impact of CBR: i) community involvement and ownership; ii) multi-sectoral collaboration in the implementation of CBR; iii) the role of disabled people's organisations in CBR; and iv) the scaling up of CBR programmes. In addition the participants discussed the evolution of CBR from a model that was often viewed as medical to one that promoted the inclusion and rights of disabled people within their respective communities.

It was agreed that creating awareness about CBR requires activities that focused on both the community and decision makers. Furthermore, awareness-raising cannot be general but must be appropriate to specific groups. Dialogue between participants must be culturally sensitive and use appropriate language. Participating states should have a national policy on disability issues. There must be a 'political will' at all levels and within all ministries for the implementation of CBR to be truly successful. This must recognise that accessibility, participation and inclusion are matters of human rights. In recognition of the fact that without Government support the 'scaling up' of CBR will not take place, disabled people's organisations and NGOs should use the media to lobby governments (WHO 2003).

All participants in the review considered CBR a useful strategy to promote the human rights of, and equal opportunities, for disabled people regardless of the nature or severity of their impairment. Highlights from the recommendations generated by the review include the following:

- All stakeholders in CBR should work to ensure the human rights of disabled people.
- Government policy and support are essential; for the development of CBR programmes including the policies that support the rights of disabled people.
- Multi-sectoral collaboration is essential to CBR, including co-ordination and co-operation between community and referral services and agencies.
- Disabled people's organisations have a key role to play in educating disabled people with regard to their rights and advocating for those rights to all stakeholders involved in the development and implementation of CBR.
- All UN agencies, international and local NGOs should collaborate with governments in the promotion of CBR as a strategy for the inclusion of disabled people in all programmes for the reduction and prevention of poverty (WHO 2003: ii).

c) Review of medical rehabilitation
The final element of DAR's strategy revision was a proposal to review medical rehabilitation and the provision of assistive devices. This is another collaborative venture involving governments, international medical organisations, and disabled people's organisations. The recommendations from the first two initiatives, outlined above, have been incorporated into the review guide. The review is currently being conducted; once complete the results will be presented to the WHO General Assembly.

As will be very evident from this discussion, the WHO's DAR does not work in isolation. Depending on the project, team members often collaborate and learn from other WHO units and groupings sharing knowledge and experience in order to provide a more comprehensive and valuable service. Important recent developments from this type of collaborative activity include the *International Classification of Functioning, Disability and Health* (WHO 2001d) finalized by the WHO's 'Classification, Assessment, Surveys and Terminology Unit' and the *Innovative Care for Chronic Conditions: Building Blocks for Action* (WHO 2002) initiative that was produced by the WHO's Health Care Team.

Unlike its predecessor, *The International Classification of Impairments, Disabilities and Handicaps* (WHO 1980), the new classification of functioning and disability addresses not only bodily functioning and structure as impairments, but also activity and participation in community, social and civic life. 'Activity' represents the execution of daily living tasks and 'participation' refers to involvement in life situations and the interaction between the individual and the community. These are all influenced by personal and environmental factors. This new classification system recognizes that when there is a facilitative environment, disability is reduced, and when the environment is hindering, disability is made worse. For further discussion of the strengths and weaknesses of this new approach see Bury (2000), Hurst (2000) and Pfeiffer (2000).

The *Innovative Care for Chronic Conditions* initiative starts from the premise that most health care systems are not prepared or equipped to cope with people who have long-term or chronic conditions. Therefore, it is argued that interventions should be directed toward the effective prevention and management of chronic conditions. This requires the shift in emphasis from an approach that is based on an acute and episodic care model in favour of one clustered around a more comprehensive system of care and support. The key aim of this approach is to give those with long-term health problems the knowledge and skills for self-management. This involves goal-setting and problem-solving linked directly to existing community resources. In order to facilitate this transformation, medical and rehabilitation teams must restructure their working practices to improve the development and delivery of the range of services needed to empower individuals and their families to live within rather than apart from the community. To this end the traditional prescriptive role of the medical professional must give way to one of consultation; doctors and associate professionals must become a community resource.

Conclusion

In this chapter, I have described my experiences as a medical physician coming to terms with the problems faced by disabled people mainly in the poorer countries of the developing world. My experiences in Africa taught me that poverty and disability go hand-in-hand and that the difficulties disabled people and their families encounter in their everyday lives cannot be solved by medical interventions alone. This awareness was strengthened after I became involved with CBR, the WHO's disability and rehabilitation programme, and disabled people's own organisations. For me, there is little doubt that CBR policies can only be successful with the full support of the entire community, and that disabled people's organisations and NGOs must work together to bring about meaningful change. Disability is a human rights issue. However, the development and recent revision of the WHO's CBR programme clearly emphasises that there is a continuing need for appropriate medical and rehabilitative interventions, and that these should complement disabled people's ongoing struggle for equal opportunities and human rights.

Bibliography

Barnes, C. and Mercer, G. 2003: **Disability**. Cambridge: Polity.

Bury, M. 2000: A Comment on the ICIDH2. **Disability and Society**, 15 (7) 1073-1078.

Finkelstein, V. 1998: **Rethinking Care in a Society Providing Equal Opportunities for All**, Invited discussion paper submitted to the World Health Organization 3rd March (available on: www.leeds.ac.uk/disability-studies/archiveuk/index).

Hurst, R. 2000: To revise or not to revise. **Disability and Society**, 15 (7), 1083-7.

Ingstad, B. 2001: Disability in the Developing World. In G. L. Albrecht, K.D. Seelman, and M. Bury (eds), **Handbook of Disability Studies**. London: Sage, 772-92.

Pfeiffer, D. 2000: 'The Devils are in the Detail': the ICIDH2 and the Disability Movement. **Disability and Society**, 15 (7) 1079-1082.

Stone, E. 1999: Disability and development in the majority world. In E. Stone (ed.), **Disability and Development**. Leeds: The Disability Press, 1-18.

United Nations 1994: **Standard Rules on the Equalisation of Opportunities for People with Disabilities**, New York: United Nations.

WHO 1978: *The Declaration of Alma-Ata*. Geneva: World Health Organization.

WHO 1998: Disability and Rehabilitation Team: proposed strategy paper 1999-2000. *Disability/Injury Prevention and Rehabilitation Department, Social Change and Mental Health Cluster*. Geneva: World Health Organization (unpublished discussion paper).

WHO 2001a: *Rethinking Care from the Perspective of Disabled People*. Geneva: World Health Organization.

WHO 2001b: *Voices*. Geneva: World Health Organization.

WHO 2001c: '*Rethinking Care' from Different Perspectives*. Geneva: World Health Organization.

WHO 2001d: *International Classification of Functioning and Disability, and Health*. Geneva: World Health Organization.

WHO 2002: *Innovative Care for Chronic Conditions: Building Blocks for Action*. Geneva: World Health Organization.

WHO 2003: *International Consultation to Review Community Based Rehabilitation (CBR)*. Geneva: World Health Organization.

INDEX (compiled by Marie Ross)

Aarts, L., 26
Abberley, P., 4, 41
Abdel Nour, M., 151-152
Abdel-Salam, S., 150
Abdi, O., 123
Abedin, M.N., 164
abnormality, 152
abortion, 4, 76
abuse, 73
accessibility, 108, 137, 204
 Europe, 100, 106
 social model, 98
 transport, 80-83, 85-87, 90
Accessible Information Directive, 86
Ackers, L., 99-100, 105, 107, 110
Action on Disability and Development, 127, 143-144
activists, 1, 8, 11, 13, 35, 65-66, 122, 124, 153, 155
 civil rights, 70
 disability rights, 4, 13, 17, 23, 193
 independent living, 66
adaptation, 58-60
agency and structure, 107, 111, 124, 133, 139-140, 142, 198-199
Ahmad, A., 117-118
Ahmed, M., 152, 156
Albert, B., 12-13, 131, 133-134
Amsterdam Treaty 1997, 9, 22, 31, 74, 98, 107
Andenæs, M., 100
Anthony, E., 117
anthropology, 160

anti-discrimination, 8-9, 21-22, 24, 26, 29, 74, 84-85, 87, 92-94, 122, 137, 203
 legislation, 8-9, 24, 29, 74, 84-85, 92-94, 122
Armstrong, F., 11, 49, 54, 57, 62, 121-122
Asian Development Bank, 135, 144
attitudes, 50, 55, 65, 69, 80, 84, 119-120, 158
 discriminatory, 164
Barnes, C., 135, 154,
 and Mercer, G., 1-2, 8, 10, 115, 119, 123, 127, 170, 192-193
 independent living, 33
 labour market, 102-103, 110
 social model of disability, 23, 55
Barton, L., 121-122
Berg, S., 11, 32, 38
Bernard v Enfield, 88
Bernstein, H., 117-118
Bettray v Staatssecretaris van Justitie, 104
bioethics, 12, 75-77
biological, 2, 70, 75, 151-153
Botta v Italy, 88
Boxall, K., 52
Boylan, E., 149-150
Britain, 17, 29, 32, 45, 111
British Council of Organisations of Disabled People, 29, 48, 77
Brown, C., 122
Bureau for Action in Favour of Handicapped People, 68
Bury, M., 135, 205
Campbell, J., 187

capitalism, 7, 41, 117-121, 123-129
Castells, M., 116
Central Agency for Mobilisation and Statistics, 155-156, 160
Centre public d'aide sociale de Courcelles v Lebon, 113
cerebral palsy, 58-59, 61
Chappell, P., 177
charity, 66, 68, 73, 77, 122, 153-154, 180
Charlton, J. I., 1, 4-5, 7-8, 115-116, 120, 125
Charter of Fundamental Rights, 25, 108, 112
children, 50, 52, 110, 149-150, 155, 157, 188, 199-200
 citizenship, 100
 Deaf, 188
 discrimination, 164
 education, 49, 54-56, 58
 learning difficulties, 27, 61, 149
 mobility needs, 186
 personal assistance, 42, 44-45
civil rights, 23, 34, 70, 81, 85, 121-123, 129, 137
Clements, L., 88
Cockburn, T., 107
Coleridge, P., 1, 3, 5, 7, 115, 120
Commission of the European Communities, 9, 17, 29, 112
Community Based Rehabilitation, 13, 169, 186, 193, 195-201, 203-204, 206-207
conflict, 7, 35, 189
consumption, 4, 110, 117
Copenhagen Conference, 136-137, 145
Corker, M., 153

Council of the European Communities, 19, 29
counselling, 71
culture, 7, 27, 40, 50, 127, 182, 200
Cunningham, S., 21
Dalley, G., 35, 42
Davis, K., 66, 122, 28, 152-153
De la Porte, C., 25
de Lorenzo, R., 26
De Schutter, O., 89
deaf, 134, 139, 155-156, 188
Degener, T., 22
demonstrations, 172, 174
Denmark (Ministry of Foreign Affairs), 26, 67, 82, 137, 140, 145
Department for International Development, 133-134, 144-145
Department of Employment and Solidarity, 51
dependency, 32-33, 38-45, 100, 105-106, 109, 112, 203
Derbyshire, H., 143
Diamantopoulou, A., 87
Diatta v Land Berlin, 105
difference, 5, 49, 53-55, 57, 65, 120, 170, 172
direct action, 73
Directive on Equal Treatment in Employment, 24
Directorate of Employment, Industrial Relations and Social Affairs, 68
disability
 activists, 4, 13, 17, 23, 193
 benefits, 55, 104-105
 children, 50, 183
 definition, 26, 65-67, 69, 133, 135, 137, 148, 151-152, 187, 205

INDEX

ICIDH, 33
development, 13, 131, 133, 136-137, 139, 141, 143
discrimination, 22, 24, 31, 85, 87
transport, 85
equality, 24, 28, 93-94, 138
experience, 1, 2, 66, 165
human rights, 9, 12-13, 65, 73, 77, 108, 132-133, 206
impairment, 2, 6-7, 13, 16, 36, 39, 44, 53, 134, 148, 152, 158
individual model, 18, 34, 148, 151, 153, 157-159, 194
medical model, 53, 136, 153-154, 159, 182
movement, 66, 77, 128, 132, 139, 146, 159
organisations, 22, 67, 72, 74, 182
policy, 8-9, 11, 19, 25-30, 36, 38, 133, 137-138, 144, 157, 159, 204
politics, 35, 70
poverty, 132, 135-136, 140, 185, 195, 199, 206
psycho-emotional, 50
rehabilitation, 13, 158, 193-195, 199-202, 206-207
relative model, 32, 35, 37, 39
research, 36
rights, 8-9, 15, 30, 47, 65-66, 154, 184-185
services, 34
social construction, 17
social model, 1, 17-18, 23, 33, 65, 80, 92, 115-116, 118, 123-124, 126, 128, 130, 132, 134, 136, 144, 153-154, 180-181, 186, 193
social relational model, 50
stigma, 195
studies, 23, 109, 115, 118, 121, 125, 152
rights-based approach, 20, 23-24, 28, 106-107, 111, 122, 164
theory, 30, 129
transport, 86, 91-92
Disability and Rehabilitation Team, 13, 193, 195-196, 198, 200-201, 203-204, 207
Disability Discrimination Act 1995, 74, 92, 137
disability equality training, 138
Disability, Poverty and Development, 133, 145
Disabled People's Parliament, 9, 21, 30, 73, 78
Disabled Peoples' International, 1, 8, 12, 29-30, 47, 65-78, 124, 184-185, 191-192
disablement, 8, 44, 110, 118-119, 129, 134-135, 151, 153-154, 157
disablism, 118, 191
discourse, 34, 64, 122
discrimination, 22, 26, 66, 93, 134, 164, 181
direct, 21, 90
education, 49
employment, 20, 24, 74
European Court of Human Rights, 90
indirect, 9, 21, 90
institutional, 18, 21, 52, 165
legislation, 74, 92, 98, 107, 109, 137
non-discrimination, 20, 22, 24, 26, 74, 81-82, 86, 106, 110, 137

positive, 169
race, 85, 93
transport, 85
disease, 33, 36, 39, 44, 70
domination, 126, 169
Douglas, M., 5
Draft Passenger Ships Directive, 86, 96
Drewett, A.Y., 122
Driedger, D., 1
dyslexia, 3
education, 9, 24, 26, 108
   accessibility, 52, 55, 189, 202
   Bangladesh, 163
   Cambodia, 188
   deaf, 188
   Egypt, 150
   exclusion, 198
   France, 49, 51, 54-56, 63
   Ministry of Education, 56
   health, 166-167, 172-174, 188, 194
   inclusion, 20, 51, 55, 64
   India, 189
   integration, 56, 108
   personal assistance, 39
   segregation, 52, 56
   special, 15, 55, 140
   state system, 54, 57-58
   visually impaired, 189
Ekensteen, V., 35, 37
El Banna, A., 149, 156
Elwan, A., 119
emancipation, 123
emancipatory research, 170
employment, 8, 10, 19, 28, 41-42, 102, 104, 155, 157, 188, 201-202
   barriers to, 45, 110
   equal opportunities, 21, 25, 74, 96
   legislation, 85, 107, 157
   migrants, 102, 104
   personal assistants, 33
   rights, 28, 74, 99
   sheltered, 18, 20, 104
Employment Framework Directive, 85, 96
empowerment, 34-35, 38, 41, 57, 181, 184
environmental barriers, 3, 9, 17, 25, 37, 44, 50, 55, 65, 69-70, 134, 136, 153, 158, 164, 182, 188, 205
equal opportunities, 21, 121, 158, 174, 194, 200, 204, 206
equality, 37, 78, 140, 183, 191
   and full participation, 8, 18, 22-23, 107, 184, 201
   disability, 24, 28, 93-94, 138
   gender, 21, 42
   legislation, 52, 74
   race, 107
   training, 138
ethnicity, 3
eugenics, 4, 12, 77
European Civil Aviation Conference, 86, 96
European Commission, 19, 22, 25, 29, 71-72, 74-75, 86-87, 96, 132, 145
European Community, 19-20, 22, 29, 31, 72, 111-112
European Conference of Ministers of Transport, 81, 95-96
European Congress on Disability, 101, 112
European Congress on Independent Living, 101, 112
European Day of Disabled People, 10, 21-22

European Disability Forum, 10, 22, 26, 71-72, 74, 77, 86-87, 92, 94, 96, 98, 100, 107-108, 112-113
European Network on Independent Living, 47, 71, 101, 112
European Parliament, 19, 29, 72-73, 75, 109
European Union, 7, 9-11, 17-18, 22, 24-28, 30, 67-68, 72-74, 76, 81, 85-87, 92, 94, 98-103, 106-108, 110-113, 132, 134, 143, 145
Eurostat, 102, 104, 112
euthanasia, 4, 75
exclusion, 18, 50, 63, 65, 88, 92, 133, 180, 190
  and disability, 12, 18, 49, 184
  education, 55, 198
  labour market, 110
  social, 1-2, 5-8, 11, 24-25, 44, 132, 143
experience
  disability, 1-2, 66, 165
  disabled people, 35, 50, 102, 153-154, 159, 191
  discrimination, 21, 49
  exclusion, 181
  gender, 142, 144
experts, 44, 76, 79, 184-185, 187, 200-201
exploitation, 29, 117, 125
Fahmy, M., 149, 152, 155-156
family, 6-7, 41-42, 52, 88-89, 100-101, 104-106, 109-110, 142, 149-150, 155-156, 158, 163, 166-167, 169, 171-174, 176, 190, 196
Fanon, F., 117, 120, 125

feudalism, 125
Finkelstein, V., 23, 34, 66-67, 118-119, 123-124, 128, 134, 193, 202
Fletcher, A., 188
Flood, T., 13, 180
Fredman, S., 93-94
French, S., 49, 53-54, 58, 105
Fundamental Principles of Disability, 30, 78, 130, 192
gender, 3, 21, 42, 45, 60, 140-145, 173-177
genetic, 59, 76, 109, 149
Ghia, A., 3-4
Giddens, A., 3
Gindin, S., 117-118
Glass, R., 164
Gleeson, B., 41, 119, 121
government
  Bangladesh, 163, 165
  bill, 38-40
  developing countries, 142, 154, 198
  Egypt, 148, 156
  Finland, 136, 144, 203
  Non-Government Organisations (NGOs), 68, 100, 115, 124, 139-140, 142-143, 145, 155, 195, 199-200, 203-204, 206
  South Africa, 189
  Uganda, 190
  UK, 74, 76, 198, 203
grassroots, 180, 184, 190
Gray, A., 4
Groce, N., 5-6, 119
Hagrass, H., 148, 150, 152, 154-156
Hahn, H., 23
Handley, P., 122
Hanks, J., 5-6

Hanks, L., 5-6
Harrison, P., 117
healthcare, 163, 172, 177, 194-198, 200, 205
Held, D., 6
HELIOS, 20, 72
Hepple, B., 93
Hertzberg, A., 140
High Speed Trains Directive, 86
Hirschl, T.A., 125
Holgersson, L., 37, 41
Holme, L., 37
Hoogvelt, A., 7, 117
Hoque, M.F., 164
Horsler, J., 118, 120, 123, 125
Hossain, M.M., 164
housing, 7, 20, 33, 71, 89, 91, 108, 110, 188, 199, 202
Hughes, B., 53
human rights, 4, 13, 21-25, 65-66, 70, 72-73, 75-76, 78, 81, 92, 94, 108, 121-122, 127, 132, 134-137, 139-140, 143-144, 146, 151, 155, 159, 165, 183, 185, 191, 204, 206
Hunt, P., 33, 35, 66, 181
Hurst, R., 12, 14, 65, 73, 125, 135, 165, 182, 188, 205
Hvinden, B., 26
identity, 27, 37, 50, 64, 69
ideology, 40, 42, 115, 121-123, 126
illness, 150, 199
images, 55
impairment, 2-7, 13-14, 16-19, 33, 36, 39, 44, 49-50, 52-55, 58-59, 65, 76, 106, 119, 148-153, 156-159, 173-175, 177, 180, 182, 184, 186, 195-196, 199, 204

imperialism, 29, 118
Imrie, R., 53
incapacity, 33, 39, 44
inclusion, 10, 22, 49, 53, 60, 77, 93, 98, 107, 110, 137-138, 141, 143, 146, 188, 203-204
independent living, 1, 32-33, 38, 66, 71, 106, 110, 169, 181, 184, 186
individual model of disability, 19, 52
inequalities, 6, 35, 55, 62, 102, 107, 126
infanticide, 5
Information on Disabled Passengers Directive, 86
Ingstad, B., 1, 5-6, 119, 140, 193, 195
injuries, 13, 157, 166, 194
institution, 60, 62, 93, 181
International Labour Organisation, 140, 145, 152, 163, 178, 198
International Monetary Fund, 4, 117-118
International Year of Disabled People, 8, 19
Inzirillo v Caisse d'Allocations Familiaties de l'Arrondissement de Lyon, 105
Jayasooria, D., 8
Johnson, R.L., 170
Justice, S., 101
Kallen, E., 65
Kalyanpur, M., 8
Kempf v Staatssecretaris van Justitie, 102
Kisanji, J., 6, 120
Labour government, 113, 140, 145, 198

labour market, 20, 26, 41-42, 44-45, 102, 104, 108, 110-111, 119
Lang, R., 123
Lansdown, G., 188
Law, J., 80, 94
Lawrie-Blum v Land Baden Wüttemberg, 101
Lawson, A., 12, 80
Leaman, D., 66, 68
learning difficulties, 2, 27, 57, 64
Lenin, V.I., 118
leprosy, 195
Levin v Staatssecretaris van Justitie, 102, 114
Leys, C., 125
Liggett, H., 23
Light, R., 189
Lister, R., 107, 110
local authorities, 189
Lundström, K., 100
Lunt, N., 102, 152-153, 157
Mabbett, D., 23, 26
Machado, S., 26
majority world, 1-4, 6-8, 11-14, 16, 29, 115-120, 124-126, 128-129, 182-183, 193, 199, 206
Malik, K., 120, 125
Malinga, J., 8, 184-185
marriage patterns, 6, 149
Martin, E., 37
Marx, K., 125
Marzari v Italy, 89
materialist model of disability, 120
Matsebula, S., 189
Matthews, B., 12, 80
McColgan, A., 90
McGlynn, C., 100

media, 7, 55, 167, 204
medical
  assessments, 54
  assumptions, 135-136
  care, 53, 58, 60, 164-165, 178, 202-203
  intervention, 167, 187, 194, 202, 206
  professionals, 53, 59, 69-70, 153, 194, 205
  rehabilitation, 3-4, 8, 69, 153, 165, 194, 201, 204-205
  services, 3-4, 8, 66, 163, 170, 174, 177, 197-198, 201-202
medical model of disability, 1, 11, 34, 36, 49, 53, 55, 63, 69-70, 134-136, 148, 151, 153-154, 157-159, 163, 194
medicine, 4, 7, 18, 75, 194
mental
  development, 149
  disability, 56
  disorder, 134
  illness, 2
  impairment, 137
Mercer, G., 1,
  and Barnes, C., 1-2, 8, 10, 14, 115, 119, 123, 170, 193
Miles, M., 5-6, 135
Miles, S., 4, 8
MIND, 95
Ministero degli Affair Esteri, 146
Momin, A.K.M., 13, 163-164, 166
Moore, K., 142
Morgan, H., 12, 28, 98
Morris, J., 33-35, 106, 152-154
Nadash, P., 34, N
National Council on Disability, 139, 146

Navarro, V., 125
Nicolaisen, I., 7
NORAD, 139-140, 146
normality, 50, 152
Nosseir, N., 149-150, 156
Novitz, T., 91
Nowak, M., 88
Office of the Deputy President, 189, 192
Oliver, M., 1, 18, 23, 32-33, 36, 41, 66, 94, 106, 110, 119, 152-154, 165, 170, 181, 186-187
Ooi, G., 8
Open Method of Co-ordination, 25
oppression, 1-2, 14, 23, 50, 63, 66, 119-120, 124-126, 181, 189, 191
Osman, A., 151
otherness, 51, 152
Oxfam, 14, 127, 140-141, 146
Panitch, L., 117-118
passivity, 37
Pearson, C., 34
Peers, S., 100
personal tragedy, 10, 152-153, 159
Peters, Y., 75
Pfeiffer, D., 34, 135, 205
Pochet, C., 25
political activism, 1, 8, 181
political economy, 12, 15, 30, 115, 120, 125, 128-129
poverty, 25, 65, 132, 135, 143, 148, 180, 190, 195, 199
　line, 3, 163
　　reduction, 132, 136, 140, 142, 185, 202, 204
Priestley, M., 11, 14, 17, 23, 51, 118
Prinz, C., 26

psychiatric system, 27
psycho-emotional, 50
Pupulin, E., 13, 193
Qandil, A., 148
quality of life, 76, 177
Quibell, R., 23, 121-123
Quinn, G., 94
R v IAT ex parte Antonissen, 113
Race Directive, 9, 85
racism, 21, 120
Rahman, M., 164
Ras-Work, B., 150
Ratzka, A., 33-34
Raulin v Minister van Onderwijs en Wetenschappen, 102, 114
Read, J., 88
recreation, 59
Reeve, D., 50, 62
rehabilitation, 66, 68, 104, 134, 141, 158, 166-167, 195-196, 198
　community based, 13, 169, 186, 193, 195-201, 203-204, 206-207
　economic, 172
　individualised, 20
　medical, 3, 8, 201, 204
　professionals, 66, 68, 174, 194, 196-197
　services, 151, 165, 172, 174, 177, 196, 201, 202
　social, 172
religion, 6, 22, 74, 90, 109, 154
Report of the First European Disabled People's Parliament, 21, 30, 78
Road Safety and Motor Vehicles Directive 2003, 85
Robertson, A., 123

Rosenthal, E., 27
Rothstein, B., 35, 38
Russell, M., 23, 119, 122, 124, 126, 182
Samoy, E., 104
Sapey, B., 152-153
Scheer, J., 5-6
Scheiwe, K., 100
Scheper-Hughes, N., 149
self advocacy, 22
Sen, A., 122
Sentges v The Netherlands, 89-90
service provision, 68, 93, 103, 166-167
Shakespeare, T., 42, 106, 119, 154
Shaw, J., 99, 115
Shaw, M., 115
Sheldon, A., 12, 115
Shukrallah, A., 156
Single European Treaty, 24
Sinha, K.C., 165-166
Sly, F., 102
social
  exclusion, 1-2, 5-8, 11, 24-25, 44, 143
  inclusion, 10, 25, 28, 112, 140, 198
  justice, 32, 34
  relations, 18, 23-24, 99, 115-116
social model of disability, 1, 17, 23, 33, 65, 80, 92, 115-116, 118, 123-124, 126, 128, 130, 132, 134, 136, 144, 153-154, 181, 186, 193
  EU model, 17
  implementation, 23-24, 27
social services, 32, 34, 37-38, 54, 177, 202
socio-economic, 19-20, 35, 140

sociology, 160
Söder, M., 37
solidarity, 25, 200
Spanish National Council of Disabled People, 22
special needs, 37, 122
spinal injury, 13, 165, 172
STAKES, 133, 136, 139, 143, 146
Stalford, H., 12, 28, 98, 100, 107
Standard Rules on Equalization of Opportunities for Persons with Disabilities, 21
Steinmeyer, H.D., 81, 84
Stienstra, D., 141
stigma, 195
Stone, E., 3, 6, 115, 119, 165, 182
Stychin, C., 100
Sundram, C.J., 27
Suntinger, W., 88
Swain, J., 154
Szyszczak, E., 100
Talle, A., 6-7
Teçke, B., 148
Thirwall, A.P., 117
Thlimmenos v Greece, 90
Thomas, A., 125
Thomas, C., 116
Thomas, P., 143
Thornton, P., 102, 123, 152-153, 157
Tomaševski, K., 125
Tomlinson, S., 123
Tøssebro, J., 8
Trägårdh, L., 41
Twimyuke, M., 190
Ulland, K.H., 137
UN Standard Rules, 21, 69, 73-74, 137, 202
unemployment, 27, 128

Ungerson, C., 35
Union of the Physically Impaired Against Segregation (UPIAS), 1-2, 16, 30, 33, 36, 44, 48, 66, 78, 118, 130, 181, 192
United Nation's Childrens Fund (UNICEF), 185
United Nations, 2, 4, 7-9, 16, 21, 68-69, 73-74, 78-79, 98, 121-123, 132, 136-137, 140, 143, 146, 159, 162, 165, 179, 183-184, 198, 201-204
  Convention, 28, 192
  Standard Rules, 21, 69, 73-74, 137, 202
United States, 24, 30, 71, 116, 118, 137, 140, 143, 164, 181
  Bill of Rights, 24
University of Leeds, 128, 178
Ursic, C., 27
USAID, 137-139, 143, 147
Üstün, B., 1
van der Mei, A., 100-101
van Oorschot, W., 26
visual impairment, 134, 139, 155, 189
Waddington, L., 24, 100-101, 104, 110
Walsh, P.N., 27
Weeks, J., 118
welfare policy, 11, 45, 155
welfare state, 25, 27-28, 37-38, 41
Werner, D., 186-187
White, S., 189
Whittle, R., 22
Wintemute, R., 100
Wolfensohn, J.D., 132
women
  disabled, 42, 110, 156, 187, 203

World Bank, 4, 117-118, 124, 131-132, 134, 140-143, 146-147, 164, 179, 182
World Health Assembly, 195
World Health Organisation, 1-2, 4, 8, 13, 16, 33, 35, 47-48, 69-70, 77, 79, 135, 147, 152-154, 162, 164-165, 179, 182, 193, 195-197, 199-207
  Declaration of Alma-Ata, 196, 200, 207
  Health for All by the Year 2000, 195
Yeo, R., 142
Young, I.M., 20, 23, 51, 121-123
Zarb, G., 34
Zehlanova and Zehnal v The Czech Republic, 89-90
Zukas, H., 70